New Medieval Literatures 17

New Medieval Literatures

ISSN 1465-3737

Editors

Dr Laura Ashe, University of Oxford
Prof. David Lawton, Washington University, St Louis
Prof. Wendy Scase, University of Birmingham

New Medieval Literatures is an annual of work on medieval textual cultures. Its scope is inclusive of work across the theoretical, archival, philological, and historicist methodologies associated with medieval literary studies. The title announces an interest both in new writing about medieval culture and in new academic writing. The editors aim to engage with intellectual and cultural pluralism in the Middle Ages and now. Within this generous brief, they recognize only two criteria: excellence and originality.

Submissions are invited for future issues. Please write to the editors:

Laura Ashe (laura.ashe@ell.ox.ac.uk)
David Lawton (dalawton@wustl.edu)
Wendy Scase (w.l.scase@bham.ac.uk)

For submission guidelines and further information please visit
http://www.english.ox.ac.uk/new-medieval-literatures

New Medieval Literatures 17

Edited by
Wendy Scase, Laura Ashe and David Lawton

D. S. BREWER

First published 2017
D. S. Brewer, Cambridge

ISBN 978 1 84384 457 0

D. S. Brewer is an imprint of Boydell & Brewer Ltd
PO Box 9, Woodbridge, Suffolk IP12 3DF, UK
and of Boydell & Brewer Inc.
668 Mount Hope Ave, Rochester, NY 14620–2731, USA
website: www.boydellandbrewer.com

A catalogue record for this book is available
from the British Library

The publisher has no responsibility for the continued existence
or accuracy of URLs for external or third-party internet websites
referred to in this book, and does not guarantee that any content
on such websites is, or will remain, accurate or appropriate

This publication is printed on acid-free paper

Printed and bound in Great Britain by TJ International Ltd, Padstow, Cornwall

Contents

Illustrations

The Idle Readers of Piers Plowman *in Print*
Spencer Strub

Figures

Maps

1

The Lives of *Nytenu*

Imagining the Animal in the Old English *Boethius* and *Soliloquies**

MICHAEL RABY

Ælfric of Eynsham had a fondness for elephants. He was unlikely to have seen one first-hand – there are no records of elephants having been imported into Anglo-Saxon England; instead, he gathered his knowledge of the creature from a variety of textual sources.[1] An excursus in his homily based on the Books of the Maccabees conveys facts about their size (larger than a house), diet (a taste for mulberries), gestation period (twenty-four months), and lifespan (300 years on average).[2] These details have been read as evidence of a zoological interest in animals that does not reduce them to mere figurative significance.[3] For all of his zoological leanings, however, Ælfric viewed the elephant – and

*   For their comments at various stages of this article's development, I would like to thank Dorothy Bray, Peter Buchanan, Leslie Lockett, Manish Sharma, and Michael Van Dussen. I am also grateful for the suggestions provided by the anonymous reviewers.

1   E. J. Christie, 'The Idea of an Elephant: Ælfric of Eynsham, Epistemology, and the Absent Animals of Anglo-Saxon England', *Neophilologus* 98 (2014), 465–79. See also J. E. Cross, 'The Elephant to Alfred, Ælfric, Aldhelm and Others', *Studia Neophilologica* 37 (1965), 367–73; Emily V. Thornbury, 'Ælfric's Zoology', *Neophilologus* 92 (2008), 141–53; Letty Nijhuis, '"Sumum menn wile þincan syllic þis to gehyrenne": Ælfric on Animals–his Sources and their Application', in *Transmission and Transformation in the Middle Ages: Texts and Contexts*, ed. Kathy Cawsey and Jason Harris (Dublin, 2007), 65–76.

2   *Ælfric's Lives of Saints*, ed. Walter W. Skeat, EETS o.s. 76, 82, 94, 114 (London, 1881–1900; repr. in 2 vols, 1966), 2:104, lines 564–76.

3   Thornbury, 'Ælfric's Zoology', 150–2. On the figuration of animals in medieval thought, see Sarah Stanbury, 'Posthumanist Theory and the Premodern Animal Sign', *Postmedieval* 2 (2011), 101–14.

nonhuman animals generally – through a thick lens of human exceptionalism. Ælfric reiterates that elephants, the greatest of beasts ('eallra nytena mæst'), can readily be trained by human skill.[4] He is invoking the widely held belief that the ability to tame larger and physically stronger animals is one of the most obvious proofs of human superiority.[5] Elsewhere, Ælfric drew the metaphysical boundaries between human and animal more explicitly. In his *Colloquy*, for instance, the students declare their distance from 'stupid beasts' ('stunte nytenu') by championing their desire for book learning.[6] And it has been noted how Ælfric returns in his work 'almost obsessively' to the question of whether animals possess souls (according to him, they do not).[7] Due in part to the prominence of animals in his writings, Ælfric's statements are often treated as representative of the Anglo-Saxon attitude towards animals.[8] But his voice, strident as it could be, was only one of many in an ongoing conversation about the relationship between human and nonhuman animals. This essay focuses on two other participants in that conversation: the Old English *Boethius* and *Soliloquies*.[9]

4   *Ælfric's Lives of Saints*, ed. Skeat, 104, line 572.
5   See, for example, Augustine, *De diversis quaestionibus octoginta tribus*, q. 13, ed. Almut Mutzenbecher, CCSL 44A (Turnhout, 1975), 20. See Gillian Clark, 'The Fathers and the Animals: The Rule of Reason?', in *Animals on the Agenda: Questions about Animals for Theology and Ethics*, ed. Andrew Linzey and Dorothy Yamamoto (Urbana, IL, 1998), 67–79 (68–9); Karl Steel, *How to Make a Human: Animals and Violence in the Middle Ages* (Columbus, OH, 2011), 33–5.
6   *Ælfric's Colloquy*, ed. G. N. Garmonsway (London, 1939), 42, lines 250–1: 'þe nellaþ þesan spa stunte nytenu [*bruta animalia*], þa nan þing pitaþ, buton ʒærs 7 pæter' ('we do not wish to be like stupid beasts, who do not know anything except grass and water'). Translations are my own unless otherwise noted.
7   Malcolm Godden, 'Ælfric and the Alfredian Precedents', in *A Companion to Ælfric*, ed. Hugh Magennis and Mary Swan, Brill's Companions to the Christian Tradition 18 (Leiden, 2009), 139–63 (151). According to Godden, Ælfric makes the claim that animals lack souls at least a dozen times in his writings: 'Anglo-Saxons on the Mind', in *Learning and Literature in Anglo-Saxon England: Studies Presented to Peter Clemoes on the Occasion of his Sixty-Fifth Birthday*, ed. Michael Lapidge and Helmut Gneuss (Cambridge, 1985), 271–98 (281). For a list of some of these passages, see Beatrice La Farge, '*Leben*' und '*Seele*' in den altgermanischen Sprachen: Studien zum Einfluß christlich-lateinischer Vorstellungen auf die Volkssprachen (Heidelberg, 1991), 59 n. 4.
8   See, for instance, Kathrin Prietzel, 'Animals in Religious and Non-religious Anglo-Saxon Writings', in *Tiere und Fabelwesen im Mittelalter*, ed. Sabine Obermaier (Berlin, 2009), 235–59.
9   Malcolm Godden has suggested that Ælfric's emphatic denials that animals

Far from being literal, word-for-word translations of their sources –
Boethius's *De Consolatione Philosophiae* and Augustine's *Soliloquia* – the
Old English versions condense, expand, omit, modify, and interpolate
material. Often these alterations are congruent with the expressed
positions of the original authors; at other times they depart in striking
ways.[10] Traditionally, the two works have been attributed to King Alfred
(849–99). The Old English *Boethius* survives in two versions – one in
prose, the other a *prosimetrum* – and the single medieval manuscript
witness of each version contains a preface claiming Alfred as the
translator.[11] The colophon appended to the twelfth-century copy of the
Old English *Soliloquies* makes a similar claim.[12] Recently, however, the
Alfredian attribution has been challenged by Malcolm Godden on a
number of grounds, including questions about the factual accuracy of

have souls might be a response to contrary views circulating in Anglo-Saxon
England: 'Ælfric's repeated insistence on this point suggests that he was
consciously taking issue with others, perhaps his contemporaries, perhaps his
patristic authorities, perhaps Alfred' ('Anglo-Saxons on the Mind', 281). Godden
develops his suggestion by examining how Ælfric modified a passage taken from
the Old English *Boethius* to stress the mortality of nonhuman animals ('Ælfric
and the Alfredian Precedents', 151). One of the goals of this essay is to shine
further light on this possibility by providing a clearer sense of how other Anglo-
Saxon authors understood the animal/human distinction.

10 A necessary caveat here: we must remain cautious in ascribing these alterations to the hand of the Old English translator(s), since we know little about the
specific manuscripts from which the translations were generated. In the case
of the Old English *Boethius*, there are occasional parallels, though not always
exact, with various extant commentaries; these may suggest that the translator
was working from a glossed copy of the *Consolatio*. The medieval transmission
history of the *Soliloquia* remains hazy, due in part to the lack of a modern critical
edition. Much has been written about the relationship between the Old English
Boethius and the Latin commentary tradition. For a recent reassessment, see
Rosalind Love, 'Latin Commentaries on Boethius's *Consolation of Philosophy*',
in *A Companion to Alfred the Great*, ed. Nicole Guenther Discenza and Paul
E. Szarmach, Brill's Companions to the Christian Tradition 58 (Leiden, 2015),
82–110.

11 Oxford, Bodleian Library, MS Bodley 180 (2079); London, British Library,
MS Cotton Otho A. vi.

12 The Old English *Soliloquies* appears in the 'Southwick Codex' – London,
British Library, MS Cotton Vitellius A. xv, fols 4–93. An excerpt drawn from the
opening prayer appears in London, British Library, Cotton Tiberius A. iii, fols
50v–51v.

these paratexts.[13] Nor is it certain that the two works were composed by a single author. The *modus operandi* is similarly free and expansive in both cases, and there are suggestive verbal parallels between the texts, but the precise textual relationship between the works has yet to be established.[14] For the purposes of this essay, I adopt an agnostic approach regarding the question of authorship, and, though it is unwieldy at times, I refer to two authors – the *Boethius*-author and *Soliloquies*-author – while leaving open the possibility that the translations were produced by the same person, perhaps even Alfred himself. By bracketing the traditional association with Alfred and attendant assumptions about the intellectual background of the translator(s) and the pedagogic purpose of the works, we are able to re-examine from a fresh vantage the arguments made in what Godden calls 'the first English works of philosophy'.[15]

Among the themes shared by the Old English *Boethius* and *Soliloquies* is the focus on the nature of the human soul and its particular properties and powers.[16] It is this focus that makes them such rich sites for

13 Malcom Godden, 'Did King Alfred Write Anything?', *Medium Ævum* 76 (2007), 1–23; Malcolm Godden, 'The Alfredian Project and its Aftermath: Rethinking the Literary History of the Ninth and Tenth Centuries', *Proceedings of the British Academy* 162 (2009), 93–122. See responses in Janet Bately, 'Alfred as Author and Translator', in *A Companion to Alfred the Great*, 113–42; and Leslie Lockett, *Anglo-Saxon Psychologies in the Vernacular and Latin Traditions* (Toronto, 2011), 360–73.
14 *The Old English Boethius: An Edition of the Old English Versions of Boethius's 'De Consolatione Philosophiae'*, ed. Malcolm Godden and Susan Irvine, 2 vols (Oxford, 2009), 1:135–6; *King Alfred's Old English Version of St. Augustine's 'Soliloquies'*, ed. Thomas A. Carnicelli (Cambridge, MA, 1969), 29–37; Godden, 'Did King Alfred Write Anything?'; Szarmach, 'Alfred's Soliloquies'.
15 In the words of Godden: 'By dropping the Alfredian narrative for these texts it is true that we lose the comforting sense of their historical moment in a particular decade and court and personality. But by freeing them from that straitjacket and from that over-familiar story of books most necessary for all men to know, emerging from a community insecure about its abilities and short on scholarship and written for the uneducated, we allow ourselves to see them in a very different light: as intellectually ambitious and learned enterprises and, in the case of the *Boethius* and *Soliloquies* at least, enterprises aiming, however hubristically, to go well beyond the range of their Latin predecessors and to attempt something remarkably adventurous – and creating in the process the first English works of philosophy' ('The Alfredian Project', 122).
16 Leslie Lockett's magisterial *Anglo-Saxon Psychologies* argues that the *Consolatio* and *Soliloquia* were translated into Old English in part to familiarize Anglo-Saxon readers with the classical model of the unitary human soul. Lockett

thinking about the nonhuman animal. As the field of critical animal studies continues to demonstrate, the outline of the human can only be discerned against the background of the nonhuman. Recent studies by medievalists such as Dorothy Yamamoto, Karl Steel, and Susan Crane have examined how the human/animal divide is drawn, enforced, and troubled in a variety of genres.[17] Much of this work concentrates on texts from the later Middle Ages. While scholars have long discussed aspects of the representation of animals in Anglo-Saxon literary culture, including in the context of riddles, the *Physiologus*, and narrative poems, some of the most pressing questions raised by critical animal studies have not yet been fully brought to bear on the study of Old English texts.[18] An example of one such question appears in Alastair Minnis's recent survey of late medieval ideas about Paradise, *From Eden to Eternity*. Minnis devotes considerable time to a concern that, until fairly recently, would have struck many readers as marginal or 'merely interesting': what will happen to nonhuman animals at the Day of Judgment? Will there be space for them in the 'new heaven' and 'new earth' foretold by the Book of Revelation (Rev. 21:1)?[19] According to Minnis, late medieval theologians almost unequivocally answered 'no'.

does not discuss in much detail how the Old English authors, or their sources, conceptualized the nonhuman soul.

17   Dorothy Yamamoto, *The Boundaries of the Human in Medieval English Literature* (Oxford, 2000); Steel, *How to Make a Human*; Susan Crane, *Animal Encounters: Contacts and Concepts in Medieval Britain* (Philadelphia, 2013). See also the essay collection *Rethinking Chaucerian Beasts*, ed. Carolynn Van Dyke (New York, 2012); Jeffrey Jerome Cohen, 'Inventing with Animals in the Middle Ages', in *Engaging with Nature: Essays on the Natural World in Medieval and Early Modern Europe*, ed. Barbara A. Hanawalt and Lisa J. Kiser (Notre Dame, IN, 2008), 39–62; David Salter, *Holy and Noble Beasts: Encounters with Animals in Medieval Literature* (Cambridge, 2001); Joyce E. Salisbury, *The Beast Within: Animals in the Middle Ages*, 2nd edn (London, 2011). This, of course, is a far from an exhaustive list of recent scholarship that discusses animals in Middle English literature. See the overview by Stanbury, 'The Premodern Animal Sign'.

18   It is important to note that Anglo-Saxonists have done valuable work in interrogating the limits of the human through studies of the monstrous. See, for instance, Katherine O'Brien O'Keeffe, '*Beowulf*, Lines 702b–836: Transformations and the Limits of the Human', *Texas Studies in Literature and Language* 23 (1981), 484–94.

19   Alastair Minnis, *From Eden to Eternity: Creations of Paradise in the Later Middle Ages* (Philadelphia, 2016), esp. 140–52. See also Steel, *How to Make a Human*, 92–118; and Franceso Santi, '"Utrum plantae et bruta animalia et

Minnis's book comes in the wake of work by thinkers such as Giorgio Agamben, who devotes a chapter to this same question in his seminal genealogy of the human/nonhuman divide, *The Open*.[20] Other scholars have attempted more comprehensive efforts to trace the development of the human/animal distinction back through the premodern period. Richard Sorabji examines how a number of philosophical innovations made by classical thinkers, particularly Aristotle, enabled the emergence of what he calls 'the crisis'.[21] Gary Steiner's treatment of Aristotle in *Anthropocentrism and its Discontents* is more attentive to the internal contradictions and inconsistencies in the philosopher's thought. Commenting on the discrepancies between Aristotle's zoological and metaphysical works, Steiner writes:

> Aristotle's conflicting comments about animals do not constitute a simple inconsistency but rather reflect Aristotle's recognition of a continuum between human beings and animals while seeking to distinguish human beings on the basis of their rational capacities.[22]

When Steiner turns to the Middle Ages, however, his analysis is less nuanced and less attuned to complications of the 'virtually unmodified' legacy of anthropocentrism that he sees stretching from the patristics to Aquinas (131). To be fair, Steiner is covering a lot of historical ground in his study and thus needs to move briskly at times, but his characterization of medieval theories of nonhuman animals is symptomatic of a historiographical tendency, even among medievalists, to reduce a body of diverse, often conflicting, statements made over the course of centuries to a unified doctrinal position, often called mainstream or orthodox Christianity.[23] When examined more

corpora mineralia remaneant post finem mundi": L'animale eterno', *Micrologus* 4 (1996), 231–64.

20 Giorgio Agamben, *The Open: Man and Animal*, trans. Kevin Attell (Stanford, CA, 2004), 17–19.

21 Richard Sorabji, *Animal Minds and Human Morals: The Origins of the Western Debate* (Ithaca, NY, 1993). See also Urs Dierauer, *Tier und Mensch im Denken der Antike: Studien zur Tierpsychologie, Anthropologie und Ethik* (Amsterdam, 1977).

22 Gary Steiner, *Anthropocentrism and its Discontents: The Moral Status of Animals in the History of Western Philosophy* (Pittsburgh, 2005), 76.

23 Steiner's genealogical project is openly polemical; in this case, he is making the argument that Christianity – viewed here in its purest (i.e.

closely, many of the medieval texts that are lumped together as ortho-
doxly Christian reveal moments of inconsistency and ambivalence
similar to those Steiner identifies in Aristotle's theorizing of the
human/animal divide.

In what follows, I examine key passages in the Old English *Boethius*
and *Soliloquies* that attempt to delineate the paradigmatic markers
of human exceptionalism – namely, reason and immortality – by
constructing a differential concept of the nonhuman animal. The first
part of the essay considers the lexicographical strategies the authors
use to translate the Latin word *animal* and its etymon *anima*, neither
of which had precise lexical equivalents in Old English. The second
part demonstrates how the Old English *Boethius* fails to replicate the
Consolatio's distinction between reason and perception upon which
the human/animal distinction is supported. The third part takes up
the question of the afterlife: what happens to nonhuman animals,
and nonhuman life more generally, at the eschaton? The Old English
Soliloquies, I argue, alludes to a tradition that envisions the end of days
differently from the more anthropocentric strain of eschatology traced
by Minnis and Agamben; in this alternative tradition, all creatures
– human and nonhuman – are promised participation in the final
restoration.

medieval) form – does not contain the resources necessary to develop an
ecologically based ethics. On the other side of the debate are modern theologians, such as David L. Clough, who draw on premodern sources in their
critique of the anthropocentrism of Christianity. See, for instance, Clough,
On Animals. Volume 1: Systematic Theology (London, 2012), esp. 149–51. Cary
Wolfe identifies traces in premodernity of what he calls a 'prehumanism' that
thinks 'the human/animal distinction quite otherwise' than the entrenched
speciesism that characterizes post-Enlightenment humanism. See Wolfe,
'Human, All Too Human: "Animal Studies" and the Humanities', *PMLA*
124 (2009), 564–75 (564). On the question of orthodoxy, see for example,
Karl Steel's *How to Make a Human*, which, in my view, overestimates the
ideological coherence of what he calls 'doctrinal Christianity' (30), as in the
following claim: 'Participating in a Western philosophical tradition that [...]
originates with Aristotle, Christian thinkers as diverse as the foundational
Augustine and the ninth-century court scholar John Scottus Eriugena, whose
Periphyseon would repeatedly be condemned as heretical, think much the
same thing on reason, humans, and animals' (31). As this essay will make clear,
there are major differences between Augustine and Eriugena when it comes
to this problematic.

Translating Anima(l)

There were no 'animals' in Old English literature. According to the *OED*, the noun 'animal' does not appear in English until John Trevisa's late fourteenth-century translation of Bartholomeus Anglicus's *De proprietatibus rerum*.[24] It is descended ultimately from Latin *animal*. Augustine and Boethius define an *animal* as the conjunction of a body (*corpus*) and a soul (*anima*).[25] In the philosophical vocabulary of late antiquity, *anima* had a wide range of meanings; in this context it refers to the vital principle that animates all living beings.[26] Augustine mines the link between *anima* and *animal* for a little comedy at the beginning of the *Soliloquia*. After 'Augustine' admits that he loves only two things in the world – God and the soul ('deum et animam') – his interlocutor Reason cheekily asks whether he then loves fleas and bugs, which are *animalia*, that is, creatures with souls.[27] 'Augustine' clarifies his position: he loves rational souls ('rationales animas'), which he and his human friends possess but fleas and bugs do not.[28] When referring specifically to nonhuman animals, though, Augustine and Boethius usually opted for terms that underscored species difference, not the commonality of life implied by *animal*. *Pecus* (herd animal) was commonly used to signify

24   *OED*, s.v. 'animal'. The *MED* provides an earlier example of 'animal' from *Sir Orfeo* (c.1330), but this is actually a misreading of 'aumal' (enamel) that has since been corrected by editors. On the word's English history, see Laurie Shannon, *The Accommodated Animal: Cosmopolity in Shakespearean Locales* (Chicago, 2013), 7–11. See also Sarah Kay, who, drawing on the work of Pierre-Olivier Dittmar, claims 'il n'y a pas d'animal au Moyen Age' (Kay, 'Before the *Animot*: *Bêtise* and the Zoological Machine in Medieval Latin and French Bestiaries', *Yale French Studies* 127 (2015), 34–51 (36)).

25   See, for example, Boethius, *Philosophiae consolatio*, III, pros. 11, ed. Ludwig Bieler, CCSL 94 (Turnhout, 1957), 57, lines 28–9. Augustine, *De civitate Dei*, IX.9, ed. Bernard Dombart and Alfons Kalb, CCSL 47 (Turnhout, 1955), 257, lines 5–6: 'Cum enim animans, id est animal, ex anima constet et corpore' ('For a living creature – that is, an animal – consists of soul and body'). The English translation is from *The City of God against the Pagans*, ed. and trans. R. W. Dyson (Cambridge, 1998), 370.

26   See the classic study by Richard Broxton Onians, *The Origins of European Thought: About the Body, the Mind, the Soul, the World, Time, and Fate* (Cambridge, 1951). See also Gerard O'Daly, *Augustine's Philosophy of Mind* (Berkeley, 1987), 11–14.

27   Augustine, *Soliloquiorum libri duo*, I.2.7, CSEL 89, ed. Wolfgang Hörmann (Vienna, 1986), 11, line 15; 12, lines 14–17.

28   Augustine, *Soliloquiorum libri duo*, I.2.7, ed. Hörmann, 12, lines 18–24.

any domesticated animal, as well as nonhuman animals in general. It was often paired with *bestia* (beast or wild animal). These two terms reflect the respective pre- and postlapsarian use value of animals, a relationship grounded either in subservience or hostility.[29] Old English developed an equivalent of the *pecus–bestia* pairing: *neat* or *nyten*, meaning a herd animal, any kind of domesticated animal, or, most broadly, nonhuman animals in general, and *deor* (deer), which was also used metonymically to refer to wild animals as a separate class.[30] Unlike in Latin, there was no single generic term that encompassed human and nonhuman. When it came to translating the references to *animalia* in the *Consolatio*, the Old English translator sometimes adopted an either/or approach: 'animal' is translated as 'mon' (human) at one point, while shortly thereafter 'animalibus' is rendered 'netenu'.[31] At other times, he employed circumlocution. In the Latin text, after hearing Philosophia define *animal*, the Prisoner agrees that all animals seek to preserve their existence, but he wonders whether inanimate creatures (*inanimata*) are also governed by this tendency.[32] The *animalia–inanimata* opposition becomes in the Old English a contrast between 'cwica wuht' (living things) and 'gesceaftum swylce nane sawle nabbað' ('creatures that have no soul', ch. 34, lines 249–53).[33] The Old English *Soliloquies* translates Augustine's witty line about *animalia* with a similar phrase: 'gyf þu þinne freond forði lufast þe he sawle hæfð, hwi ne lufast þu þonne ælc þing þe sawle hæfð? hwi ne lufast þu mys and flæa?' ('If you love your friend because he has a soul, why then do you not love everything that has a soul? Why don't you love

29   Pierre-Olivier Dittmar, 'Le Seigneur des animaux entre "pecus" et "bestia": Les Animalités paradisiaques des années 1300', in *Adam, le premier homme*, ed. Agostino Paravicini Bagliani, Micrologus' Library 45 (Florence, 2012), 219–54. See also Kay, 'Before the *Animot*', 37; and Clark, 'The Fathers and the Animals', 68.

30   On this nomenclature, see Earl R. Anderson, *Folk-Taxonomies in Early English* (Madison, 2003), 425–9.

31   *The Old English Boethius*, ed. Godden and Irvine, B-text, ch. 34, lines 239, 309. Subsequent references to chapter and line numbers are cited parenthetically.

32   Boethius, *Consolatio*, III, pros. 11, ed. Bieler, 57, lines 45–6.

33   The phrase 'cucra wuhta' is used in *Genesis A* to describe nonhuman animals in opposition to humans ('folc'). *Genesis A*, in *The Junius Manuscript*, ed. George Philip Krapp, The Anglo-Saxon Poetic Records: A Collective Edition 1, (New York, 1931), 41, lines 1296–9a.

mice and fleas?')[34] *Animalia* becomes 'ælc þing þe sawle hæfð', losing the *animal/anima* joke in translation.

Both texts use Old English *sawol* to translate Latin *anima*. The Old English word is more circumscribed in its semantic range than its Latin counterpart, more anthropocentric in its connotations. As Leslie Lockett and others have demonstrated, *sawol* in the corpus of Old English literature primarily refers to the transcendent soul that departs the body at death and participates in the afterlife; it refers, that is, primarily to the human soul.[35] An awareness of the narrower semantic range of *sawol* is apparent in the Rushworth Gospel glosses of Matthew: in cases where *anima* refers to the soul as the principle of life and not as a transcendent, immortal entity, the glossator opts for *feorh* (life-force) instead of *sawol*.[36] The Old English *Phoenix* makes this distinction as well. In the source, Lactantius's *Carmen de ave phoenice*, the phoenix releases its *anima* when overcome by flames, but in the Old English poem, the bird gives up its *lif* and *feorhhord* (life-treasure).[37] The *Phoenix*-author restricts the application of *sawol* to the immortal human soul for which the bird is merely the figure. The bifurcation of *sawol* and *lif* undergirds

34 *Soliloquies*, ed. Carnicelli, 57, lines 18–20. Subsequent references to page and line numbers are cited parenthetically. Translations of the Old English *Soliloquies* are my own, but they have been made in consultation with the translations of Henry Hargrove and Simon Keynes and Michael Lapidge: *King Alfred's Old English Version of St Augustine's 'Soliloquies' Turned into Modern English*, trans. Henry Lee Hargrove, Yale Studies in English 22 (New York, 1904); *Alfred the Great: Asser's 'Life of King Alfred' and other Contemporary Sources*, ed. Simon Keynes and Michael Lapidge (Harmondsworth, 1983), 138–52.

35 Lockett, *Anglo-Saxon Psychologies*, 51; La Farge, '*Leben' und 'Seele'*, 108–9. According to Michael Joseph Phillips, 'even when *sawol* is considered as "the principle of life", the fact that it is the immortal part of man is never lost sight of' (Phillips, 'Heart, Mind, and Soul in Old English: A Semantic Study', PhD diss. (University of Illinois at Urbana-Champaign, 1985), 260).

36 *The Holy Gospels in Anglo-Saxon, Northumbrian, and Old Mercian Versions*, ed. Walter W. Skeat (Cambridge, 1871–87; repr. Darmstadt, 1970), 25–242. See Phillips, 'Heart, Mind, and Soul', 256–60; and Lockett, *Anglo-Saxon Psychologies*, 51–2. On *feorh*, see Lockett, *Anglo-Saxon Psychologies*, 43–53; and La Farge, '*Leben' und 'Seele'*.

37 Lactantius, *Carmen de aue phoenice*, ed. Samuel Brandt, CSEL 27.1 (Vienna, 1893), 141, lines 93–4; *The Phoenix*, in *The Exeter Book*, ed. George Philip Krapp and Elliott Van Kirk Dobbie, The Anglo-Saxon Poetic Records: A Collective Edition 3 (New York 1936), 100, lines 220b–221a. See La Farge, '*Leben' und 'Seele'*, 110–1.

Ælfric's repeated articulations of species difference: humans have *sawla*, nonhumans have *lif*. Indeed, it is quite possible that his insistence on this point was a corrective response to Anglo-Saxon authors who were using *sawol* to translate *anima* in cases where *lif* or *feorh* may have been more in line with conventional usage, including perhaps the translator of the Old English *Boethius*, a text with which Ælfric was familiar.[38] The Old English *Boethius* and *Soliloquies* are more forward looking in their usage: they anticipate the broadening of the semantic range of *sawol* in the later Middle Ages, when it is more commonly used to translate *anima* in the Aristotelian sense of an animating or organizing principle, such as in the case of the vegetative and sensible 'souls' associated with plants and animals respectively.[39] For contemporary readers, though, the claim that mice and fleas possess *sawla* would have unsettled the species-particular connotations of the term.

Between Reason and Perception: Modelling the Soul in the Old English Boethius

The Old English *Boethius* provides two models of the soul, which divide the human from the nonhuman along different lines. The first appears in the reworking of the *Consolatio*'s infamous *metrum* 'O qui perpetua' (III, met. 9).[40] In rendering this linguistically and doctrinally difficult section,

---

38   On the possibility that Ælfric is deliberately responding to the Old English *Boethius*'s use of *sawol*, see Godden, 'Ælfric and the Alfredian Precedents', 151. See also Kurt Otten, *König Alfreds Boethius*, Studien zur englischen Philologie, neue Folge 3 (Tübingen, 1964), 175. A notable nonhuman exception occurs in *Beowulf*: the Danes are said to seek the soul ('sawle') of Grendel (*Klaeber's Beowulf and the Fight at Finnsburg*, ed. R. D. Fulk et al., 4th edn (Toronto, 2008), 29, line 801a). In *Genesis A*, God forbids Noah from eating the soul-blood ('sawldreore') of animals (47, line 1520b). On this prohibition, see Mary Clayton, 'Blood and the Soul in Ælfric', *Notes & Queries* 54 (2007), 365–7.

39   *OED*, s.v. 'soul'. La Farge, '*Leben*' und '*Seele*', 118–21.

40   On the Old English version of the metre, see Whitney F. Bolton, 'How Boethian is Alfred's *Boethius*?', in *Studies in Earlier Old English Prose*, ed. Paul E. Szarmach (Albany, NY, 1986), 153–68; Paul E. Szarmach, 'Alfred, Alcuin, and the Soul', in *Manuscript, Narrative, Lexicon: Essays on Literary and Cultural Transmission in Honor of Whitney F. Bolton*, ed. Robert Boenig and Kathleen Davis (Lewisburg, PA, 2000), 127–48; and Peter Dronke, *The Spell of Calcidius: Platonic Concepts and Images in the Medieval West* (Florence, 2008), 56–67.

the Old English *Boethius* replaces the Platonic concept of the world-soul
with the human soul:

> For þi ic cwæð þæt sio sawul wære þriofeald forþam þe uðwitan secgað
> þæt hio hæbbe þrio gecynd. An ðara gecynda is þæt heo bið wilnigende,
> oðer þæt hio bið irsiende, þridde þæt hio bið gesceadwis. Twa þara
> gecyndu habbað netenu swa same swa men; oðer þara is willnung, oðer
> is irsung. Ac se mon ana hæfð gesceadwisnesse, nalles nan oðru gesceaft;
> forði he hæfð oferþungen ealle þa eorðlican gesceafta mid geðeahte and
> mid andgite.

(ch. 33, lines 217–23)

> (I said that the soul was threefold because philosophers say that it has
> three natures. One of those natures is concupiscible, the second irascible,
> the third rational. Animals have two of these natures, like men: one of
> those is concupiscence, the other is anger. But man alone has reason, not
> the other creatures, and so he has surpassed all the earthly creatures with
> thought and understanding.)

The ultimate source of the threefold model of the soul is Plato.[41] Among
the various *uðwitan* who transmitted the doctrine to the Middle Ages,
the author of the Old English *Boethius* was likely counting Alcuin,
whose treatise *De ratione animae* contains a similar passage:

> Triplex est enim animae, ut philosophi volunt, natura: est in ea quaedam
> pars concupiscibilis, alia rationalis, tertia irascibilis. Duas enim habent
> harum partes nobiscum bestiae et animalia communes, id est, concupis-
> centiam, et iram. Homo solus inter mortales ratione viget, consilio valet,
> intelligentia antecellit.[42]

41   See, for instance, Plato, *The Republic*, IV, 436a–444e, ed. G. R. F. Ferrari,
trans. Tom Griffith (Cambridge, 2000), 131–43. Although Plato identifies the
rational part of the soul with the human, it does not necessarily follow that
nonhuman animals lack rationality. His theory of the transmigration of the soul
presupposes that the rational part of the soul – which, unlike the lower parts,
survives death and thus preserves identity – can be reborn into nonhuman
animals. On Plato's equivocation regarding animals and reason, see Steiner,
Anthropocentrism and its Discontents, 55–7; and Sorabji, *Animal Minds and
Human Morals*, 9–12.
42   Alcuin, *De ratione animae*, PL 101:639–40. Translations are modified
from J. J. M. Curry, 'Alcuin, *De ratione animae*: A Text with Introduction,

(The nature of the soul is threefold, as the philosophers maintain: there is one part that is concupiscible, another that is rational, and a third that is irascible. Beasts and animals have two of these three parts in common with us, namely the concupiscent and the irascible. Among mortal creatures, man alone lives through reason, thrives in deliberation, and excels in intelligence.)

Note how Alcuin uses *animalia* as a synonym for *bestiae*, thus eliding the connection to *anima* as the vital principle shared by human and nonhuman alike.[43] Alcuin gestures toward this etymological link when he lists the various names by which the soul is known: the first is *anima*, because the soul gives life ('vivificat').[44]

Alcuin's ultimate definition of the soul, however, is rooted not in the vivifying function common to all living organisms, but in a form of life available only to rational (i.e. human and angelic) beings:

> Quid sit anima, nil melius occurrit dicere quam spiritus vitae; sed non ejus vitae quae in pecoribus est, sine rationali mente: sed vita nunc minor, quam angelorum, et futura quidem angelorum, si ex praecepto sui Creatoris hic vixerit.[45]

(I can think of no better way to describe the soul than as the spirit of life; not of that life which beasts have, without rational thought, but a life which, now lesser than the angels', will be the same as theirs, if it has lived its life here according to the command of its Maker.)

Critical Apparatus, and Translation', PhD diss. (Cornell University, 1966). Curry identifies parallels with Isidore's *De differentiis rerum* and Cassian's *Collationes* (7). On Alcuin's influence on the Old English *Boethius*, see Godden, 'Anglo-Saxons on the Mind', 274. As Godden observes, the Old English translator may have drawn on the commentary tradition instead of, or in addition to, *De ratione animae*. For the parallels with the commentary tradition, see Szarmach, 'Alfred, Alcuin, and the Soul', 135–9; and *The Old English Boethius*, ed. Godden and Irvine, 2:384–6. On the influence of *De ratione animae* more broadly, see Lockett, *Anglo-Saxon Psychologies*, 283–98.

43 The use of Latin *animal* to signify 'nonhuman animal' in contradistinction to humans was not uncommon in the Middle Ages: Steel, *How to Make a Human*, 20 n. 69.

44 Alcuin, *De ratione animae*, PL 101:644.

45 Ibid., 645.

The meaning of *anima* has narrowed considerably. As Godden puts it, 'after the initial obeisance to Plato, Alcuin takes the soul as more or less identical with the conscious, rational mind'.[46] Godden goes on to point out how the Old English *Boethius* sometimes follows Alcuin in conflating soul and mind, as on occasions when the translator uses *sawol* to translate *mens* (mind).[47] In this case, though, rationality is simply one component, albeit the most privileged one, in a model of the soul that shares the other capacities with nonhuman animals.

The picture of reason as the unique preserve of the human becomes more complicated when we turn to the second model of the soul. In *Consolatio* V, pros. 5, Philosophia attempts to demonstrate that everything is known according to the nature of the knower. She does so by adducing the various types of cognition:

> Sensus enim solus cunctis aliis cognitionibus destitutus immobilibus animantibus cessit, quales sunt conchae maris quaeque alia saxis haerentia nutriuntur; imaginatio uero mobilibus beluis, quibus iam inesse fugiendi appetendiue aliquis uidetur affectus; ratio uero humani tantum generis est sicut intellegentia sola diuini.[48]

> (For sense and sense alone, deprived of all other modes of cognition, has been allotted to animate creatures without self-motion (to the shellfish of the sea, for example, and to other such things as cling to rocks); while imagination is allotted to beasts with self-motion, who seem to have within them already some desire for what must be avoided and what must be chosen. But reason is the property of the human race only, just as understanding alone is the property of the divine.)

There is some overlap here with the Platonic tripartite model: humans share desire, but not reason, with (mobile) animals.[49] Unlike the Platonic

46   Godden, 'Anglo-Saxons on the Mind', 272.
47   Ibid., 275–7; Otten, *König Alfreds Boethius*, 173; Lockett, *Anglo-Saxon Psychologies*, 317–25.
48   Boethius, *Consolatio*, V, pros. 5, ed. Bieler, 99, lines 11–17. The English translation is modified from *Consolation of Philosophy*, trans. Joel C. Relihan (Indianapolis, 2001), 142.
49   The account of the Platonic model of the soul in the prosimetric version of the Old English *Boethius* reveals evidence of an attempt to synthesize the two models; it claims that concupiscence and irascibility are found in 'unrim wuhta' ('a countless number of creatures') and 'welhwilc neten' ('nearly every animal'),

model, though, Philosophia's hierarchy of cognition is based on a recognition, albeit a limited one, that different species of nonhuman animals have different capabilities, that there is, in other words, no such thing as *the* animal.[50] Non-moving animals are restricted to sensation (*sensus*), while moving animals also possess imagination (*imaginatio*), the ability to form mental images from traces of sensation.[51] The distinction between the respective capabilities of moving and non-moving animals is Aristotelian. In his account of the faculties of the soul, which he explicitly frames as a corrective to Plato's tripartite model, Aristotle posits a close link between imagination and locomotion. In order to move toward (or away from) a specific end, the creature must view that end as desirable (or undesirable). The faculty of the imagination in nonhuman animals fulfils this propositional function.[52] Aristotle's account of perception is complicated and difficult to parse, but, as Richard Sorabji demonstrates, it provides an opening to explain how nonhuman animals can seemingly act in calculative, deliberate ways without attributing to them the faculty of reason.[53] Perception and the related faculty of imagination pick up the slack. As Boethius would later do, Augustine took advantage of the expanded domain of perception

with the proleptic implication that the exceptions are immobile animals (ch. 20, lines 190–1).

50   On the 'asininity' of the designation 'the animal', with its corralling definite article, see Jacques Derrida, *The Animal that Therefore I Am*, ed. Marie-Louise Mallet, trans. David Wills (New York, 2008).

51   See Gerard O'Daly, 'Sense-Perception and Imagination in Boethius, *Philosophiae Consolatio* 5 m. 4', repr. in *Platonism Pagan and Christian: Studies in Plotinus and Augustine* (Aldershot, 2001), 327–40; John Marenbon, *Boethius* (Oxford, 2003), 130–5. Boethius offers a slightly different account of imagination in animals in his commentary on Porphyry's *Isagoge* (*In Isagogen Porphyrii commenta, editio secunda*, 1.1, ed. Samuel Brandt, CSEL 48 (Vienna, 1906), 136–7).

52   Aristotle, *De anima*, III.10, 433a9–433b30, trans. J. A. Smith, in *The Complete Works of Aristotle: The Revised Oxford Translation*, ed. Jonathan Barnes (Oxford, 1984), 689. Steiner, *Anthropocentrism and its Discontents*, 66. Aristotle distinguishes between the sensitive and the calculative imagination, the latter being particular to humans (433b). Despite repeated assertions that perception necessarily entails desire and imagination, Aristotle is unclear about whether all animals possess imagination (413b20–3; cf. 428a8; 433b). On this point see, Michael V. Wedin, *Mind and Imagination in Aristotle* (New Haven, 1988), 41–2.

53   Sorabji, *Animal Minds and Human Morals*, esp. 17–20. See also Steiner, *Anthropocentrism and its Discontents*, 64–6.

in order to preserve the human/animal divide. He did not deny that animals sometimes act in ways that seem to imply a kind of knowledge; as Gerard O'Daly puts it, animals, according to Augustine, 'are capable of building up a stock of empirical experience which will influence their instinctive behaviour: they can remember, recognize, anticipate'.[54] But Augustine maintained that these cognitive capacities represent only a 'semblance of knowledge' and can be better understood as evidence of the often-impressive perceptual powers exercised by animals.[55]

The Old English *Boethius* translates the hierarchy of cognition as follows:

> He hine ongit þurh þa eagan, synderlice þurh þa earan, synderlice þurh his rædelsan, synderlice þurh gesceadwisnesse, synderlice þurh gewis andgit. Monige sint cucere gesceafta unstyriende, swa swa nu scylfiscas sint, and habbað þeah sumne dæl andgites, forþam hi ne mihton elles libbon gif hi nan grot andgites næfdon. Sume magon gesion, sume magon gehyron, sume gefredon, sume gestincan. Ac styriendan netenu sint monnum gelicran forþam hy habbað eall þæt þa unstyriendan habbað and eac mare to, þæt is þæt hio hyrigað monnum, lufiað þæt hi lufiað and hatiað þæt hi hatiað, and flyð þæt hi hatiað, and secað þæt hi lufiað. Þa men þonne habbað eall þæt we ær ymb spræcon and eac toeacan þam micle gife gesceadwisnesse. Englas þonne habbað gewiss andgit.

> (ch. 41, lines 128–40)

(He perceives him through the eyes, in a different way through the ears, in another way through his imagination, in another way through reason, in another way through perfect understanding. Many living creatures are motionless, as shellfish are, and yet have some portion of perception, for they could not otherwise live if they did not have a speck of perception. Some can see, some can hear, some can feel, some can smell. But moving animals are more like men because they have all that the motionless creatures have and also more as well, that is, that they resemble men, loving what they love and hating what they hate, and they flee what they

---

54   O'Daly, *Augustine's Philosophy of Mind*, 98. For instance, Augustine argues from personal experience that fish have memories: *De Genesi ad litteram*, III.8.12, ed. Joseph Zycha, CSEL 28.1 (Vienna, 1894), 71.

55   Augustine, *De civitate Dei*, XI.27, ed. Dombart and Kalb, 347, lines 42–59. See also Augustine, *De Trinitate*, XII.2, ed. W. J. Mountain and F. Glorie, CCSL 50 (Turnhout, 1968; repr. 2001), 356–7.

hate and seek what they love. Then men have all that we have mentioned before and also in addition to that the great gift of reason. Then angels have perfect understanding.)

The first sentence indicates that the Old English version will not map neatly onto the conceptual vocabulary of the Latin; the symmetry of Philosophia's fourfold categorization of *sensus–imaginatio–ratio–intellegentia* is scuttled by the inclusion of two representatives of sensation, seeing and hearing. The invocation of specific sense modalities suggests an awareness on the part of the translator of the difficulty of lexicalizing perception as an abstract concept in Old English.[56] The *Boethius*-author uses Old English *andgit* to translate Latin *sensus*, but *andgit* meant 'understanding' as well as 'perception'.[57] In the preceding forty chapters of Old English *Boethius*, whenever *andgit* has appeared – nine times – Irvine and Godden have translated the word as 'understanding' or (in one case) 'insight'.[58]

In fact, *andgit* has twice referred to the understanding as a faculty that distinguishes humans from nonhuman animals:

> Hwæt, ge þonne þeah hwæthwega godcundlices on eowerre saule habbað, þæt is andgit and gemynd and se gesceadwislica willa þæt hine þara twega lyste.

(ch. 14, lines 76–8)

> (Indeed, you men have something godlike in your soul, that is understanding and memory and the rational will that takes pleasure in those two things.)

> Ac se mon ana hæfð gesceadwisnesse, nalles nan oðru gesceaft; forði he hæfð oferþungen ealle þa eorðlican gesceafta mid geðeahte and mid angite.

(ch. 33, lines 221–3)

---

56   Otten, *König Alfreds Boethius*, 177–8.
57   *Dictionary of Old English*, s.v. 'andgyt'. See Phillips, 'Heart, Mind, and Soul', 55–7; and Soon Ai Low, 'The Anglo-Saxon Mind: Metaphor and Common Sense Psychology in Old English Literature', PhD diss. (University of Toronto, 1998), 13–15.
58   Old English *Boethius*, ch. 13, line 4 (*ondgit*); ch. 14, line 77; ch. 18, line 105; ch. 26, line 7; ch. 26, line 8 (*angite*); ch. 33, line 223; ch. 34, line 344 ('insight'); ch. 39, line 97 (*andget*); ch. 39, line 100 (*godcund andgit*).

(But man alone has reason, not the other creatures, and so he has surpassed all the earthly creatures with thought and understanding.)

Given this established usage, the choice of *andgit* to render *sensus* might obscure, if only temporarily, the very distinction the text is attempting to reproduce. As Kurt Otten points out, the translator does seem aware of this potential for confusion, as he immediately lists the various sense modalities as a way to delimit the intended meaning of *andgit*.[59] This clarification is shortly followed, though, by the claim that angels have 'gewiss andgit' (*intellegentia* in the *Consolatio*). Even though 'understanding' is intended here, the framing of the hierarchy – the lowest creatures have some degree of *andgit*, the highest creatures have perfect *andgit* – gives the impression of a continuum structuring the taxonomy rather than, as in the Latin, strata of discrete classifications.

The treatment of moving animals also deserves comment. The Old English translator omits the reference to *imaginatio*, which he earlier translated as *rædelse*, while preserving the claim that mobile animals move toward what they desire and flee from what they hate. He likely had trouble – as modern commentators do – unpacking the *Consolatio*'s account of the mechanics of perception. As a consequence of this omission, the seeking and avoiding behaviour of moving animals is no longer understood through the Aristotelian paradigm of perception, and thus the link between moving and non-moving animals is severed. The *Boethius*-author observes twice that moving animals resemble humans ('sint monnum gelicran') in their seeking and avoiding tendencies. These additions, along with the dropping away of imagination and the consequent decoupling of moving and non-moving animals, leave us with a taxonomy more aligned with modern biological thought, in which certain nonhuman animals (e.g. primates) are considered to be closer to humans than they are to other nonhuman animals (e.g. molluscs).

The distinction between perception and understanding is further blurred when the *Boethius*-author attempts to recapitulate the hierarchy:

> Forþi is hiora gearowito swa micle betra þonne ure gesceadwisnes se, swa ure gesceadwisnes is betere þone nytena andgit sie, oððe þæs gewittes ænig dæl þe him forgifen is, auþer oððe hrorum neatum oððe unrorum.
>
> (ch. 41, lines 152–5)

---

59   Otten, *König Alfreds Boethius*, 178.

(So their [the angels'] full understanding is as much better than our reason is, as our reason is better than the perception of animals is, or than any portion of intelligence that is granted to them, whether to moving animals or to unmoving ones.)

The passage interjects an ambiguous third term – 'þæs gewittes ænig dæl þe him forgifen is' – between the polarities of reason and perception, human and beast. The Bosworth–Toller *Anglo-Saxon Dictionary* defines *gewit* as 'perception', as well as the 'faculty of knowing', and, for the latter sense, subdivides the illustrative quotations into two categories that replicate the language of medieval taxonomies – 'rational beings' and 'animals'; the passage quoted above is the only representative of the second category.[60] Indeed, the application of *gewit* to nonhuman animals is rather anomalous. For Ælfric, as well as the Anglo-Saxon poets, the word is 'distinctive of the human species'.[61] The Old English *Boethius* largely follows this usage. Like *andgit*, *gewit* is repeatedly used within the text to denote a particularly human endowment. In the Circe episode, Ulysses's thegns are turned into an assortment of beasts and lose all likeness to human beings except for their *gewit* (ch. 38, lines 38–9). Earlier in the Old English *Boethius* nonhuman animals are described as 'ungewittigan gesceafta' ('irrational creatures', ch. 36, line 129; ch. 36, line 139). Now, the *Boethius*-author admits that animals do possess some manner of *gewit*. This phrase could be an attempt to reconstitute Philosophia's excised claim that some animals do more than simply sense – that is, they imagine – but the Old English translator goes on to elide the distinction between moving and nonmoving animals upon which Philosophia's categorization was based. In his view, the *gewit* granted to nonhuman animals may differ in kind from the *gewit* possessed by humans, but, if so, his terminology is unable to register the difference; on the contrary, the language of portioning once again implies a distinction of degree in which animals share a portion of a faculty that is elsewhere associated with the human.

60   *An Anglo-Saxon Dictionary*, ed. Joseph Bosworth and T. Northcote Toller (Oxford, 1898); *Supplement*, ed. T. Northcote Toller (Oxford, 1921), s.v. 'ge-wit'. The dictionary is available online at http://www.bosworthtoller.com. See also Antonina Harbus, *The Life of the Mind in Old English Poetry* (Amsterdam, 2002), 45.
61   Hans-Jürgen Diller, '"Emotion" in Old English – a Lexical Gap?', in *Metamorphosen: Englische Literatur und die Tradition*, ed. Hugo Keiper, Maria Löschnigg, and Doris Mader (Heidelberg, 2006), 17–32 (25).

The Old English *Boethius* reiterates throughout that reason and understanding are the sole prerogative of humans. Lady Philosophia's hierarchy forces the translator to test this axiom against a finer-grained model of cognition. He struggles to articulate the difference between human and nonhuman cognition. Part of the problem is the limited philosophical vocabulary of Old English; it is easier in Latin to lexicalize reason and perception as two distinct faculties. But the Old English *Boethius*-author is not simply translating; he is concerned with more than just adequacy, with replacing a given Latin word with its closest Old English equivalent.[62] He is thinking through the philosophical problems alongside Boethius, modifying at times the original premises and conclusions. The impreciseness of his third term – 'þæs gewittes ænig dæl' – reflects an uncertainty about where to draw the line between perception and reason, human and animal, that cannot entirely be written off as the result of an impoverished lexicon.

The Old English Soliloquies and the Preservation and Restoration of Creation

At the outset of the Old English *Soliloquies*, Agustinus (the translator's rendering of 'Augustinus') states his desire to know two things: God and the nature of his own soul. With the help of his interlocutor, Gesceadwisnes (Reason), he soon establishes the rationality of the human soul. The other exceptional property of the human soul – immortality – remains more elusive. Although Agustinus acknowledges the immortality of the human soul in his opening prayer, he is subsequently beset by uncertainty and forgetfulness, and he enjoins Gesceadwisnes to convince him beyond doubt. In the Latin *Soliloquia*, Reason demonstrates the soul's immortality through a series of arguments grounded in dialectic and Platonic metaphysics. As various scholars have pointed out, the Old English translator takes a different tack, replacing Augustine's scaffolded logical argument with his own proofs. Offering a provisional assessment of the alterations, Milton McC. Gatch writes: 'the Old English substitutes an argument from authority for the Augustinian

---

62 On the translation strategies of the Old English *Boethius*, and the issue of adequacy in particular, see Nicole Guenther Discenza, *The King's English: Strategies of Translation in the Old English 'Boethius'* (Albany, NY, 2005).

logical and metaphysical demonstration of the immortality of the soul.'[63] This is largely true, but there is an important exception. Gesceadwisnes's clinching demonstration, the one that convinces Agustinus above all others (90, line 15), takes the form of a 'logical and metaphysical demonstration':

> Ic wundrige hwi ðu efre þæs wenan mahte be manna sawlum þaet hy næran æca, forðam ðu genoh geare wistes þæt hyt is seo ealra hehsta and seo seleste godes gesceafta; and ðu wast æac genoh geare þæt he nane gesceafta ne forlet eallunga gewitan swa þæt hy to nawuihte weorðe, ne furðum þa ealra unweorðlicostan; ac he gewlitegað and gegerað æalle gesceafta, and æft ungewliteað and ungerað, and æft edniowað. Swa wrixliað ealle genu þæt hy farað, and instepe æft cumað, and weorðað eft to ðam ylcan wlite and to þære ylcan winsumnesse manna bearnum, þe wæron ærþamðe Adam gesingode. Nu ðu miht geheran þæt nan gesceaft swa clene on wæg ne gewit þæt hi æft ne cume, ne swa clæne ne forwyrð þæt hi to hwanhwugu ne weorðe. Ac hwi wænst þu þonne, nu þa wacestan gesceafta eallunga ne gewitað, þæt seo selest gescaft myd ealle gewite?

> (90, lines 1–12)

(I wonder why you could ever believe that men's souls were not eternal, for you clearly knew that the human soul is the highest of all and the best of God's creatures; and you also clearly know that he does not allow any creature to pass away entirely so that it comes to naught, not even the most unworthy of all; but he forms and adorns all creatures, and again unforms and unadorns them, and again renews them, so they all change again that they go away, and suddenly come again, and return to the same form and to the same beauty for the children of men, in which they were before Adam sinned. Now you can grant that no creature so fully passes away that it does not come again, nor so entirely perishes that it does not become anything. But why then do you suppose, now that the weakest creatures cannot entirely pass away, that the best creature should similarly depart?)

Gesceadwisnes's argument for the immortality of the soul appeals to a doctrine that is less axiomatic than the premise it is meant to verify – the

---

63   Milton McC. Gatch, 'King Alfred's Version of Augustine's *Soliloquia*: Some suggestions on its Rationale and Unity', in *Studies in Earlier Old English Prose*, 17–45 (34). See also Malcolm Godden, 'Text and Eschatology in Book III of the Old English *Soliloquies*', *Anglia* 121 (2003), 177–209.

belief that God preserves all creatures from destruction and will in the future return them to their paradisal forms. The claim is enigmatic: what is the nature of this preservation and restoration? How does the *reditus* of all creatures differ from the resurrection of human bodies that will occur at Judgement Day? In this section, I unpack the metaphysical premises condensed in Gesceadwisnes's argument and locate them within a wider medieval eschatological tradition.

Thomas A. Carnicelli, the most recent editor of the Old English *Soliloquies*, points out that the Old English translator could have found the doctrine of preservation elsewhere in the Latin *Soliloquia* or in the *Consolatio*.[64] In the opening prayer of the *Soliloquia*, 'Augustine' praises God, 'qui ne id quidem quod se inuicem perimit, perire permittis' ('who does not allow to perish even that which is mutually destructive', 1.2.8–9). The Old English version reads: 'þu hy hæfst æalle gesceapene gebyrdlice and gesome, and to þam geþwære þæt heora nan ne mæg oðerne mid ælle fordon' ('You have shaped them all orderly and peaceably, and in such a way that none of them may entirely destroy another', 50, lines 20–2). That God has ordered the universe so as to preserve his creatures from perishing is a recurrent theme in Augustine's account of providence. In *City of God*, Augustine writes that all humans, including robbers and murderers, are sustained by a natural principle of order that he calls *pax*. Even savage animals (*saeuissimae ferae*) seek to live their lives according to the laws of *pax*.[65] These laws continue to obtain after the creature dies:

> Etsi mortuorum carnes ab aliis animalibus deuorentur, easdem leges per cuncta diffusas ad salutem generis cuiusque mortalium congrua congruis pacificantes, quaqua uersum trahantur et rebus quibuscumque iungantur et in res quaslibet conuertantur et commutentur, inueniunt.[66]

> (Even when the flesh of dead animals is devoured by other animals, it still finds itself subject to the same laws: to the laws which are distributed

---

64   *Soliloquies*, ed. Carnicelli, 99, 104. The entry in *Fontes Anglo-Saxonici* cites the presence of loose parallels with *City of God*, and occasional parallels with the *Consolatio*, the latter of which 'may show use of Boethius as a source, in the original Latin or the Old English version, or the effect of the same Old English author rewriting Latin texts in similar ways'. Malcolm R. Godden, 'The Sources of Augustine, *Soliloquies*', *Fontes Anglo-Saxonici*, 2001.

65   Augustine, *De civitate Dei*, XIX.12, ed. Dombart and Kalb, 677, line 71.

66   Ibid., 678, lines 126–30, trans. Dyson, 937.

throughout the universe for the preservation of every kind of mortal creature, and which give peace by bringing suitable things suitably together. This is true no matter where it is taken, no matter with what substances it is joined, and no matter what substances it is converted and changed into.)

The postmortem perdurance of substance is an important principle for Augustine's theory of resurrection, which, among other logistical difficulties, must explain how a human body that has been consumed by wild animals can be resurrected.[67] I will have more to say about Augustine's theory of resurrection shortly. Boethius's account of providence similarly emphasizes the preservative function of God's ordering of the universe, though at times he attributes the harmonizing and bridling of conflict to the intermediary agencies of *amor* and *natura*. Without *amor*'s conciliatory intervention, creatures would be locked in a cycle of perpetual enmity and destruction; later in the *Consolatio*, it is *natura* that is described as the binding force that prevents animals from reverting to a primordial condition of strife and antagonism.[68] *Natura* works diligently to keep creatures from destruction, on the level of both the individual and, through the propagation of offspring, the species.[69] While it is likely, as we will see, that the *Soliloquies*-author was influenced by the *Consolatio*'s account of providence, there is a more exact parallel to Gesceadwisnes's argument in a less obvious source.

In his masterwork, the *Periphyseon* (c.867), a dialogue between a master and his disciple, John Scottus Eriugena expounds his theory of primordial causes, a variation on the Platonic doctrine of the forms. When a body perishes, the theory holds, it dissolves into the elements and, from there, returns to the primordial causes from which it originated.[70] By passing into the primordial causes, a creature passes out of time. Or, as the Master succinctly puts it, death is 'the death of

---

67   See, for instance, Augustine, *De civitate Dei*, XXII.20, ed. Dombart and Kalb, 839–40. On the logistics of resurrection in Augustine and other premodern theologians, see Carolyn Walker Bynum, *The Resurrection of the Body in Western Christianity, 200–1336* (New York, 1995).

68   Boethius, *Consolatio*, II, met. 8, ed. Bieler, 36; III, met. 2, ed. Bieler, 40. On the representation of nature in *Consolatio*, see Gerard O'Daly, *The Poetry of Boethius* (Chapel Hill, NC, 1991), 104–77.

69   Boethius, *Consolatio*, III, pros. 11, ed. Bieler, 58, lines 53–64.

70   John Scottus Eriugena, *Periphyseon*, III, ed. Édouard A. Jeauneau, 5 vols, CCCM 161–5 (Turnhout, 1996–2003), 3:110, lines 3196–209 (696B). Translations

death' ('mors mortis').[71] Thus, no nature can destroy another nature.[72] The imperishability of substantial beings is one of the premises that underpins Eriugena's remarkable argument that the souls of nonhuman animals do not perish with their bodies.[73] The Master takes issue with the Fathers, who, he argues, got it wrong when they claimed, as Ælfric will later, that animal souls are reducible to their bodies. He repurposes the same evidence that patristic texts used to assert the superiority of humans – the 'natural powers' ('naturales uirtutes') exercised by nonhuman animals, such as the memory of Ulysses's dog, the chastity of widowed griffins, the piety of storks – in order to argue that animal souls are immaterial.[74] But he also invokes the imperishability of animal bodies to argue for the perdurance of animal souls:

> Et si omnium animalium corpora, quando soluuntur, non ad nihilum rediguntur, sed in elementorum qualitates, quarum concursu materialiter facta sunt, redire naturalis ratio perspicue perhibet, quomodo eorum animae, cum profecto sint melioris naturae – qualiscunque enim anima sit, meliorem esse omni corpore nemo sapientum denegat – omnino perire possunt, dum rationi non conueniat quod deterius est manere et saluari, quod uero melius corrumpi et perire [...].[75]

> (And if the bodies of all animals, when they are dissolved, are not reduced to nothing but, as the natural reason clearly allows, return to the elemental qualities by the concourse of which they were materially made, how can their souls perish entirely, seeing that they are certainly of a superior nature – for none of the wise deny that any soul is superior to every body –, when it is not consistent with reason that what is inferior

are from *Periphyseon*, trans. I. P. Sheldon-Williams, rev. John J. O'Meara (Montreal, 1987).

71 Eriugena, *Periphyseon*, V, ed. Jeauneau, 5:23, line 669 (875C).

72 Ibid., 135, lines 4356–7 (956C).

73 On the place of animals in Eriugena's metaphysics, see Peter Dronke, 'La creazione degli animali', repr. in *Intellectuals and Poets in Medieval Europe*, Storia e Letteratura 183 (Rome, 1992), 193–217 (199–202); and Peter Dronke, *Imagination in the Late Pagan and Early Christian World: The First Nine Centuries A.D.* (Florence, 2003), 182–4.

74 Eriugena, *Periphyseon*, III, ed. Jeauneau, 3:171, line 5050 (738D). See Dronke, 'La creazione degli animali', 199.

75 Eriugena, *Periphyseon*, III, ed. Jeauneau, 3:170, lines 5013–21 (738A–738B); trans. Sheldon-Williams, 375.

should remain and be preserved while what is superior is destroyed and perishes?)

The logic here closely resembles Gesceadwisness's demonstration of the immortality of the human soul: if no creature is ever entirely destroyed, not even bodies, surely the soul, which is superior to every body, will perdure as well. Although there remains little evidence to support the traditional legend that King Alfred invited Eriugena to England, or even that Eriugena's works were known to the Anglo-Saxons, other parallels between the *Periphyseon* and the Old English *Boethius* and *Soliloquies* have been adduced in recent years.[76] Noting 'unusual' affinities, Peter Dronke has called for a reconsideration of Eriugena's possible influence on the Alfredian corpus.[77] Such a task exceeds the scope of this essay. My intention here is to propose for consideration another parallel with the thinker whose work emphasizes, to a degree unprecedented in medieval philosophy, what Dronke calls 'the connaturality between human and animal.'[78]

According to Gesceadwisness, creaturely life is preserved through a process of regeneration and renewal, through a dialectic of forming, unforming, and renewing. Here too we find echoes in the Old English *Boethius*, particularly in the following account of divine providence.

> Godcunda foreþonc [...] styreð þone rodor and þa tunglu and þa eorþan gedeð stille and gemetgað þa feower gesceafta, þæt is wæter and eorðe and fyr and lyft. Þa he geþwærað and gewlitegað, hwilum eft unwlitegað and on oðrum hiwe gebrengð, and eft geedniwað and tydreð ælc tudor, and hi eft gehyt and gehelt þonne hit forealdod bið and forsearod, and eft geeowð and geedniwað þonne þonne he wile.
>
> (ch. 39, lines 198–204)

76   Michael Treschow, 'Echoes of the *Periphyseon* in the Third Book of Alfred's *Soliloquies*', *Notes & Queries* 238 (1993), 281–6; Dronke, *Spell of Calcidius*, 65–9; Jean Ritzke-Rutherford, 'Anglo-Saxon Antecedents of the Middle English Mystics', in *The Medieval Mystical Tradition in England: Papers Read at the Exeter Symposium, July 1980*, ed. Marion Glasscoe (Exeter, 1980), 216–33. Compare Gatch: 'Although there was undoubtedly some literary contact between the Carolingian scholars and the court of Alfred, both directly and via Welsh churches, there are no strong arguments to suggest that Alfred and his advisers knew the work of Eriugena in dialectics or metaphysics or that they knew the colleagues of John Scotus' (Gatch, 'King Alfred's Version of the *Soliloquia*', 19–20).

77   Dronke, *Spell of Calcidius*, 68.

78   Dronke, 'La creazione degli animali', 201–2.

(Divine providence [...] moves the firmament and the stars and keeps the earth still and governs the four elements, that is water and earth and fire and air. He harmonizes and forms them, sometimes unforms them again and brings them forth in a different form, and again renews and fosters every new growth and hides them again and preserves them when they are old and withered, and shows them again and renews them when he wishes.)

This passage departs from the Latin *Consolatio* by ascribing the movement of the heavenly bodies and the governing of the elements to divine providence, instead of to the sequence of Fate ('fati series').[79] In limiting the scope and heuristic value of the concept of fate (Old English *wyrd*), Old English *Boethius* comes closer to the position of Augustine, who viewed *fatum* as an unnecessary, distinctly pagan mediation.[80] For Augustine, God is directly responsible for nurturing the development of even the tiniest of creatures.[81] Up to a point, at least. Although Augustine claims that the earth will be transformed, not destroyed, at the Day of Judgement, he gives no indication that any life-form other than humans will survive the conflagration that ushers in the 'new heaven' and 'new earth'.[82] In the words of Andrea Nightingale: 'There are no plants or animals in the City of God. The resurrected saints are the only remaining earthly species.'[83] Augustine eschewed figuring the resurrection with images of organic growth and fecundity in order to emphasize the difference between natural processes of change and the final transformation that will endow the human body with its incorruptible spiritual body; such is the chasm between the evergreen tree's simulacrum of eternity and the true immortality granted to the inhabitants of the City of God.[84] The *Consolatio* does not specify what will happen to nonhuman creatures at the end of days, but the Old English version makes an oblique reference:

79   Boethius, *Consolatio*, IV, pros. 6, ed. Bieler, 80, lines 69–72.
80   Augustine, *De civitate Dei*, V.1, ed. Dombart and Kalb, 128–9. Much has been written about *wyrd* in Old English *Boethius*. For an overview, see Jerold C. Frakes, *The Fate of Fortune in the Early Middle Ages: The Boethian Tradition* (Leiden, 1988), 83–100.
81   Augustine, *De civitate Dei*, V.11, ed. Dombart and Kalb, 142, lines 18–25.
82   Augustine, *De civitate Dei*, XX.16–18, ed. Dombart and Kalb, 726–30.
83   Andrea Nightingale, *Once Out of Nature: Augustine on Time and the Body* (Chicago, 2011), 49–50.
84   Augustine, *De civitate Dei*, XXII.1, ed. Dombart and Kalb, 806, lines 6–12. See Bynum, *Resurrection of the Body*, 94–104.

Ealla gesceafta he hæfde getiohhod þeowe buton englum and monnum. Forþi ða oðre gesceafta þeowe sint, hi habbað hiora þenunga oð domes dæg.

(ch. 41, lines 74-6)

(He had intended all creatures to be servants except angels and men. Because the other creatures are servants, they have their service until doomsday.)

Having fulfilled their service, will nonhuman, nonangelic creatures necessarily be reduced to nought?

A more expansive, if not entirely clear, account of who – or what – will arise on Judgement Day is added to the Old English *Soliloquies*. In his opening prayer, Agustinus praises God for preserving the various species on earth through the generation of offspring in the way that a withered tree is replaced by a fresh, green one. Such manner of change, he explains, extends to all beasts and birds ('nytenu and fugelas', 53, line 22). From trees and beasts, Agustinus moves to humans and the special manner of preservation-through-change that occurs at Judgement Day:

Ge furþum manna lichaman forealdiað, swa swa oðre gescæaftas ealdiat. Ac swa swa hy ær wurðlicor lybbað þonne treowu oðþe oðre nytenu, swa hy eac weorðfulicor arisað on domes dæge, swa þæt nefre syððam þa lichaman ne geendiað ne ne forealdiað; and þeah se lichaman er were gemolsnod, þeah wæs seo sawl simle lybbende siððam heo ærest gesceapen wes.

(53, lines 22-7)

(So too human bodies grow old, just as other creatures do. But just as they live more worthily than trees or other animals, so too they will arise more worthily on Judgment Day, so that never afterward shall their bodies decay nor grow old. And even though the body had decayed before then, yet the soul was always alive since it was first created.)

As Gatch observes, Agustinus appears to be making the Augustinian point that humans differ from trees and animals in so far as they will undergo a different manner of change on the last day.[85] They will arise 'more worthily' ('weorðfulicor'). The *-lic* element in *weorðfulicor*

---

85 Gatch, 'King Alfred's Version of the *Soliloquia*', 28.

makes it well suited to pair with *lichaman*, and the aural parallelism is
heightened by the chiastic structure – 'lichaman [...] wurðlicor lybbað
[...] weorðfulicor arisað [...] lichaman'. But, on the semantic level, the
phrasing implies a distinction of a degree, not kind: human bodies will
arise 'more worthily' than trees and other animals, which suggests that
these nonhuman creatures will arise too, albeit 'less worthily', whatever
that might mean. The terminological distinctions are blurry as well.
With his claim that humans live more worthily than 'other animals'
('oðre nytenu'), Agustinus curiously refers to humans as a class of *nyten*,
the Old English word for 'cattle' and nonhuman animals generally. The
lack of an Old English equivalent for *animal* is glaring here, as, in order
to preserve the parallelism with 'oðre gescæaftas', the *Soliloquies*-author
relies on 'oðre nytenu', a phrase that highlights the very thing that in
the Augustinian tradition is eradicated at the eschaton, what Agamben
calls the 'unredeemable remnant' in the physiology of the blessed, the
nytennes (bestiality) within the human.[86]

Although Gesceadwisnes does not explicitly mention the eschaton in
her argument about the immortality of the human soul, she alludes to
an alternative theological tradition, one that postulated that the end of
days would restore creation – and not just humanity – to a primordial
condition of perfection: God, she explains, will suddenly return to all
creatures the beauty they possessed before Adam sinned ('ærþamðe
Adam gesingode'). Whereas Augustine's eschatology was more future-
oriented, less premised on returning to a Golden Age, Greek fathers
such as Origen and Gregory of Nyssa envisioned a universal restoration
(Gr. *apokatastasis*) based on the principle that the end contains the
beginning.[87] A version of Origen's teachings was condemned in the sixth

---

86 Agamben, *The Open*, 19.
87 Bynum, *Resurrection of the Body*, 97. An important aspect of Augustine's
mature eschatology is his rejection of millenialism, the belief that the Second
Coming of Christ will usher in an interim period of earthly harmony preceding
the Last Judgment. See Paula Fredriksen, 'Tyconius and Augustine on the
Apocalypse', in *The Apocalypse in the Middle Ages*, ed. Richard K. Emmerson and
Bernard McGinn (Ithaca, NY, 1992), 20–37. On *apokatastasis*, see Brian E. Daley,
The Hope of the Early Church: A Handbook of Patristic Eschatology (Cambridge,
1991); and Ilaria Ramelli, *The Christian Doctrine of Apokatastasis: A Critical
Assessment from the New Testament to Eriugena* (Leiden, 2013). Some patristic
thinkers specified that nonhuman animals would be returned to their prelap-
sarian state of docility and harmony. See, for instance, Theophilus of Antioch,
Ad Autolycum, 2.17, quoted in Ramelli, *Christian Doctrine of Apokatastasis*, 65.

century, but apokatastatic ideas continued to influence eschatological currents through the Carolingian period. Drawing on Origen and other Greek sources, Eriugena described a general return (*reditus generalis*), in which creation would be restored to a transcendent condition figured by Eden.[88]

The Disciple in the *Periphyseon* struggles to accept the inclusion of nonhuman creatures: 'Num irrationabilia animalia, ligna etiam et herbae omnesque huius mundi partes a summo usque deorsum in uerbo dei incarnato restaurata sunt?' ('Are we to say that irrational animals, and even trees and plants, and all parts of this world from the highest to the lowest, are restored by the Incarnation of the Word of God?')[89] The Master assures him that when Christ assumed and restored human nature, he assumed and restored the form of every creature in heaven and on earth, since all modes of being (e.g. body, motion, sense) are contained within the human. At the general return, animals will not resurrect their earthly bodies; they will pass into the primordial causes through the restoration of human nature. Only rational creatures can participate in the special return (*reditus specialis*) that follows the general restoration and beatifies and deifies the elect. Still, even if all creatures are not permitted to eat of the Tree of Life, each one gains – or rather regains – entrance to Paradise, the state in which God will be 'all in all' (*omnia in omnibus*).[90] The *Periphyseon* is structured around a sophisticated theory of *apokatastasis*, but there were other variations on the idea circulating in contemporary texts, including some composed in Anglo-Saxon England.

The seventh-century Hiberno-Latin treatise *De ordine creaturarum*, once thought to be the work of Isidore of Seville, contains an influential description of the sun and moon.[91] Originally created to minister to the needs of Adam and Eve, the luminaries also suffered at the Fall by losing

88   On Eriugena's eschatology, see the essays in *History and Eschatology in John Scottus Eriugena and his Time*, ed. Michael Dunne and James McEvoy (Leuven, 2002), esp. José Luis Cantón Alonso, '*Deus omnia in omnibus*: Les *exempla naturalia* dans le discours eschatologique de Jean Scot Érigène', 333–46.
89   Eriugena, *Periphyseon*, V, ed. Jeauneau, 5:76, lines 2411–14 (913B); trans. Sheldon-Williams, 586.
90   Eriugena, *Periphyseon*, V, ed. Jeauneau, 5:98, lines 3998–9 (929A). Cf. 1 Corinthians 15:28.
91   On *De ordine creaturarum*, see the introductory material in Marina Smyth, 'The Seventh-Century Hiberno-Latin Treatise *Liber de ordine creaturarum*: A Translation', *Journal of Medieval Latin* 21 (2011), 137–222 (137–63).

some of their brightness. By claiming that the luminaries did not endure
this undeserved punishment without sorrow, the author imputes some
degree of agency, or at least animation, to the stars.[92] When humans
are restored at the end of days so too will be the luminaries: 'Sed quia
per redemptoris aduentum humano generi pristinae beatitudinis in
melius restauratio promittitur, etiam creatura suum antiquum decorem
acceptura non dubitatur.' ('But because through the coming of the
Redeemer restoration into a state better than its original happiness has
been promised to the human race, it cannot be doubted that creation
itself will receive its former beauty.')[93] Quoting Isaiah 30:25–6, the author
specifies that the restored moon will be as bright as the sun currently
is and the sun will be seven times brighter. The sublunary world will
also be restored, liberated from the cycle of growth and decay: 'cum
enim nascendi et moriendi in hominibus condicio cessauerit, tunc
etiam uiriditatis et ariditatis suae incrementa et damna ipsa terra non
habebit' ('For when birth and death will cease among men, the earth
will no longer experience the increases and decreases of its greenness
and dryness').[94] Motivating the author's discussion of earthly renewal is
twice-cited Romans 8:20–2:

> For the creature was made subject to vanity, not willingly, but by reason
> of him that made it subject, in hope: Because the creature also itself shall
> be delivered from the servitude of corruption, into the liberty of the glory
> of the children of God. For we know that every creature groaneth and
> travaileth in pain, even till now.[95]

In his exegesis of the Pauline text, Augustine had scoffed at the possibility that the phrase 'every creature' could encompass trees, vegetables,
stones, or nonhuman animals, insisting that the term applied to humans

---

92   Smyth, '*Liber de ordine creaturarum*', 174–5 n. 46. On patristic debates about
the animation of stars, see Alan Scott, *Origen and the Life of Stars: A History of
an Idea* (Oxford, 1991).

93   *Liber de ordine creaturarum: Un anónimo irlandés del siglo VII*, 5, ed. Manuel
C. Díaz y Díaz, Monografías de la Universidad de Santiago de Compostela 10
(Santiago de Compostela, 1972), 114, lines 23–5. The translation is from Smyth,
'*Liber de ordine creaturarum*', 175.

94   *Liber de ordine creaturarum*, 11, ed. Díaz y Díaz, 170, lines 24–7; trans.
Smyth, 196.

95   *Liber de ordine creaturarum*, 5, ed. Díaz y Díaz, 114, lines 22–3; 116, lines
47–9.

alone.[96] Aquinas would expand the orbit of redemption to include heavenly bodies and the elements as well as humans, but he states unequivocally that plants, minerals, and nonhuman animals cannot, and will not, participate in the final renewal of creation.[97] The author of *De ordine creaturarum* took a more inclusive view, extending redemption to the luminaries and the earth below.

Close parallels with the description of the sun and moon in *De ordine creaturarum* have been identified in later texts, including the ninth-century *Old English Martyrology* and homilies by Ælfric.[98] The *Old English Martyrology* has been linked by scholars to the same Alfredian milieu out of which the Old English *Boethius* and *Soliloquies* may have originated.[99] Interspersed with the hagiographic material for the month of March is a hexameral account of creation. On the fourth day of

---

96 Augustine, *Expositio quarundam propositionum ex epistola ad Romanos*, 53, in *Augustine on Romans: Propositions from the Epistle to the Romans; Unfinished Commentary on the Epistle to the Romans*, ed. and trans. Paula Fredriksen Landes (Chico, CA, 1982), 23, lines 34–9. Cf. Augustine, *Enarrationes in Psalmos*, XXXV.12, ed. D. Eligius Dekkers and Johannes Fraipont CCSL 38 (Turnhout, 1956), 331, lines 1–31.

97 Thomas Aquinas, *Summa theologiae*, Supplement, q. 91, a. 5, ed. P. Caramello (Turin, 1956), 359–60; Aquinas, *Summa contra Gentiles*, IV.97, ed. P. Marc, C. Pera, and P. Caramello, 3 vols. (Turin, 1961–7), 3:416–17. On Aquinas's views regarding animals and the eschaton, see Santi, 'L'animale eterno'; Steel, *How to Make a Human*, 106–7; and Minnis, *Creations of Paradise*, 147. Minnis discusses other late medieval accounts of the restoration of prelapsarian solar and lunar radiance (160–5).

98 Smyth, 'Liber de ordine creaturarum', 156–60; J. E. Cross, 'De ordine creaturarum liber in Old English Prose', *Anglia* 90 (1972), 132–40; Christine Rauer, 'Usage of the *Old English Martyrology*', in *Foundations of Learning: The Transfer of Encyclopaedic Knowledge in the Early Middle Ages*, ed. Rolf H. Bremmer, Jr., and Kees Dekker (Paris, 2007), 125–46 (135). Irvine Homily 6 also contains parallels: Irvine suggests that Irvine Homily 6 and the *Old English Martyrology* may have been influenced by an intermediary text that drew on *De ordine creaturarum* (*Old English Homilies from MS Bodley 343*, ed. Susan Irvine, EETS o.s. 302 (Oxford, 1993), 152–3).

99 *The Old English Martyrology: Edition, Translation and Commentary*, ed. and trans. Christine Rauer, Anglo-Saxon Texts 10 (Cambridge, 2013), 11–13. According to Rauer, the earth-as-egg image found in the metrical version of the Old English *Boethius* may have derived from the *Old English Martyrology*, which in turn likely borrowed the image from *De ordine creaturarum* (Rauer, 'Usage of the *Old English Martyrology*', 135–6).

creation – commemorated on March 21 – God placed the sun and the moon in the firmament:

> Ac þa Adam ond Eua on neorxnawonge gesyngodan, ða wæs þæm tunglum gewonad heora beorhtnes, ond hi næfdon na siððan butan þone seofoðan dæl heora leohtes. Ac on domesdæge, þonne ure Drihten edniwað ealle gesceafte, ond eall mænnisc cynn eft ariseð, ond hi næfre ma ne gesyngiað, þonne scineð seo sunne seofon siðum beorhtre ðonne heo nu do, ond heo næfre on setl gangeþ.[100]

(And when Adam and Eve sinned in Paradise, the brightness of the heavenly bodies was then dimmed, and since then they have only had one seventh of their former brightness. And on Doomsday, when our Lord will renew all of creation, and all humankind will be resurrected and they will sin no more, the sun will then shine seven times brighter than it does now, and it will never set.)

The *Old English Martyrology* follows *De ordine creaturarum* in taking the renewal of the sun and moon as paradigmatic of the restoration of the whole of creation ('ealle gesceafte'). In one of his homilies, Ælfric envisions a similar sevenfold restoration of solar radiance occurring at the eschaton, the moment when Christ will suddenly renew all ('færlice eall geedniwod').[101] It is not clear, though, whether the 'eall' actually encompasses all, as Ælfric goes on to state that the only inhabitants of the 'new heaven' and 'new earth' will be the elect. Although Gesceadwisnes does not explicitly mention the sun or the moon, her supposition that all creatures will suddenly be restored to their Edenic beauty has affinities with the exegetical tradition represented by *De ordine creaturarum* and the Anglo-Saxon works it influenced.

Near the end of the first book of the Old English *Soliloquies*, Gesceadwisnes states that God made two – and only two – eternal 'æca'

100   *Old English Martyrology*, ed. Rauer, 68. The translation is Rauer's.
101   Ælfric, 'Sermo ad populum, in octavis pentecosten dicendus' (Homily 11), in *Homilies of Ælfric: A Supplementary Collection*, ed. John C. Pope, 2 vols, EETS o.s. 259–60 (London, 1967–8), 1:407–52 (443, lines 512–3). There is no equivalent passage in Ælfric's main source, Julian of Toledo's *Prognosticon futuri saeculi*. See also Ælfric, 'De falsis diis' (Homily 21), in *Homilies of Ælfric*, ed. Pope, 2:667–724 (679, lines 56–65). On Ælfric's eschatology, see Milton McC. Gatch, *Preaching and Theology in Anglo-Saxon England: Ælfric and Wulfstan* (Toronto, 1977), esp. 66–104.

creatures: angels and human souls (82, line 15). Her demonstration of this doctrinal point, though, is predicated on assigning some manner of renewed existence to all creatures, a category that presumably includes nonhuman animals, as well as plants, stars, minerals, and elements. Indeed, her insistence that even the most unworthy of creatures will be renewed functions as a counterpoint to those who would exclude animals or other nonhuman mixed bodies from the universal salvation promised in Romans 8:21–2. She posits a nonfigurative continuity between the renewal that sustains organic life in its earthly existence and the renewal that restores creation to its paradisal beauty. Even if humans arise 'more worthily' at the end of days, even if they alone can undergo beatification (as Eriugena maintains), the Old English *Soliloquies* imagines a final end for nonhuman creatures beyond oblivion.

The human/animal divide is sustained in Anglo-Saxon culture through a sub-network of distinctions: soul and life-force, reason and perception, immortality and mortality. I have examined passages in the Old English *Boethius* and *Soliloquies* that destabilize these distinctions by plotting their terms onto a spectrum, by converting differences of kind to differences of degree. To be sure, some of the instability can be attributed to the limited philosophical lexicon of Old English. But we discount the translations as philosophical endeavours in their own right if we chalk up the contradictions and incongruities solely to unskilful translation practice or the lexical fuzziness of the target language. Ælfric, for one, demonstrates how the vocabulary of Old English can be pressed into the service of maintaining a firm boundary between human and nonhuman. We would also risk overlooking the possible influence of other medieval texts and traditions that view the human/animal divide differently from Augustine and Boethius. Rather, I see the passages discussed here as structured by an imperative to reconcile the distinctiveness of humans with a recognition of the continuum that binds all animate creatures and, for that matter, inanimate creatures too. At once proclaiming and denying human exceptionalism, these moments in the Old English *Boethius* and *Soliloquies* lay bare the difficulties entailed in producing the concept of the human and its equally notional corollary, the animal.

2

Disruptive Things in *Beowulf**

AARON HOSTETTER

> It is not normal today to think of 'inanimate objects' as possessing a lively capacity to do things to us and with us, although it is quite normal to experience them as such.[1]
>
> Jane Bennett, 'The Powers of the Hoard' (2012)

When the spring comes to Friesland and the ice blocking the harbours finally thaws, a Danish thane brings his leader a powerful message, a call to violent and immediate action after a long, tense winter. Yet he does not do so through the powers of oratorical persuasion. Rather he makes a simple gesture: he places the sword of Hnæf, the Dane's fallen war-leader, onto the lap of his successor, Hengest, who responds by attacking his former hosts and avenging his predecessor's death. This is an intriguing moment within an Anglo-Saxon poetics that frequently creates drama through speeches and conversations – for example, in hagiographic narratives like *Andreas* or *Guthlac A*. However, in the *scop*'s account of the fight at Finnsburh, the object is eloquent and compelling, and moves human actors to decision and response. Speech is substituted with the presence of an important relic of the slain lord. As Gillian Overing reminds us, a sword is a complex signifier culturally and linguistically, which can stand in for many things: battle, glory, political power, masculinity, even the man himself.[2] In the case of the Danes in

*   I would like to thank Ellen Malenas Ledoux, Lyra Hostetter, James Brown, Jr., Jillian Sayre, and *NML*'s two anonymous readers for their probing questions, keen insights, and timely critiques of this article in its draft stages.

1   Jane Bennett, 'The Powers of the Hoard: Further Notes on Material Agency', in *Animal, Vegetable, Mineral: Ethics and Objects*, ed. Jeffrey Jerome Cohen (Washington, DC, 2012), 237–69 (263).

2   One synonym for 'man' is *secg*, which has a homonym (inflected differently and

the Frisian springtime, this synecdoche, the sword, has been converted into a painful metaphor – the *hildeleoma* (the battle-bright blade) that remains when its owner has been taken away in death.[3] And the fact of this final substitution demands swift, bloody action. By giving Hengest the symbolic authority over their expedition, the Danes have also given him responsibility for prosecuting the loss of Hnæf. The sword in this instance speaks in a louder and more irresistible voice than any human could – its unforgettable history of possession and inheritance calls out for savage retribution. And so the Danish warriors, with Hengest at their van, shatter the fragile truce and attack their former hosts. All because of the exchange of a sword. Objects in *Beowulf* can be perilous things.

This essay will explore the power of the so-called inanimate realm in *Beowulf*, and the para-subjective effects its things create within its milieu. Certain material objects – for example, the glorious torque given to Beowulf by Wealhtheow (1195–1214) – divert the course of the story, momentarily capturing the narrative and forcing it to recognize their fascination. Powerful things are not inert and static, rather they are fictional occasions: they are continuous moments of material being that often seem to stand in the way of the story and its actors. They interrupt the legend of the greatness of human deeds, in favour of a meditation on the status of the material world that suffuses the story of *Beowulf*. We may want to read a story about ideals and motivations, yet the poem insists that we apprehend these by way of the objects that surround and permeate the institutions it celebrates.

Criticism and reception of *Beowulf* have often been materially inflected. For example, it is not uncommon for a translation of the poem to be illustrated with photographs of northern European artefacts, which affirm that the goods and commodities in the poem had a basis in the lived world of its Anglo-Saxon audience, though John Hines has criticized the straightforwardly illustrative aspects of the practice.[4] Just as often scholars examine literary issues in light of archaeological

feminine in gender) meaning 'sword' (*Bosworth–Toller Anglo-Saxon Dictionary*). For Gillian R. Overing, see *Language, Sign, and Gender in Beowulf* (Carbondale, IL, 1990), 37–8 and 45–6.

3   All quotations from *Beowulf* are taken from Klaeber's *Beowulf and the Fight at Finnsburh*, 4th edn, ed. R. D. Fulk, Robert E. Bjork, and John D. Niles (Toronto, 2008). Brackets and diacritical marks are removed for ease of reading. Translations are mine.

4   John Hines, *Voices in the Past: English Literature and Archaeology* (Cambridge, 2004), 29.

remnants, as Gail Owen-Crocker does in *The Four Funerals in Beowulf*, which supports its arguments on the centrality of funerals as a structuring device in the poem with ample reference to the burial practices and recovered grave-goods of medieval Scandinavia and Anglo-Saxon England.[5] Other studies scour records and documents to obtain an idea of how the cultural and political institutions of *Beowulf*'s world modulated how its audience would have understood it, and by extension how we should invest the poem with meaning; an example is John M. Hill's *The Cultural World of Beowulf*.[6] In *Landscape of Desire*, Gillian Overing and Marijane Osborn take the materiality of place as their starting point, attempting to understand the world of *Beowulf* by sharing its spaces, such as sailing seas similar to those Beowulf travelled.[7] The material world of the Anglo-Saxons has even influenced and inspired poetic studies of the text, such as John Leyerle's immensely useful 'The Interlace Structure of *Beowulf*', which posits the numerous Anglo-Saxon artefacts that feature interlaced design-work as an aesthetic parallel to *Beowulf*'s winding poetics.[8]

I endeavour to accomplish a very different sort of materialist intervention from these previous studies: I explore what the objects of *Beowulf* are themselves capable of achieving, and how the poet responds to their potency as he weaves them into his narrative frame. This represents a turn in the status of the material thing as represented by poetry, at least, a turn to us as modern people. As Kellie Robertson suggests, following Bruno Latour, the divide between subject and object was less rigid before the seventeenth century, and the world of things was often regarded as having greater influence on the ideas and thoughts of humans.[9] *Beowulf* is a prime example of this relationality of the material – in the poem's lines, objects are powerful, able to organize the poet's language around them and dictate their story. Sometimes this

5   Gail Owen-Crocker, *The Four Funerals in Beowulf, and the Structure of the Poem* (New York, 2000).

6   John M. Hill, *The Cultural World in Beowulf* (Toronto, 1995).

7   Gillian R. Overing and Marijane Osborn, *Landscape of Desire: Partial Stories of the Medieval Scandinavian World* (Minneapolis, 1994).

8   John Leyerle, 'The Interlace Structure of Beowulf', *University of Toronto Quarterly* 37 (1967), 1–17.

9   Kellie Robertson, 'Medieval Things: Materiality, Historicism, and the Premodern Object', *Literature Compass* 5/6 (2008), 1060–80 (1063). For Bruno Latour, see *We Have Never Been Modern*, trans. Catherine Porter (Cambridge, MA, 1993).

representation creates a weird exterior for the object, communicating its excessive nature beyond the human. This outside to human desires for legible narrative and historiography is the focus of James Paz, who also connects New Materialisms to certain objects in *Beowulf*. He identifies the presence of 'riddle-like things' that resist human efforts to interpret them – and sometimes, as in the case of Grendel's mother, resist violently.[10] Paz's reading of things in the poem emphasizes their hostility to interpretation, and even suggests the ultimate impossibility of inter- pretation, arranging poetic objects in opposition to the humans who try to make sense of them. Although I share Paz's sense of material recal- citrance in *Beowulf*, my approach recognizes an inherent cooperation between physical matter and human representation, a mutual influence that often guides the poet in communicating these objects' capacities.

This puissance of objects in the poem leads me to speculate upon their 'vibrancy', to borrow the term from Jane Bennett, who recog- nizes an 'active, earthy, not-quite-human capaciousness' in inanimate matter that extends beyond humanity's assumed prerogative to order the world's materials and assign them meaning: a strange power of objects to influence or even to resist the designs of human actors.[11] She explores the political implications of this understanding – how it should alter our view of the material world of which we are a part.[12] The force of vibrant matter can be understood as 'thing-power', a quality that lies largely in the unknowable space beyond and prior to our subjectivity, a quasi-agentic force which at times mirrors the opera- tions of a conscious will, an impetus that affects and changes the things around it (including ourselves). These are not wholly new ideas, and Bennett traces the concept of 'thing-power' back to Baruch Spinoza, who famously claims, 'Each thing, as far as it can by its own power, strives to persevere in its own being.'[13] These 'conative' bodies are found

---

10   James Paz, 'Æschere's Head, Grendel's Mother, and the Sword that isn't a Sword: Unreadable Things in Beowulf', *Exemplaria* 25 (2013), 231–51 (249).

11   Jane Bennett, *Vibrant Matter: A Political Ecology of Things* (Durham, NC, 2010), 3.

12   This is the essential common ground for a host of closely related, though not identical, approaches that I will refer to as New Materialisms, which include work by Graham Harman, Bruno Latour, Ian Bogost, Levi R. Bryant, and Timothy Morton. The diversity of these approaches is showcased in the collection *New Materialisms: Ontology, Agency, and Politics*, ed. Diana Coole and Samantha Frost (Durham, 2010).

13   Baruch Spinoza, *Ethics* (1677), trans. Edwin Curley (London, 1996), pt. 3,

throughout *Beowulf*, powerful objects that bend the world of the poem around their undeniable presence, 'striving' to maintain their material destiny in a world of transitory values and fragile human lives.

Beowulf, however, is not alone in the Old English poetic corpus in regarding its objects as vibrant. In the hagiographic romance *Elene* the story is driven by a material fascination that leads Constantine to possess the actual cross of Christ. These objects are more than just holy symbols, things supplemented by God, especially in the case of the nails of the Cross. Upon their discovery, Judas Cyriacus repurposes their metal, creating a blessed bit for the emperor's horse, extending the material destiny of these sacred relics by an act of translation. Objects come into focus in *Andreas*, too, a poem very much about the consumable materiality of the body. In this legend, stone is shown to be powerful through the intervention of God, on one occasion becoming animated to walk and talk, on another, bursting open to produce a flood upon command. In either case the stones are hardly inert, and become fascinating in their potential for activity and response.[14] The most vibrantly material poems in the Anglo-Saxon corpus are the Exeter Book Riddles, which feature speaking objects that playfully invoke their own thing-power once they are isolated from the faceless assemblage of household items. They fashion themselves as something more than just one object out of many, and they spin playful, sometimes lurid, fictions about their existence and purpose in the web of the human world. This is not meant to be an exhaustive list of vibrancy, but it shows that Anglo-Saxon poetry has a deep regard for things, and often explores the implications of materiality.

The objects in *Beowulf* are vibrant and they exert their thing-power upon the narrative strategies of the poet, allowing us to conceptualize a material world that pervades and even at times dominates human existence. The dependence of *Beowulf* upon the fabricated world of important commodities implies a derivative nature for human ideals in an immense material universe, implies that humanity requires the presence of objects in order to create ideals in the first place. 'Against the subjectivity of men stands the objectivity of the man-made world', Hannah Arendt observes, positing an innate relationship between people and the enculturated world around them, shot through with mutual

prop. 6, and quoted in Bennett, *Vibrant Matter*, 2.
14   For a view of ancient stone as useful and alluring, see Denis Ferhatović, 'Spolia-Inflected Poetics of the Old English *Andreas*', *Studies in Philology* 110 (2013), 199–219.

needs.[15] As Ian Hodder suggests, humans and things are 'entangled' – existing together in strands of dependence, both altering each other and engaged in each other's survival.[16] *Beowulf* suggests such a world: the poem may recreate and celebrate fine, socially instantiating values and emotions, such as the excellence and loyalty that prop up its exemplary kingships and social orders. However, it uses the complex existence of objects to do more than just reimagine the glories of this long-dead world – it also uses them to introduce a powerful theme of the fragility of human endeavour. The objects speak a counter-story to Beowulf and Hrothgar's glory, emphasizing the vanity of heroic deeds. What endures, these things seem to say, is the material world itself, while human societies and ideals constantly shift and change within it.

Beowulf, though more than a thousand years old, is a text that proceeds from an understanding of the power of the material, that explores a political world expressed through and thoroughly permeated by the vibrant objects that circulate within its milieu. The author of the poem uses that imaginative framework of an idealized and nostalgic social world to examine the resonances of the commodities that give meaning to human action and emotion. The use of objects in *Beowulf* reveals a precocious understanding of thing-power, in that material objects often have effects on both the actors of the poem and the narrative that contains them, effects which show them to be more than just an inert presence.

Advocating the vibrancy of the material world re-enfranchises the power of the objects that surround us, freeing them from philosophical mindsets that locate agency and truth in Platonic forms – the abstract, intangible, universal exemplar of what every individual thing should be. These attitudes towards the material often assume that the concrete world is secondary to the abstractions that govern its phenomena. To argue that the object should be considered vibrant is to revivify this material object of idealist presuppositions, and locate an ontological priority of a thing outside our thoughts.[17]

15   Hannah Arendt, *The Human Condition* (Chicago, 1958), 137.
16   Ian Hodder, *Entangled: An Archaeology of the Relationships between Humans and Things* (Malden, MA, 2012), esp. 88–112.
17   This is not to say that idealist philosophies have been mistaken in their views on the nature of reality, only that they are focused on other matters. For an important balance to the New Materialist tendency to dismiss competing, more traditional theories and argue for the radical innovation of its proponents' ideas, see Andrew Cole's, 'The Call of Things: A Critique of Object-Oriented

Bennett argues that the things all around us, the objects of the material world, cannot be relegated to the status of second-class citizens by virtue of being non-alive or seemingly inert or passive. She states instead, by invoking as an example the complex behaviour of things such as decomposing trash, that even so-called inanimate objects have a power to influence, even thwart, contradict, and complicate human designs. They 'create' effects in the world beyond and outside those intended by the humans who exist around and try to use them.[18] Bill Brown, who coined the term 'thing theory' and first called for a 'new materialism', describes this recalcitrance:

> We begin to confront the thingness of objects when they stop working for us [...] when their flow within the circuits of production and distribution, consumption and exhibition, has been arrested, however momentarily. The story of objects asserting themselves as things, then, is the story of a changed relation to the human subject.[19]

Objects become things when they do not quite work the way that they should, when they seem somewhat out of our control, and they confound or frustrate our designs in using them. The human subject must admit that it is not the only actor in the system. The battery in the trash heap that refuses to moulder quietly, instead leaking poisonous fluid, is an example of thing-power's relentless ability to spark changes in this world. Another instance of the strange wilfulness of objects can be found when the Geatish warriors attempt to hack at Grendel in Heorot: they soon find that 'þone synscaðan / ænig ofer eorþan irenna cyst, / guðbilla nan, gretan nolde' ('no battle-blade, / none of the choicest iron upon the earth, / wished to bite that sinful scather', lines 801b–3). A similar construction occurs when Beowulf attempts to strike Grendel's mother with the sword Hrunting: 'Ða se gist onfand / þæt se beadoleoma bitan nolde, / aldre sceþðan' ('Then the guest in the hall discovered / that the

Ontologies', *Minnesota Review* 80 (2013), 106–18. By reminding us of the work of idealist philosopher Johann Fichte and the medieval mystic Meister Eckhart, Cole's essay reveals that the idea of para-subjective objects has a hoary lineage of its own. Cole's admonition to remember the medieval is well intentioned and well taken, as it enables a more fleshed-out approach to the deep history of the Western intellectual tradition, and promises to build bridges between generations of theorists sometimes inclined to treat one another with suspicion.

18   Bennett, *Vibrant Matter*, 1–3.
19   Bill Brown, 'Thing Theory', *Critical Inquiry* 28.1 (2001), 1–22 (4).

battle-bright blade did not wish to bite, / to harm her life', lines 1522b–24a). In both cases the narrator makes a careful distinction between ability and volition, specifying that these are tools that do not wish to work (*nolde* = *ne* + *wolde*, the preterite singular form of *willan*, 'to wish or want to'). Most translators render the modal verb as 'could', as if the idea itself is too bizarre to be thought, and so this obstinacy becomes unconsciously suppressed by everyday habits of speech.[20] Yet the weird agency of the intractable object remains, filled with, as Bennett notes, a 'lively capacity to do things to us and with us'.[21] In this case, the reluctant sword acts according to an innate disobedience which announces its agency in the system within which it operates.

The presence of this force, this thing-power, demands that we perceive the material world in a more capacious way, as a family of interrelated phenomena that do not depend on human action and belief to give them meaning and purpose. This ontological under-standing of vibrancy advocated by the New Materialists is intended to complicate and challenge the dialectical materialism of the Marxist tradition, which locates its own sense of vibrancy in the relationship between human acts of production and the natural world, forming an epistemology of how we perceive those objects (as commodities) in a political economy.

Vibrancy signifies an uncanny surplus inherent in the material object, something that exceeds the human social activity that constitutes the commodity. As Bennett cautions, this surplus is not due to anything supernatural or animistic. Instead, it derives from an identification of the persistent sense of material existence that escapes or eludes the account of everything the object seems to do in its environment. That something extra explains the volatility and energy of what seems to be a stable object, constantly being tried and tested in an endless series of environ-mental reactions and changes. This surplus, however, also is evident even in traditional Marxist analysis, which locates a social life of objects *qua* commodities, able to be fetishized, placed into distorted comparison with other commodities by way of extrinsic exchange values, and which

---

20   For a typical example, see R. M. Liuzza's version of 801–3: '[...] that no sword, / not the best iron anywhere in the world, / could even touch that evil sinner [...]' (*Beowulf*, trans. R. M. Liuzza, 2nd edn (Toronto, 2013), 73). Other instances are easily found among the numerous translations that have been produced over the years.

21   Bennett, 'Powers of the Hoard', 263.

become, in short, 'citizens' of a world of political economy.[22] This sense of citizenship, however, is historical and driven by political forces and pressures. There is vibrancy to the object in the Marxist understanding, due to human intervention, which bathes the object 'in the fire of labour' as it transmogrifies it from a use value into a commodity.[23] There is a place, however, in *Capital*'s analysis where thing-power surfaces, where the object seems to act on its own within its environment. Fetishization, unavoidably a conscious, human act, imbues the object with some sort of reanimated, extra agency:

> Nevertheless the table continues to be wood, an ordinary, sensuous thing. But as soon as it emerges as a commodity, it changes into a thing which transcends sensuousness. It not only stands with its feet on the ground, but, in relation to all other commodities, it stands on its head, and evolves out of its wooden brain grotesque ideas, far more wonderful than if it were to begin dancing of its own free will.[24]

The fetishized commodity recognizes its sorcerous life through human endeavour which sets economic forces into motion. At the same moment it kindles this existence, it begins to act contrary to its design – it exceeds its usefulness, and advocates new relations between itself and the world of objects. In short, commodities act as actual citizens, with political agency and a will that is capricious and sometimes non-productive. The Marxist focus on human history as the mover of objects is the main area of contention with the New Materialists, who would prefer to understand the object of its own accord. There does not need to be, however, any disagreement on this account: things and humans depend upon one another in meshes of involvement, as has been shown by Hodder and others, and the traditional notion of the commodity form is just one way of explaining this entanglement we experience every day.

The active citizenry of *Beowulf*'s material realm seems to be exclusive to things made from gold and steel, items of sufficient cultural value to be considered vibrant. The food, for instance, which must be ample during Hrothgar's several feasts, is not shown by the poet. Mead, however, is shown in plenty. This is not just because, as Hugh Magennis

---

22   Karl Marx, *Capital: A Critique of Political Economy*, vol. 1 (1867), trans. Ben Fowkes (Harmondsworth, 1976), 155.

23   Ibid., 289.

24   Ibid., 163–4.

argues, the act of eating invokes anxieties about bodily functions, shared
with animals, while drinking signifies the social values of the human
realm.[25] Rather, the difference may be located in the heritability of its
serving objects – mead is noble, while food is everyday. A drink might
be served in a golden chalice or a richly decorated horn, something that
can be handed down to one's descendants, while food was often eaten
from a trencher made of wood or even stale bread. What about the tools,
probably made of wood, of the many peasants and servants who no
doubt surround the story's main actors? These items and their users are
not even relatable in the aesthetic strategies of the storyteller. Materiality
in *Beowulf*, it would seem, is separate from the quotidian, and is aligned,
counter-intuitively, with the eternal and the enduring. These are values
that, in Platonically influenced schemes, tend to be associated with
spirit, soul, and *forma*, yet here are linked to the undeniably present, to
things that can be transferred across time into the hands of the future.
Those objects that will survive their bearers are vibrant to the *Beowulf*
poet.

An important exception to the rule of gold and steel is the
mead-hall itself, a vastly important cultural edifice made of wood. This
undoubtedly powerful object is a primary location in the Anglo-Saxon
poetic imaginary, the scene of communal identity and the focus of
many of its threats.[26] The visitor to the hall is a fascinating, repeated
motif in *Beowulf*, even when monstrously inverted (such as the *nið-sele*
of Grendel's mother (1513) or the dragon's *eorð-sele* (2232)). However,
the hall itself as a building often only becomes visible in moments of
danger, when its end is in sight, such as at the creation of Heorot, which
forecasts its burning (67–85), the breaking open of the *recedes muþan*
(the mouth of the hall) by Grendel (723–4), the view of the destroyed

25 Hugh Magennis, *Anglo-Saxon Appetites: Food and Drink and their
Consumption in Old English and Related Literature* (Dublin, 1999), 59–60.
26 The nature of the mead-hall's exceeding its object status is most effectively
explored by Edward B. Irving, Jr.'s 'The Hall as Image and Character', where
he describes Heorot as an actual participant in the drama of the poem (in his
Rereading Beowulf (Philadelphia, 1989), 133–66). Alvin A. Lee's *The Guest-Hall
of Eden* (New Haven, 1972) presents another image of the hall transcending the
mundane, though it is not materialist at all in its focus or purposes. Magennis
identifies the mead-hall as a social nexus and source of identity in his *Images of
Community in Old English Poetry* (Cambridge, 1996); and Stephen Pollington
relates the hall in literature to archaeological evidence in *The Mead-Hall: The
Feasting Tradition in Anglo-Saxon England* (Norfolk, 2003).

interior of Heorot (997–1002), or at the destruction of Beowulf's
own hall by the dragon (2324–7). The vibrancy of wood in this case
is complicated by its supplementation with other materials: Heorot
is described as 'horngeap' ('horn-wide', 82), decorated perhaps with
antlers, and it is both bound by iron bands (*irenbendum*, 774), which
preserve it from falling down during the Grendel fight, and spangled
with gold (*goldfah*, 308 and 1800), which causes it to sparkle brilliantly
in the sun. Heorot is a compelling object in the panoply of *Beowulf*, a
wooden thing that exceeds mere substance due to the complexity of its
entanglements in the world of the story's actors – a thing that establishes continuity across time, a fit setting for the socially instantiating
rituals of the Danes.

The lengthy scenes of celebration, where Beowulf is honoured for his
extraordinary deeds by the receipt of rich gifts, sometimes exasperate
first-time readers of the poem. How would these readers' experience
of the often-protracted instances of treasure exchange be transformed
if these objects of value were not perceived as inert things imposed
upon by human agents, but as bearers of active political and social
meaning in their own right? This would recast the political drama from
the interplay and complications arising from the very human desire for
so-called 'transcendent' values, such as enduring glory, and place it into
a realm where objects wield real political power over human designs.
No longer the possessors of fantastic wealth, humans are re-envisioned
as its temporary shepherds, lucky enough to keep a culturally significant object for a limited time. The main body of *Beowulf* would then
accord with its opening, where the glory and power of Scyld Scefing is
expressed primarily as a function of his influence over the material – his
power described by his ability to overthrow mead-benches ('meodosetla
ofteah', 5) – and driven home, pushed into legend, by the account of his
funeral ship laden with the most valuable treasures possible (36b–42).
Scyld, as exemplary king, is a warden of economic assets, and his son,
the little Beowulf, is notable for his willingness to distribute those goods
to his thanes (20–5). To apply this paradigm to the rest of the poem,
these commodities must be reconceived to square with the way that the
characters in the story imagine them.

The economic predominates over the world of *Beowulf*, where
treasured items circulate in exchange for loyalty and great deeds.
Materiality dominates its framework, and the object vibrates within this
enriched social context. The object has to be more than passive if the
story is to function as a statement of worldly experience, and so these

commodities should be reinvested with political and social presence arcing through time. A precious artefact, for instance a ring or bracelet, is given in the past to guarantee future action. It endures as a symbol of the legal obligations and emotional relationships between human actors that bind together a social body. This material relationship can be detected linguistically as well: often the *Beowulf*-poet chooses to represent a sword with the word *laf* (2611 etc.), which usually means 'heirloom' or 'relic.' This metonymic relationship shows the sword to be something more than just a weapon, a glorious tool of warfare. Rather, it designates the sword as a continuity between the past, present, and future, the linchpin that holds together the entire agnatic social order. The family is manifested and remembered through its ability to pass down heritable objects. Yet this materialist focus in the language of *Beowulf* goes even further than that. Among the epithets used to signify a lord are *goldwine* (gold-friend, 1171 etc.), *brytta* (distributer, 35 etc.), and *beag-gyfa* (giver of rings, 1102), while the subordinate warrior, a thane, is so named for the act of receiving the largesse of the lord (*þegn* is derived from the verb *þicgan*, which means to receive, accept, or consume). Materiality influences the way that political and social structures are described, and the object shapes the way we perceive human institutions and interpersonal relationships.

The poem's valorization of human glory and social praise would mean very little without the material objects given from lord to thane, and so economic exchange is among the most important ideas conveyed in *Beowulf*. While it is true, as R. M. Liuzza argues, that it is not a simple desire for the object itself that impels the story, that neither 'greed or economic necessity' are motivators of heroic action, it would be incorrect to extend this observation any further and say that the poem valorizes ideal qualities, such as praise or glory, in and of themselves, to the exclusion of the material.[27] Material objects, glittering rings and wave-patterned swords, are guarantors of the ideal. The honour of men and the glory of action are crystallized and memorialized in the exchange of valuable objects. One possesses *lof* (praise) because one bears an object in which that praise inheres: all who see the object know the terms by which that praise was acquired, and, as a result, the social order can be constituted upon the tangible evidence of these idealistic

---

27 R. M. Liuzza, '*Beowulf*: Monuments, Memory, History', in *Readings in Medieval Texts: Interpreting Old and Middle English Literature*, ed. David F. Johnson and Elaine Treharne (Oxford, 2005), 91–108 (94).

qualities.[28] In the world of *Beowulf*, the pursuit of glory is inseparable from the pursuit of material goods, as long as the intentions of the seeker are honourable.[29]

Sometimes capricious and destructive, like Hnæf's sword, the material object in *Beowulf*, usually a precious commodity of some sort, a worked artefact of gold or steel, falls into Bennett's category of vibrant matter. As a result of this powerful, fascinating presence, the story becomes diverted in order to closely observe that thing and to witness its effects in the poem's time and space. Though these sorts of details abound in the poem, I would like to focus upon those items which seem to warp and challenge the progress and purpose of the story. Three important objects in *Beowulf* stand out most distinctly: the torque that Wealhtheow gives to the hero; the melted sword-hilt that Beowulf rescues from the lair of Grendel's mother; and the collection of precious artefacts found in the dragon's hoard.

The first of these powerful objects is introduced as Hrothgar's court celebrates the victory of the hero over Grendel. The queen of the Danes, Wealhtheow, enters the festivities both to reward Beowulf and to bind him to her cause, to support her sons' claims to the Danish throne. She enforces her impassioned plea by presenting the Geatish warrior with not only a cup full of mead, but also several valuable treasures: a pair of bracelets, another mail-shirt, and more rings. On top of those more common items comes something truly extraordinary, a precious torque that freezes the narrative in order that it may be described in some detail:

> [...] healsbeaga mæst
> þara þe ic on foldan   gefrægen hæbbe.
> Nænigne ic under swegle   selran hyrde
> hordmaððum hæleþa   syþðan Hama ætwæg
> to þære byrhtan byrig   Brosinga mene,
> sigle and sincfæt –   searoniðas fleah

---

28   Although at times this inherent memory can be unwelcome and destructive to the social bonds it is intended to create, as with the disrupted nuptials of Freawaru and Ingeld (2032–69a).

29   In the majority of cases within *Beowulf*, this is true. The failed Danish king Heremod, whose reign was disrupted by his destructive possession and avaricious acquisition of material goods, should be read as an important antithesis to Scyld Scefing, Hrothgar, and Beowulf (901–14, 1709a–1722a).

Eormenrices,   geceas ecne ræd.
Þone hring hæfde   Higelac Geata,
nefa Sweartinges   nyhstan side,
siðþan he under segne   since ealgode,
wælreaf werede;   hyne wyrd fornam
syþðan he for wlenco   wean ahsode,
fæhðe to Frysum.   He þa frætwe wæg,
eorclanstanas   ofer yða ful,
rice þeoden;   he under rande gecranc.
Gehwearf þa in Francna fæþm   feorh cyninges,
breostgewædu,   ond se beah somod.
Wyrsan wigfrecan   wæl reafeden
æfter guðsceare;   Geata leode
hreawic heoldon [...]

(1195–214a)

([...] The greatest of all neck-rings
which I have ever heard of on the earth.
I have heard of none better under the sky
in hoard-treasures of heroes since Hama carried away
to that bright city the necklace of the Brosings,
the jewel and the precious thing – fleeing the crafty hatred
of Eormenric, obtaining his own enduring good.
Hygelac the Geat, the nephew of Swerting,
possessed that torque, on his final journey,
when he defended the treasure under his banner,
protected his battle-spoils. Ill chance seized him
when he for his pride sought trouble,
a feud with the Frisians. He wore that ornament,
those precious stones across the cup of waves,
prince of the realm. He fell under his shield.
He passed on then into the grasp of the Franks, the spirit of the king,
his mail-shirt and that torque together.
A lesser warrior plundered the kill
after the war-shearing; Geat men
kept the corpse-field [...])

The beauty and value of the neck-ring are so amazing that the poem imitates the observing eye: both stare at it in astonishment. The narrator stutters in his admiration for the torque, repeating the formulaic statement of how he has never heard of better (1196–7). This attention to its resplendence, however, is never allowed to become a mere catalogue of its physical characteristics. We do not end up knowing much about the neck-ring except that it is adorned with precious stones (*eorclanstanas*) and that it exceeds all other possible necklaces (*healsbeaga mæst*). What we are told indicates that its precious nature is expressed best as a function of its existence through time, as an object of history. The torque analogously reaches backwards into the mythological and historical past: it is like something made by the blacksmithing dwarves of Germanic legend (*Brosinga mene*), and also like something famously stolen by a hero from the wealthy and powerful king of the Eastern Goths (who died in the 370s). This description links a sense of the distant, mythological past to more recent events, at least within human memory, to create an image of desirability and value.[30] The purpose of these metaphoric comparisons is to pin down the glorious nature of the neck-ring and to express its worth in historical terms. Wealhtheow's torque has the potential to be an eternal good (*ecne ræd*), something that extends forwards and backwards through time, and bears the memory and identity of its possessors.

Possession of this glorious torque, however, is not just a function of the past. The moment of Beowulf's great honour at being given such a treasure is suddenly tempered by a grim future, interrupted by the intimation of terrible events to come. For the hero will give this neck-ring to Hygd, the Geatish queen (2172–3), who presumably will give it in turn to her husband, Hygelac, sometime afterwards. Here the unfortunate consequences of that possession are made clear: Hygelac will bear the torque to his approaching doom. The long view of the history of the fabulous neck-ring suggests that within victory lies defeat, and that defeat is of a more profound and enduring nature than any possible victory. Hama might successfully steal a similar torque from Eormenric, to his everlasting glory, but Beowulf's own beloved lord will die ignominiously in a foreign land, and the neck-ring fall into the hands of a 'wyrsa wigfreca'. Possession of the artefact, and its attendant pride, might even be responsible for Hygelac's death, according to one possible reconstruction of the nodes of history in the torque's legend.

---

30   The connection between myth and present is made also when Beowulf instructs Hrothgar on how to dispose of his chain-mail byrnie in the case of his death: 'þæt is Hrædlan laf, / Welandes geweorc' ('It is an heirloom of Hrethel, / the work of Weland', 454–5).

The torque compresses time into a single experience; it becomes 'untimely matter', according to a model proposed by Jonathan Gil Harris. The *Beowulf* author here, like Harris, recognizes 'how matter, like palimpsest, exhibits a temporality that is not one'.[31] The breathless experience of the object, seen through the narrator's polychronic eye, moves from past glory to the 'ill chance' (my translation of *wyrd* in line 1205) that takes Hygelac's life in the future. Yet these multiple time-frames are overwritten, one on top of the other, equally discernible and mutually influential upon each other. The *ecne ræd* of the torque is an eternal promise, but one that will elude its future possessors, who bear it to their destruction and loss. A historical lesson is expressed through the power of the object, a compelling statement of the role of the material in the story of *Beowulf*. The precious thing opens up the spaces in the narrative required for the subtlety of theoretical speculation, which is absolutely congruent with the way that these objects create the stability upon which emotional relationships can be built. Ideas do not only follow things in *Beowulf*: they are also given opportunity to be manifested in the spaces that these objects hollow out.

The complex temporality of objects recurs in the poem, and the vibrancy of the material will again be thrust into prominence. After the hero returns from the lair of Grendel's mother, he brings with him only the enormous head of Grendel and the equally oversized hilt of the giant sword he used to decapitate the terrifying monsters. Despite the presence of numerous valuable treasures in the underwater cave into which Beowulf had been dragged, the warrior chooses to bear only these two items back with him. One is restorative and retributive, the final trophy in a game of deadly swapping, as noted by Paz[32] – itself a gruesome reminder that bodies are material too, and liable to be rendered into fetishized objects themselves. Grendel's head is a political statement, proof positive that the feud between the monsters and men has been ended.

The sword hilt is something else entirely, having come to Beowulf unlooked-for though just in the nick of time. It is a surplus that attests to several facts. First, it proves Beowulf's story: Hrunting would not bite the mother's neck and the desperate battle could only be resolved by the fortuitous intervention of the monstrous sword. Second, it bears witness to the supernatural power of the Grendelkin and magnifies the exceptionality

31 Jonathan Gil Harris, *Untimely Matter in the Time of Shakespeare* (Philadelphia, 2009), 24.
32 Paz, 'Æschere's Head', 239.

of Beowulf's deeds in defeating them. Only he could wield the *eotenisc* sword (1560–1), the only weapon that could harm both the mother and the son, even though it was destroyed in the process. Third, and most importantly, the hilt brings into focus a strand of historical narrative that sits on the fringes of the story, introducing a new theme in the history of conflict the poem portrays. To access this historical narrative one must read the *runstafas* etched in the side of the huge sword-hilt:

> Hroðgar maðelode;   hylt sceawode,
> ealde lafe.   On ðæm wæs or writen
> fyrngewinnes;   syðþan flod ofsloh,
> gifen geotende   giganta cyn,
> frecne geferdon;   þæt wæs fremde þeod
> ecean dryhtne;   him þæs endelean
> þurh wæteres wylm   waldend sealde.
> Swa wæs on ðæm scennum   sciran goldes
> þurh runstafas   rihte gemearcod,
> geseted ond gesæd,   hwam þæt sweord geworht,
> irena cyst   ærest wære,
> wreoþenhilt ond wyrmfah.

                                                            (1687–98)

> (Hrothgar spoke, examining the hilt,
> the ancient heirloom. On that the start was written,
> the olden struggles; when the flood destroyed,
> the ocean rushing, the kindred of giants –
> they were made fearful; that was a people estranged
> from the Eternal Lord. The Sovereign gave them
> their final reward through the whelming of waters.
> Thus was marked upon that sword-guard,
> bright of gold, correctly through rune-staves,
> set down and spoken, from those who had wrought that sword,
> the best of iron, which was previously
> hilt-twisted and snake-patterned.)

It seems strange that the giants' sword would contain the story of their own destruction at the hands of the Lord.[33] Yet this is not the only

---

33   Gillian R. Overing states that the runes on the sword-hilt contain the story of the 'or fyrngewinnes' (origin of ancient strife), but does not say who or what

instance of eerie residue we encounter in the case of the hilt: more compellingly, it attests to the existence of an outside, of cultures alien to humanity, clinging to survival, and which nonetheless engage in activities – the creation of treasured objects and the use of written language – that have formerly been seen as solely human occupations. The sword-hilt is literally extra-human, an artefact from another race of creatures 'exiled not only from the hall', as Seth Lerer points out, 'but from the matter of hall-poetry', creating a history only expressible through 'cryptic documents' conveyed through acts of private reading.[34] Paz identifies the sword-hilt as a terrible surplus, an indecipherable code challenging Hrothgar to respond in some legible fashion.[35] This lingering message communicates an exterior to the community of Heorot, in runic letters legible to the knowing observer yet speaking of experiences beyond the pale of humanity.

This sword is described as an 'old heirloom' (*ealde lafe*), which on the one hand feels like the use of habitual language. On the other hand, diction is never idle or automatic, even in formulaic schemes of oral composition. By calling the giant sword an ancient relic, the ideas of inheritance and time are thrust into prominence, asserting the sword's existence as another palimpsest. The sword-hilt bears meaning across the ages, from the past to the future, bearing witness to a story of origins. In this case, it is the beginnings of violence, committed when one race of creatures struggles against their ordained place in the world, and is destroyed by overwhelming force. Hostility and resistance in the story on the sword-hilt beget only more hostility, and so the legend incised into the gold is about the initiation of the cycles of rebellion and retribution. This is a story that would be very familiar to an Anglo-Saxon audience conditioned to respond to

made the markings (Overing, 'Swords and Signs: A Semiotic Perspective on Beowulf', *The American Journal of Semiotics* 5 (1987), 35–57 (56)). Michael R. Near stops short of saying the writing is giant-made, suggesting that the sword's inscription comes to its human readers as evidence of an 'alienated' perspective and art that is extra-human and 'supernatural' (Near, 'Anticipating Alienation: *Beowulf* and the Intrusion of Literacy', *PMLA* 108 (1993), 320–32 (324)). Dennis Cronan states firmly that the 'or fyrngewinnes' refers only to Cain's fratricide and that the account of the giants' destruction is merely a parenthesis (Cronan, 'The Origin of Ancient Strife in Beowulf', *North-Western European Language Evolution* 31/32 (1997), 57–68 (57)).

34 Seth Lerer, *Literacy and Power in Anglo-Saxon Literature* (Lincoln, NE, 1991), 179.

35 Paz, 'Æschere's Head', 246–7.

historical narratives of presumption and punishment such as the poems in the Junius Manuscript (especially the recurring cycles of *Christ and Satan*). These are stories that are not told merely as entertainment, but as education, as a warning to those who would act with such presumption. It is reasonable to assume that the audience of *Beowulf* would interpret the brief legend in a similar way. Another reader of the runic inscription does react in that way: Hrothgar, who is arguably literate enough to decipher its runes, proceeds immediately from the inscription to his famous 'sermon', his lengthy admonishment to the younger Beowulf on the dangers of human pride and avarice (1700–84).

Beowulf brings the sword-hilt back into the light where its meaning can once again be interpreted, rescuing it from the silence and stasis of the Grendelkin's hoard. Hoarding items, as the dragon does later in the poem, demonstrates a fascination with the object in and of itself – a fascination which reaches beyond economic calculations of use or exchange, and pushes the object beyond the experience of time and activity. The thing in the hoard, part of an assemblage, is sufficient as an object of desire. How it objectively functions is not important, and no one is more surprised than Grendel's mother when her own collected sword bites her throat. In its enforced separation from its congeries, the sword-hilt is given back its purpose and returned to legibility so that it may bear witness to its own position in history. It becomes the epic equivalent of one of the speaking objects of the Exeter Book Riddles, articulating its own polychronic existence.

The sword-hilt inscription is more than just a reminder to humanity to remain humble. It warns the reader about the impotence of the mortal realm against historical inevitability. Even its status as an object, the hilt of a huge sword that melts through its proper use, testifies to the powerlessness of all mortal creatures despite the obvious vigour of Beowulf. In the sword's dissolution, the narrator invokes higher powers than the strength of humans and the durability of patterned steel:

> Þa þæt sweord ongan
> æfter heaþoswate   hildegicelum,
> wigbil wanian;   þæt wæs wundra sum
> þæt hit eal gemealt   ise gelicost,
> ðonne forstes bend   fæder onlæteð,
> onwindeð wælrapas,   se geweald hafað
> sæla ond mæla;   þæt is soð metod.

> (1606–11)

(Then that sword began
after the sweat of war into battle-icicles,
the war-bill to wane. That was some miracle
that it all melted much like the ice
when the Father releases the bonds of frost
and unwinds the choking ropes, the one who wields power
over the seasons – that is the true Measurer.)

The simple order of the seasons annihilates the forged blade and the martial values it underscores, even when magnified beyond reckoning by the sword's tremendous size. The progression of time takes the slaughtering, binding cold of the icy seas in winter and melts them into water by the ordaining power of God. The hilt's inscription drives home the overwhelming force of water in comparison with the military strength of mortal creatures. The natural world's supremacy renders negligible the armed resistance of creatures, even creatures as magnificent as an army of giants. The rushing ocean (*gifen geotende*) and the flooding waters (*wæteres wylm*), the preponderance of *materia* itself, suffice to chastise their pride and destroy their resistance. If the Flood obliterates the mighty giants, how can mere humanity resist the way of the world, the tides of history?

In this way, the sword-hilt resists and thwarts the intentions of human actors – that is, it exerts its thing-power. If swords signify power, glory, force, even humanity itself, then the broken sword means the opposite, no matter how impressive the relic. The blade that melts away like water pronounces the insignificance of human military values in the face of a nonpersonifiable history that passes over mortals like the seasons. The author of *Beowulf*, by adding the legible inscription of another version of the lesson, ensures that the hilt communicates the proper message. Here the artefact and its inscription bend towards the same purpose. And even though it contradicts the immediate context of Beowulf's indomitable martial force, it invokes a meaning central to the greater purpose of the narrative. The giants are destroyed by the waters of the flood, a sign of the overwhelming ascendancy of the material world. Beowulf, and by extension humanity, are left wanting in the comparison. The hilt, itself an object that has endured inexorable changes, speaks the awful truth of the fragility of human power in this world.

So far precious objects have catalysed the historical impulses of the poem with their palimpsestic, vibrant, physical presence: torque and sword-hilt alike both thwart and enrich the narrative's focus on the present time with intimations of past and future. The final instance examined here will address a special case in the materialist understanding of *Beowulf*. Objects literally absent within the poem spontaneously create historical awareness and instigate the poem's subtlest meditation on what physical things actually mean to its narrative world. I am speaking about the treasure-trove buried in the dragon's barrow, which for much of its existence in the final third of the poem consists of mere reputation and hidden presence, something which is inaccessible to the actors of the poem. The precious cache is literally held outside the world of *Beowulf*, alienated from the desires and values of its materialist society, kept purposefully remote from that social order's need to affix emotional and political value to things and lend them meaning. The hoard represents what objects might become without humans there to interpret them.

The barrow treasure bursts onto the scene of *Beowulf* as its secrecy and long rest are violated by the entrance of an escaped thrall, and, in a passage marked by heavy corruption and manuscript damage, the audience sees briefly what the fugitive sees. The shadowy hoard is rich with precious items, the quick appearance of which sparks a recognition of the treasure's history and a vision of the archaeological substrata lying below the surface of Geatland:

> Þær wæs swlycra fela
> in ðam eorðsele   ærgestreona,
> swa hy on geardagum   gumena nathwylc,
> eormenlafe   æþelan cynnes,
> þanchycgende   þær gehydde,
> deore maðmas.   Ealle hie deað fornam
> ærran mælum,   ond se an ða gen
> leoda duguðe,   se ðær lengest hwearf,
> weard winegeomor,   wende þæs ylcan,
> þæt he lytel fæc   longgestreona
> brucan moste.

(2231–41)

> (There were many such things there
> in that earthen hall, ancient treasures
> just as I-know-not-which men in days gone by
> had hidden there, a tremendous legacy
> of a noble kindred taking meditation

upon their precious treasures. Death had seized them all
in earlier times, and he who was yet alone,
a man of the multitude who went longest there,
a friend-miserable guardian, he expected the same
so that he would be allowed to enjoy
that long-owned treasure for a little time.)

The darkened intimations of treasure not only recall the plethora of valuable objects (*eormenlafe*) buried there, but also invoke the fading presence of a forgotten people (*gumena nathwlyc*) lost to the ravages of time. Again, the word *laf* in the kenning invokes their possible legacy – this time, however, the anonymity of those from whom the treasure derives creates obscurity in the transmission of objects. The chain of inheritance is broken, leaving the hoard divested of human social meaning. These things have become lost in history. The spaces of the Wedermark open up in time, suggesting a past that clings to the present in shadowy spaces, which inheres in objects that these lost races have left behind without an heir. The *Beowulf*-poet becomes for a moment an archaeologist; he ponders how the immensity of time destroys the continuity of the precious object as an anchor of society. He foreshadows the possibility that a similar fate may await the present keepers of the land. History here reveals that the ownership of a homeland is fleeting – that time is too big and humankind too small.

In fine interlaced fashion the dramatic revelation of the forgotten tribe puts the narrative urgency on hold for a moment to invoke the words of its final memorial, the 'one who went longest there' (*se ðær lengest hwearf*). The so-called 'Lay of the Last Survivor', the sudden intervention of the dramatic monologue in the narrative epic, is often recognized as an example of the elegiac mood of Old English poetry, a poem-within-a-poem perhaps constructed according to the model of the great Exeter Book lyrics such as *The Wanderer* or *The Wife's Lament*.[36] However, like those poems, this lament is more than a meditation on death and mourning. It is instead a poetic study of objects and their relationship to the human actors who create and value them. The speaker's words ponder a world of materiality in the absence of humanity, and wonders

---

36   For a thorough and convincing challenge to the long-received notion that the Exeter Book monologues are examples of Anglo-Saxon elegy, see Kathleen Davis, 'Old English Lyrics: A Poetics of Experience', in *The Cambridge History of Early Medieval English Literature*, ed. Clare Lees (Cambridge, 2012), 332–56.

what the artefacts of his society will become after his people have passed
away:

> Heald þu nu, hruse,   nu hæleð ne mostan,
> eorla æhte.   Hwæt, hyt ær on ðe
> gode begeaton;   guðdeað fornam,
> feorhbealo frecne   fyra gehwylcne
> leoda minra,   þone ðe þis lif ofgeaf;
> gesawon seledreamas.   Nah hwa sweord wege
> oððe forð bere   fæted wæge,
> dryncfæt deore;   duguð ellor sceoc.
> Sceal se hearda helm   hyrstedgolde,
> fætum befeallen;   feormynd swefað,
> þa ðe beadogriman   bywan sceoldon;
> ge swylce seo herepad,   sio æt hilde gebad
> ofer borda gebræc   bite irena,
> brosnað æfter beorne.   Ne mæg byrnan hring
> æfter wigfruman   wide feran,
> hæleðum be healfe.   Næs hearpan wyn,
> gomen gleobeamas,   ne god hafoc
> geond sæl swingeð,   ne se swifta mearh
> burhstede beateð.   Bealocwealm hafað
> fela feorhcynna   forð onsended.
>
>   (2247–66)

> (Keep now, earth, what heroes may not,
> the possessions of earls. So, it was obtained
> from you earlier by good men. War-death has seized them,
> a fearful killing-blow, every man
> of my people, who have given up their lives
> and looked upon the hall-joys. I do not have anyone to bear the sword
> or carry forth the gold-plated flagon,
> the precious drink-vessel. The people have passed elsewhere.
> The hard helmet must be, decked with gold,
> deprived of its decoration. Its attendant sleeps,
> who should polish the war-mask.
> Likewise the mail-coat that experienced battle
> over the breaking of boards and the bites of iron
> decays with its warrior. Nor can the ringed byrnie
> go about widely after its war-chief,

upon the back of the hero. There is no joy of the harp,
the diversion of glee-wood, nor the excellent hawk
flying through the hall, nor the swift steed
stamping in a sheltered stead. A baleful death has
destroyed many living peoples.)

The most startling thing about this meditation is that objects are the chief subject of its sorrow, not people. The items of aristocratic finery lie abandoned, which indicates the triumph of the *bealocwealm* that has seized the tribe. The Last Survivor does not lament the owners of all this splendour: rather it is the missing servants whose absence imperils the world of the warrior caste. It is the loss of the *feormynd*, the attendant or the one who polishes or cares for the war-mask, not the absence of the one who wears it to glory that threatens the continued existence of society. This suggests that it is the material presence of the object that is most vital. It is no longer considered a marker of heroic glory or martial prowess, which is fleeting and liable to loss. Rather it is the thing as it behaves in its environment that ultimately determines its worldly significance. The 'Last Survivor' knows that without the servant to bear the sword or carry the pitcher, these things will be returned to the earth from whence they came; they will become objects with no relation to the social structures and political economy that interpret them and give them human life. The 'Lay' becomes more than a lament for the dead and those destined to be forgotten – it is a moment of speculation about what life remains in the commodity without human social action to animate it. This observer does not see life in objects beyond the human, only their suspension in uselessness and oblivion, though the audience of the poem knows that they will survive nonetheless down there in the barrow, seized hundreds of years later by the dragon. Objects will again become citizens of their own private world, vibrantly enduring the physical transformations which even the most durable substances, noble materials like gold and steel, undergo. Their thing-power goes on, uninterrupted by human endeavour.

The metamorphosis of seemingly permanent things gives poignancy to the contemplation of the immensity of time. This brooding vision of human transience shares its poetic force with the climax of *The Wanderer*, which observes that 'Ongietan sceal gleaw hæle hu gastlic bið / þonne eall þisse worulde wela weste stondeð' ('The wise warrior must understand how ghostly it will be / when all this world's wealth

stands wasted').[37] Just as the halls of aristocratic glory, the houses of the
good life, stand broken and desolate at the end of the human world, the
barrow treasure lies ravaged by the years, as is revealed when Wiglaf
finally lays eyes upon it:

> Him big stodan   bunan ond orcas,
> discas lagon   ond dyre swyrd,
> omige þurhetone,   swa hie wið eorðan faeðm
> þusend wintra   þær eardodon,
> þonne wæs þæt yrfe   eacencræftig,
> iumonna gold   galdre bewunden,
> þæt ðam hringsele   hrinan ne moste
> gumena ænig,   nefne God sylfa,
> sigora soðcyning   sealde þam ðe he wolde
> – he is manna gehyld –   hord openian,
> efne swa hwylcum manna   swa him gemet ðuhte.
>
> (3047–57)

> (Beside [the dragon] stood cups and pitchers,
> dishes lying there, and precious swords,
> rusty and eaten through, just as they had dwelt there
> one thousand winters in the earth's embrace.
> Then was that enormous inheritance,
> the gold of ancient men, wound with a spell,
> so that no man would be allowed to touch
> that hall of rings, unless God himself,
> the truth-king of victories, gave it to them who he wished
> – he is the protector of men – to open up the hoard,
> even to any human as seemed worthy to him.)

The truth is laid bare, the state of the hoard is finally revealed: after a
thousand years the valuable items of treasure, the *bunan ond orcas*, the
discas and *dyre swyrd*, lie in the barrow, decayed and useless, corroded
by the passage of time and the inexorable changes that even solid,
precious matter must endure. They are rusted and eaten through (*omige
þurhetone*), changed into something other than they were intended

37 For *The Wanderer*, see *The Exeter Anthology of Old English Poetry: An
Edition of Exeter Dean and Chapter MS 3501*, ed. Bernard J. Muir (Exeter, 1994),
lines 73–4. Translation mine.

to be. The toll of the *feormynd*'s absence is clear, without someone to care for and maintain these precious artefacts they have become transformed according to their material destiny. They have exceeded human intentions through long disuse. They exist solely as a collection, an assemblage pulsing with its own secret life, superfluous to calculations of use and exchange, magnetic in and of itself.

The spell (*galdre*) that lies upon the treasure trove, though it is expressed as magic, is actually the sense of strange, extra-human life that inheres in all matter, given a subjective, articulable form by a narrator awestruck by the hoard's amazingly long existence. These once-valued objects have been left alone to dwell in their own private existence, outside of human interference for a thousand years. Something must have held them in place, frozen in time, corroding and metabolizing in their subterranean environment. When Wiglaf looks upon the buried treasure, the first to do so for a millennium, he (and we) can only explain that continued existence as magical. Marked by long isolation, the dragon's hoard becomes a metonym for the vast grinding movement of time, a force under which humanity cannot even be seen as *læne*, or transitory, loaned an existence on this earth. The curse does not ward off human interference: it only communicates the distance and remoteness of history to those who are sensitive enough to hear its cold and terrible call.

Conventional wisdom would seem to limit the degree to which we can consider *Beowulf* a vibrantly materialist poem. The epic's closing words do not appear to celebrate the vitality and thing-power of the many objects that have spangled its lines and played pivotal roles in the drama. The poem instead seems to dismiss their value. In the closing moments, the Geats abandon the dragon's treasure – hard-won and dearly bought – to the earth that previously held it. Traditional views of these lines suggest a dimly limned sort of *contemptus mundi* topos, a stereotypical idea of early medieval culture which devalues the physical realm in favour of an eternal one. The wreckage of Geatish culture projected by the poem's historical consciousness stands in for the eventual failure of everything glorious yet worldly. The centrepiece of this dreary perspective on a dreary moment is the narrator's seeming dismissal of the importance of the dragon's hidden treasure – the reward for fighting the beast in the first place – with the terse statement assessing the 'gold on greote, þær hit nu gen lifað, / eldum swa unnyt swa hyt æror wæs' ('gold on the gravel, where still it lives on, / as unavailing to humanity, as it was before', 3167–8). But even this mineral pessimism contains a sense of material possibility, expressing that the reburied treasures 'lifað' – literally 'live on' or 'endure' in the present tense – and accompanied by the adverb 'gen' or 'still'. They may be 'unavailing to humanity', beyond the purposes of exchange, unusable in their current condition – yet that is hardly the only destiny for things to assume. Time and the world have their own purposes to put things to, and even their corrosions are articulations of a secret material existence beyond us, a palimpsest that is actually a *mise-en-abyme*, endlessly written over in languages no one even knows.

Objects and things abound in the Anglo-Saxon epic *Beowulf*, and these material phenomena reveal the extent to which people and things are entangled, drawn together into chains of mutual dependence in the world. The world of Beowulf and Hrothgar is delineated by the material, and there are few, if any, avenues of escape from its relentless physicality. Even death itself becomes an acknowledgment that the body is one sort of thing among others. In death, both Scyld Scefing and Beowulf – even if their souls pass into the keeping of some sort of 'Frea' (Lord, 27) or seek a place of 'soðfæstra dom' ('glory of the truth-fast', 2820) – are just another adornment in the treasure-hoards committed to oblivion in their passing, whether the poem celebrates or mourns that undeniable fact. Heaven and Hell, the idealistic outside to material existence, are underemphasized during the course of the narrative, if they exist at all for the pagan warriors and heroes of the poem.[38] These exorbitant places are inaccessible according to the very tangible terms that the story has created for itself. The materiality of the world overwhelms any attempt by humanity to ascribe a beyond to it. For example, the miserable song of the Geatish woman at Beowulf's funeral does not even fall on deaf ears: 'heofon rece swealg' (3155), the poem says. The sky just swallows the smoke that is the carrier of her grim predictions for the future; if the world is altered by the smouldering corpse-fire that consumes the best hopes of the Geats, the alteration is almost insignificant.

38 These places may exist for the narrator, who, perhaps anachronistically, ventriloquizes his belief in the beyond through the words of Beowulf, who promises an infernal future to Unferth for the slaying of his own kin (588–9). (Though the word 'helle' in the transcription, which is missing in the manuscript in its current condition, may be the Thorkelin scribe's misconstrual of 'healle': see Fred C. Robinson, 'Elements of the Marvellous in the Characterization of *Beowulf*: A Reconsideration of the Textual Evidence', in *Old English Studies in Honour of John C. Pope*, ed. Robert B. Burlin and Edward B. Irving, Jr. (Toronto, 1974), 119–37 (129–30); and Andy Orchard, *A Critical Companion to 'Beowulf'* (Cambridge, 2003), 252–3.)

The idea is grim, though coldly reflective of the poem's materialist implications – yet the relationship does not have to be so alienating. For most of the poem, the vibrant realm of matter has meshed with the human. We intertwine with the material world, mutually dependent for not just preservation but also for meaning. We are fascinated by the operation of things, even when they exceed our grasp and control, when they fall apart and fail. Thing-power, the conative impetus within all matter, demands a political realignment, a renewed recognition that we are not the sole occupants of the planet. *Beowulf*, although written down 1,000 years ago, provides a compelling model for how people and objects interpenetrate and cooperate. It is not unique among Old English poetry for this secular sense of material presence, of speculation upon the physical ecology of its narrative of heroism and loyalty, but it is alone in its perception of the often-harsh lessons of the material realm. Although ideal human qualities are fleeting, and Beowulf's glory cannot last, the world that contextualizes that glory endures – it will survive us. Palimpsestic items, 'untimely matter', not only read the complex existence of things among us; they also intimate the tenuousness of human possession and care of these things. Objects that persist to be changed over the centuries remind us that it is our own destiny to be altered by time. We must lose our grip upon these polychronic things – give them up to their own destiny of change. However, the partnership between human and object, the 'som-wist' (meal together, as the Anglo-Saxons might have called it), is powerfully constitutive, even if extremely brief.[39] The actors in *Beowulf* build their lives in partnership with a material world, dining together for as long as they may, yet all things sleep after the feast.

---

39 'Som-wist' is found poetically in *Guthlac B* (150 and 359) and *Genesis A* (2282), where all three times it refers to the living unity of body and soul, the joining of the material and spiritual.

3

Pidgin Poetics

Bird Talk in Medieval France and Occitania*

ELIZA ZINGESSER

A mon ops chant et a mos ops flaujol,
Car homs mas ieu non enten mon lati;
Atretan pauc com fa d'un rossinhol
Entent la gent de mon chant que se di.

('I sing and play the flute for myself.
For no man except me understands my language.
As little as they understand the nightingale
do the people understand what my song says.')[1]

                    Peire Cardenal, 'Les amairitz, qui encolpar las vol'

'Pa. Pa pa. Pa pa pa. Pa pa pa pa pa pa pa pa, pa pa pa pa pa pa pa pa.' These monosyllabic interjections, inarticulate yet instantly recognizable to opera lovers everywhere, represent Papageno and Papagena's expressions of delight upon their belated unification in Mozart's *Die Zauberflöte*.[2] At first, they sound like something akin to an emotion-induced speech impediment. It is easy to imagine that the two bird-like characters, gazing into each other's eyes at long last, attempt lovingly to enunciate each other's names, but make it no further than the initial

---

*   I am indebted to Matilda Tomaryn Bruckner and Eleanor Johnson for their extremely helpful comments on an early draft of this piece, to Sias Merkling for the title, and to *NML*'s two anonymous readers.
1   Peire Cardinal, *Poésies complètes du troubadour Peire Cardenal*, ed. and trans. René Lavaud (Toulouse, 1957), 366. My translation.
2   *Wolfgang Amadeus Mozart: Die Zauberflöte*, ed. A. Csampai and D. Holland (Reinbek, 1982), 111.

two syllables.[3] In deconstructing their names in this way, Mozart's librettist, Schickaneder, reveals two aspects of avian language, at least as perceived by human animals. First, he flags up the imitative nature of many birds' names.[4] Second, the scene's proliferation of disjointed '*pa*'s draws attention to the act of acoustic reduplication at the heart of most avian vocalizations. Even in the case of birds with complex songs or with a large repertory, birds are likely to repeat each song, or song section, a certain number of times.[5] And this propensity for repetition is not limited to songbirds: as anyone who has lived in the vicinity of a blue jay's nest knows, vocalizations that would more likely be described as calls rather than songs are often repeated at brief intervals. Moreover, that Papageno and Papagena call out *the same syllables* to each other may be intended to conjure up the highly mimetic nature of parrots' vocalizations – an interpretation reinforced by the musical echoes in Mozart's dialogue. In any case, the framing of the duet as a series of calls and responses can be read as an evocation of the antiphonal duetting common in many bird species.

I dwell on this scene in *Die Zauberflöte* because it demonstrates how repeated iterations of a syllable invite us to hear that syllable differently. With each successive '*pa*', through a process sometimes called semantic satiation, we hear the syllable less as a constitutive link in the differential matrix of human language, and more as nonlinguistic sound. To use Reuven Tsur's terminology, we switch from a 'speech mode' of listening to a 'poetic mode', one in which acoustic signals are perceptible even through referential language.[6] This hearing of the '*pa*'s in nonspeech mode is facilitated by Mozart's rhythmic acceleration, which trades quarter notes for eighth notes several bars into the duet, evoking something analogous to squawking. What particularly

3   Papageno and Papagena's names obviously allude to the word for parrot in a variety of languages (e.g. German *Papagei*, Italian *pappagallo*).
4   Isidore of Seville comments on how often animal names are onomatopoeic in origin. See Isidore, *The Etymologies of Isidore of Seville*, trans. Stephen A. Barney (Cambridge, 2006), Book IX.9. On onomatopoeia specifically in birds' names, see Jacques André, 'Onomatopées et noms d'oiseaux en latin', *Bulletin de la Société linguistique de Paris* 61 (1966), 146–56.
5   J. Jordan Price, 'Why is Birdsong so Repetitive? Signal Detection and the Evolution of Avian Singing Modes', *Behaviour* 150.9–10 (2013), 995–1013.
6   Reuven Tsur, *What Makes Sound Patterns Expressive?: The Poetic Mode of Speech Perception* (Durham, NC, 1992), 11–14. Tsur argues that the 'poetic function' of language invites us to rematerialize language, to hear it as sound.

interests me about this moment in *Die Zauberflöte* is its simultaneous legibility both as human language – as the partial trace of Papageno and Papagena's names – and as a rendering of nonlinguistic avian vocalization of the sort on which Papageno and Papagena's echoic names are based. The contribution of this article is to show that this hermeneutic indeterminacy is not without medieval precedent. I will argue here, via two case studies, that medieval French and Occitan lyric poets conjured up the language of birds in similar ways, using various sound effects – especially those based on repetition – to evoke avian vocalization. The two poets on whom I will focus here – Marcabru and Richard de Fournival – practise what Aaron Moe terms zoopoetics – that is, composition whose formal properties are inflected by an attentiveness to the poesis of a nonhuman animal.[7] In so doing, I contend, they craft a type of language that straddles the boundary between two widespread medieval categories of *vox*: meaningful and meaningless. Through these poets' evocations of bird vocalizations, we hear anew the raw sound that is the medium of all spoken human language.

My analysis will draw on the insights of past work in animal studies and sound studies, including that of Aaron Moe, Elizabeth Eva Leach, and Jean-Marie Fritz, the latter two of whom have studied birdsong extensively (Fritz within a broader framework of soundscapes).[8] My work also heeds Emma Dillon's recent plea to attend to 'song's sound' beyond the melodic; it shows – I hope – the potential fruits of such a line of enquiry.[9] This essay's main contribution lies in its demonstration that formal experimentation constituted both fertile ground for engagement with the nonhuman animal and a laboratory in which to put pressure on linguistic theory as taught in the medieval schoolroom: Marcabru

7   See Aaron Moe, *Zoopoetics: Animals and the Making of Poetry* (Lanham, MD, 2013), 10. Moe acknowledges that he has taken the term from Derrida, who used it especially in relation to Kafka. Moe's use of the term links it specifically with form, which is why I have adopted it here. As he explains: 'Zoopoetics is the process of discovering innovative breakthroughs in form through an attentiveness to another species' bodily poesis.'

8   See Elizabeth Eva Leach, *Sung Birds: Music, Nature, and Poetry in the Later Middle Ages* (Ithaca, NY, 2007); Jean-Marie Fritz, *La Cloche et la lyre: pour une poétique médiévale du paysage sonore* (Geneva, 2011); and Jean-Marie Fritz, *Paysages sonores du Moyen âge: le versant épistémologique* (Paris, 2000).

9   Emma Dillon, 'Unwriting Medieval Song', *New Literary History* 46.4 (2015), 595–622 (606).

and Richard de Fournival's lyric *voces*, as described above, occupy a category that is not conceptually available in grammatical treatises but that resonates with much current scholarship in both lyric theory and sound studies.[10]

Theorizing Birdsong

Most medieval thought on bird vocalizations placed them in a different category from other animal language. As Leach has amply demonstrated, questions of whether birdsong was rational, grammatical, or even musical, were repeatedly raised throughout late antiquity and the Middle Ages.[11] Bird vocalizations were often granted a particular status by late antique and medieval theorists as one category of *vox* – itself a subset of the broader category of *sonus*, or sound. A *vox*, according to Boethius, is a sound emitted from the mouth or windpipe of an animal; the notion corresponds to what we might today call a vocalization.[12] Some grammarians distinguished between, on the one hand, *vox discreta* – understood either as *vox* capable of being transposed in writing or as *vox* that signified according to semantic conventions – and, on the other, *vox confusa* – *vox* that resisted transcription in writing.[13] Later thinkers, beginning with Priscian, distinguished more systematically between meaningfulness and writeability. This led to the categories of *articulata* and *inarticulata*, on the one hand (potentially meaningful or not meaningful), and *litterata* and *illitterata* (writeable or unwriteable), on the other.[14] As both Elizabeth Leach and Umberto Eco have demonstrated, the placement of the sounds of various species

---

10   Anna Zayaruznaya has recently come to similar conclusions regarding formal experimentation and the monstrous in the *ars nova* motet. See *The Monstrous New Art: Divided Forms in the Late Medieval Motet* (Cambridge, 2015). Regarding resonances in contemporary theory, I am thinking in particular of Reuven Tsur (quoted above), of Mutlu Blasing (quoted below), and of Mladen Dolar, whose work touches on the tension between sound and sense in song (Dolar, *A Voice and Nothing More* (Cambridge, MA, 2006)).

11   Leach, *Sung Birds, passim.*

12   Boethius, *On Aristotle, On Interpretation 1–3*, trans. Andrew Smith (London, 2010), Book I.1, 15.

13   *Vox discreta* was also sometimes called *articulata*.

14   Priscian, *Prisciani grammatici Caesariensis Institutionum grammaticarum libri XVIII; Prisciani Opera minora*, ed. Martin Hertz (Leipzig, 1855), Book I.1–2.

within this grid varied.[15] Most theorists, however, placed bird vocalizations, as opposed to other animal noises, in the category of *vox* that is *inarticulata* but *litterata* (meaningless but writeable).[16] Although some troubadours emphasize birdsong's association with incomprehensibility rather than writeability, as did Peire Cardenal in this article's epigraph, this categorization makes birdsong most proximate to referential human language among all non-human vocal utterances.

I want to argue here that at least two medieval French and Occitan writers explored this conceptual proximity between human and avian languages, especially, and not coincidentally, in a corpus of lyric poetry.[17] Like Mozart's *Die Zauberflöte*, I will argue, these poems effect an avian turn especially via formal devices – such as repetition – that foreground the sense-perceptibility of language. Such figures are, of course, a constitutive feature of much lyric poetry, whether formally via refrains, repeated rhyme sounds or rhyme schemes, or in common poetic devices such as assonance and alliteration. I aim to show here, via my case studies, that the most common way of evoking avian languages was *not* to frame them as incomprehensible, as in Chaucer's famous 'Kek kek, cokkou, quek quek' from *The Parliament of Fowls*, but instead to foreground various forms of sonic recursiveness in otherwise comprehensible discourse. In so doing, these poets rethink the boundary between human and avian languages posited by grammarians, suggesting instead that song is radically avian. We might, I would suggest, take more seriously the various troubadours who describe songbirds as a source of inspiration, with some even going so far as to posit songbirds as their tutors. Jaufre Rudel, for instance, makes this claim in 'Pro ai del chan essenhadors' (PC 262.4): 'Pro ai del chan essenhadors / entorn mi et ensenhairitz:

15   Leach, *Sung Birds*; Umberto Eco et al., 'On Animal Language in the Medieval Classification of Signs', in *On the Medieval Theory of Signs*, ed. Umberto Eco and Constantino Marmo (Amsterdam, 1989), 3–41.

16   Leach, *Sung Birds*, 34. In the category of *vox* that is both *inarticulata* and *illitterata*, theorists often mention the lion's roar and the ox's lowing. Contrary to what I describe above, some thinkers placed birdsong in this same category. Leach thinks this has to do with the discrete pitches (or lack thereof) of the bird vocalizations in question. See 'Grammar and Music in the Medieval Song-School', *New Medieval Literatures* 11 (2009), 195–211 (202).

17   Christopher Davis has recently noted the use of 'lati' (Latin) as a descriptor both for birdsong and for the language of troubadour composition. See Davis, '"Chascus en lor lati": Guilhem IX, Birdsong, and the Language of Poetry', *Tenso: Bulletin de la Société Guilhem IX* 30.1–2 (2015), 2–24 (3, 12, 19).

/ pratz e vergiers, albres e flors, / voutas d'auzelhs e lais e critz / per lo dous termini suau' ('I have plenty of song masters and song mistresses around me: fields and orchards, trees and flowers, trills of birds and lays and cries, because of the sweet, gentle season').[18] Giraut de Calanso even suggests that a jongleur should be capable of imitating birdsong.[19] The mimetic relationship between bird and poet is often implied in formulations such as 'When I hear the birds sing, so I begin my song'. Bertran de Born identifies himself as a bird in 'Qan la novella flors par el vergan' (PC 80.34). There he announces that he sings like the *other* birds (!) and that he shares several qualities with them: 'chant atressi cum fant li autr'ausel; / car per auzel mi teing e maintas res' ('I sing, as do the other birds; / for I take myself for a bird in many things').[20] Building on this proximity between birdsong and human lyric poesis, the composers I describe here forge a contact or 'pidgin' language language that is neither *articulata* nor *inarticulata*, neither human nor nonhuman, but always both simultaneously. It is, to appropriate Jonathan Hsy's term, *ambilingual*, a language deployed not to shore up an imagined boundary between species but one that instead 'resonates across species difference'.[21]

Sounding the Starling: Marcabru's Sound Poems

I begin here with two songs by the twelfth-century Occitan troubadour Marcabru. Marcabru's corpus demonstrates a remarkable attentiveness to the soundscape of nonhuman animals.[22] Alongside the expected

18 *The Poetry of Cercamon and Jaufre Rudel*, ed. George Wolf and Roy Rosenstein (New York, 1983), 1:1–5. PC numbers, used throughout this essay, refer to Alfred Pillet and Henry Carstens, *Bibliographie der Troubadours* (Halle, 1933).

19 Guiraut de Calanson, 'Fadet juglar', in *Recherches sur les connaissances littéraires des troubadours occitans et catalans des XIIe et XIIIe siècles; les 'sirventes-ensenhamens' de Guerau de Cabrera, Guiraut de Calanson et Bertrand de Paris*, ed. François Pirot (Barcelona, 1972), 563–95 (verse 22).

20 Bertran de Born, *The Poems of the Troubadour Bertran de Born*, ed. William D. Paden, Tilde Sankovitch, and Patricia Stäblein (Berkeley, 1986), 285, verses 3–4.

21 Jonathan Hsy, 'Between Species: Animal–Human Bilingualism and Medieval Texts', in *Booldly Bot Meekly: Essays on the Theory and Practice of Translation in the Middle Ages in Honour of Roger Ellis*, ed. Catherine Batt and René Tixier (Turnhout, forthcoming).

22 All references are to *Marcabru: A Critical Edition*, ed. Simon Gaunt, Ruth

evocations of birdsong, Marcabru alludes to the croaking of frogs (songs III, XI), the snarling and barking of dogs (IX, XVI), and curiously, in one piece, expresses anxiety over being mistaken for an owl (XII). Even what appear to be merely topical allusions to birdsong reveal nuances that suggest an acute interest in their poesis: Marcabru distinguishes between the 'critz' ('cries') of birds and their 'chanton' ('song', II.8), and elsewhere between their 'lays e voutas e chans' ('lais and chirping and songs', XXXIV.3). His nightingale does not just sing; its song more specifically 'trills' ('del chant que grazilla', XXI.6). What is more, these nonhuman animal vocalizations are framed as akin to analogous human vocal productions. Kings and dukes make noise ('fag gran nauza', XI.43); people whistle ('sioulan', XIX.65) and bray (XXXII.26). And in one instance Marcabru draws a direct parallel between his own act of composition and that of the birds, whose songs pour forth from their beaks: 'Bel m'es can s'esclarzis l'onda / e qecs auzels pel jardin / s'esjauzis segon son latin; / lo chanz per lo[r] becs toronda, / mais eu trop miels qe negus' ('It pleases me when the wave grows bright and each bird in the garden rejoices in its own language; the song pours forth from their beaks, but I compose [songs] better than any of them', XII.1–5).[23]

The details of Marcabru's nonhuman soundscape are well worth further attention – particularly in relation to Marcabru's well-known forging of rhyme words and his deployment of unusual or unique rhyme sounds. Like Emily Dickinson's whippoorwill, Marcabru's soundscape and all of its creatures 'break [...] in bright Orthography', arguably rendering within what appears to be *vox articulata et litterata* sounds that were traditionally thought of as inarticulate and unscriptable.[24] It is perhaps no coincidence that Marcabru describes his art of *trobar* or composition as 'naturau' ('natural', XXXIII.6), and that he identifies on more than one occasion with various avian species. For instance, Marcabru declares in song XVI that he is the bird who has its young fed by starlings ('ieu soi l'auzels / c'als estornels / fauc los mieus auzeletz

Harvey, and Linda Paterson (Cambridge, 2000). Unless otherwise indicated, translations are theirs. In using the term 'attentiveness', I am indebted to Moe, *Zoopoetics*, 7 and *passim*.

23   Gaunt, Harvey and Paterson read 'toronda' as a form of *torondar*, and I follow them here (*Marcabru*, 172).

24   Emily Dickinson, *The Complete Poems of Emily Dickinson*, ed. Thomas H. Johnson (Boston, 1961), 126, poem 276.

noirir', lines 58–60), referring to the phenomenon described by ornithol-
ogists as brood parasitism.

I want to turn here specifically to Marcabru's famous starling songs:
'Estornel, cueill ta volada' (XXV, PC 293.25) and 'Ges l'estornels no·n
s'ublida' (XXVI, PC 293.26). This is because I think their attentiveness to
starlings' poesis – and their imitation of that poesis – is exceptional even
within the humming, braying, and trilling ushered in by Marcabru's
collected songs.[25] The two poems tell the tale of a starling who serves as
a messenger between a lover and his beloved, a woman who is simultaneously courting other suitors. The rhyme scheme of these two lyrics is
as follows:[26]

a7' a7' a7' b7' c3 c3 c3 c3 c3 c3 b5'

Throughout each of the starling poems, the 'a' and 'b' rhymes are
unisonnans or constant (-*ada* and -*ia* in the first song, and -*ida* and
-*ensa* in the second) while the 'c' rhyme is *singulars* – that is to say that
it changes in each stanza. While Marcabru is generally known for his
feats in rhyming, the short lines in the *cauda* of each stanza represent
a particularly remarkable accomplishment.[27] As Ruth Harvey puts it:
'the task of finding a sequence of six three-syllable lines, all with the
same sound and which make sense in the context, is quite a steep one.'[28]

25   The first of the starling songs appears in two manuscripts: Paris, Bibliothèque
nationale de France, MS fr. 856 (also known as troubadour songbook C), fol.
174v; and Paris, Bibliothèque nationale de France, MS fr. 1749 (also known as
troubadour songbook E), fol. 154. The second appears only in BnF, MS fr. 1749,
fols. 154–5. It would be thrilling to know if Marcabru's sturnine poesis extended
to his melodies, but unfortunately neither manuscript transmits music notation.
26   Catherine Leglu points out, following A. R. Nykl, that a *muwashshah* shares
its structure with Marcabru's starling songs. See Leglu, *Between Sequence and
Sirventes: Aspects of Parody in the Troubadour Lyric* (Oxford, 2000), 36; and
A. R. Nykl, *Hispano-Arabic Poetry, and its Relations with the Old Provençal
Troubadours* (Baltimore, 1946), 245–6.
27   I take the anonymous reader's point that the 'rules' which Marcabru is
following or bending in his songs were not yet fully established, Marcabru
being among the earliest troubadours, but it remains that his experimentation,
particularly on the level of rhyme sounds, far exceeds that of his predecessors
and contemporaries (few though they may be).
28   Ruth Harvey, 'Rhymes and "Rusty Words" in Marcabru's Songs', *French
Studies* 56.1 (2002), 1–14 (2). Aileen MacDonald remarks of this feature that it
'produce[s] an incantatory effect which reflects [the speaker's] obsession'. See

I would further note that this poetic structure is one in which the 'c' rhyme is given exceptional prominence in its materiality as a signifier, given both that it is the only rhyme sound that changes in each song, and that it is encapsulated in three-syllable lines (a fact that makes the rhyme sound almost constant in the fifth through to the tenth line of each stanza). In the first poem, the speaker invites the starling to take flight and visit his mistress, while the second recounts the starling's visit to the *amia*.[29] In the second poem, the starling and the beloved actually converse, and the starling's direct speech is reported (lines 23–33, 69–84).

Matilda Bruckner has argued that the metrical structure of the two songs mirrors the pattern of the starling's song. In her assessment: 'the starling's screechy voice is made abundantly audible in sounds and rhythms.' She further invites us to '[c]onsider the metrical pattern of the stanzas with a pick-up in tempo when the four seven-syllable lines of the *frons* give way to the series of short three-syllable lines in the *cauda*', pointing out that 'the bird's calls, like the lover's desires, sound out a rapid, insistent drum beat, quickly pile up over six lines, and then slow down with a longer, five-syllable line to make a smooth transition to the next *frons* before the abrupt jump to the *cauda* begins again.'[30] I find this idea quite compelling, and would add that, beyond the question of tempo, the starling's song pattern displays a remarkable similarity to the poetic form of many medieval lyrics. In the words of one ornithologist: '[in the starling's song bouts], many distinct units [...] are repeated once, twice, or several times before the next unit is introduced.'[31] One could compare these units – which Eens calls 'phrases' – either to individual verses of the same rhyme sound, or instead to a succession of *coblas*. Although repetition is a defining feature of most birdsong, the complexity of starling song and its interweaving of many different acoustic patterns make it especially analogous to troubadour song, and this proximity, I will argue, was exploited by Marcabru.

MacDonald, 'Warbled Words: The "Starling" and "Nightingale" Poems', *Tenso: Bulletin de la Société Guilhem IX* 10.1 (1994), 18–36 (20).

29   Matilda Tomaryn Bruckner has recently discussed the complexity of determining the speakers in these songs. See her 'Marcabru's Estornel: On Ventriloquists; or, The Art of Putting Words in your Belly', *French Studies* 68.4 (2014), 451–64.

30   Ibid., 459.

31   M. Eens, 'Understanding the Complex Song of the European Starling: An Integrated Ethological Approach', *Advances in the Study of Behavior* 26 (1997), 355–434 (359).

Building on Bruckner's observation that the rhyme sounds of the
second starling song, taken globally, reflect the sounds of the starling, I
want to suggest that Marcabru's imitation is in fact much more specific.[32]
I aim to show here that Marcabru's imitations of the starling's vocalization patterns are most extreme – unsurprisingly – in the direct speech
of the starling. The starling speaks directly only in three stanzas (III,
VII and VIII, all in the second song). In III, it introduces the rhyme
sound *-ic*, and in VII and VIII, its 'c' rhymes are *-utz* and *-i*. I believe
the two sounds in /i/ (III and VIII) are intended to call to mind the type
of repeated screeching in starling song that might best be transcribed
with the sound /i/. What is more, the 'c' rhymes of stanzas VII and
VIII, in *-utz* and *-i*, evoke another distinctive feature of starling vocalization: mimicry.[33] The rhyme sound *-utz* follows the pattern established
elsewhere in the song in the sense that it is, strictly speaking, *singulars*
(no other stanza in the two songs deploys this rhyme sound). I would
note, however, that the rhyme sound *-utz* is an amalgamation of almost
all of the rhyme sounds specific to the mistress's direct speech elsewhere
in the song (*-ui* in II, *-u* in IV, and *-atz* in V). Like a real starling,
Marcabru's bird riffs on the sounds produced around it.[34] The only one of
the starling's rhyme sounds that does not fit into the pattern established
in *-utz* is its last rhyme sound, *-i*. And in fact, rather than amalgamating
the sounds of the mistress's speech, here the starling instead imitates her
directly: 'Vai e·l di / qu'el mati / s'i aisi, / que sotz pi / farem fi / sotz lui
mi, / d'esta malvolensa' ('Go and tell him to approach in the morning, for

32 Bruckner proposes that the bird's chirping is 'reflected in the sharper, high-
pitched vocal and consonantal play in XXVI (-et, -ui, -ic, iu, -atz, -i, -utz, -i)'
(Bruckner, 'On Ventriloquists', 459).

33 The starling's capacity for mimicry was registered as early as Pliny the Elder.
See Pliny, *Natural History*, trans. H. Rackham (Cambridge, MA, 1940), vol.
X.LIX. For other allusions to starlings in the ancient world, see Geoffroy Arnott's
catalogue, *Birds in the Ancient World from A to Z* (London, 2007), 199–200 (I
am grateful to Isabel Köster for this reference). Eugenius II of Toledo lists the
starling among those birds capable of reproducing human language: 'Psittacus
et corvus, cornix et garrula pica, / graculus et sturni verba referre solent' ('the
parrot and the *corvus*, the *cornix* and the magpie, the chough and starlings
habitually repeat words') (quoted in Fritz, *Paysages*, 199). As Jean-Marie Fritz
has noted, Évrart de Conty makes his starling capable of singing a large section
of a *virelai* (*Paysages*, 220).

34 West and King have noted the starling's practice of recombinatory poetics.
See Meredith J. West and Andrew P. King, 'Mozart's Starling', *American Scientist*
78 (1990), 106–14 (108).

beneath a pine we shall put an end to this ill will, with me beneath him', lines 60–6). This act of imitation, I would contend, explains the serious formal anomaly of stanza VIII, which is in fact a *tornada*. Most Occitan *tornadas* repeat the *cauda* of the stanza they immediately follow, but this one instead repeats the rhyme sounds of the *penultimate* full stanza. This means that, rather than reproducing the rhyme sounds of its own speech, the starling instead imitates the rhyme sounds of the woman's speech (lines 60–6). This pattern is unique in Marcabru's corpus. While his first starling song also has an unusual *tornada* in that it introduces a new rhyme sound (*-ei*), only the *tornada* of the second starling song repeats the rhyme sounds of any stanza other than the immediately preceding one. This formal pattern is rare not just in Marcabru's corpus, but also in the troubadour corpus as a whole. Marcabru's second starling song is one of a handful of deviations from the traditional model Mölk identifies.[35]

And, in fact, the starling's imitation in the *tornada* extends beyond the *sounds* of this portion of the woman's speech to its content: 'eu·s mandi / qu'es ardi- / d'el jardi' ('I bring you word that she is getting bold in the garden', lines 81–3), the starling reports, also repeating the fact that the meeting is to take place in the morning (lines 61, 78). The starling thus 'mimics' the woman both in that it reports the content of her speech and in that it redeploys her rhyme sounds, directly in one instance (*-i*), and through amalgamation in another (*-utz*).

The unusual rhyme scheme of the starling's speech is not the only aspect of the poem that can be explained as avian in origin. As one might expect of a non-native Occitan speaker, the starling breaks linguistic rules as well as poetic ones, following on from its unusually imitative rhyme scheme in the *tornada*. Like many second-language learners, it

---

35 In his list of exceptions, Mölk also notes Peire d'Alvernha's 'Cui bon vers agrad'a auzir' (PC 323.16), which omits one of the rhyme sounds from its *tornada*. All other deviations from the pattern on Mölk's list introduce a new rhyme sound into the *tornada*. These are Marcabru's first starling song, Bernart de Ventadorn's 'Bel m'es can eu vei la brolha' (PC 70.9), and Guilhem IX's 'Farai chansoneta nueva' (PC 183.6). Mölk incorrectly includes Marcabru's second starling song in this group, failing to realize that it repeats an earlier rhyme sound. Mölk also fails to acknowledge Marcabru's 'D'aiso laus Dieu' (PC 293.16), whose two *tornadas* each introduce a new rhyme sound (in addition to maintaining the *b* rhyme, which is stable throughout the poem). See Ulrich Mölk, 'Deux remarques sur la tornada', *Metrica* 3 (1982), 3–14 (11–12).

has particular trouble with accentuation. Here are the offending last stanza and *tornada*:

66 Gent ha la razon fenida.
     Estornels cui l'aura guida
     son senhor [di]: 'Conquerida
     vos ai amor de valensa;
70   c'als mil drutz
         ha rendutz
         mil salutz,
         e pagutz –
         per c'os dutz ses traütz –
75   de falsa semensa.
         S'al mati
         les aqui
         on vos di,
         eu·s mandi
80   qu'es ardi-
         d'el jardi,
         e que-us mat e·us vensa!'

(She finished her speech graciously. The starling, guided by the breeze, said to its lord: 'I have conquered a love of value for you, for she has returned a thousand greetings to the thousand lovers, and fed them on false seed – because she brings you there without tributes (for free).

If in the morning there is an opportunity in the place which I am telling you about, I bring you word that she is getting bold in the garden, in which let her checkmate and vanquish you!')

In line 79 ('eu·s mandi'), the starling mispronounces 'mandi', placing the stress not on the first syllable but instead on the second, deploying both *rim accentual* (*mandí* instead of *mándi*) and systole (the lengthening of /i/). And shortly thereafter (lines 80–1), it displays a blatant disregard for word boundaries, splitting the word 'ardid' over two lines.[36] This procedure of splitting, known as *rim trencat* (making the rhyme sound

---

36 Both of these anomalies are have been documented by Ruth Harvey, who does not consider their location in the starling's direct speech (Harvey, 'Rhymes', 3).

internal to a word), is fairly rare among the troubadours, and much more so among the *trouvères*, though we will see the procedure used again in conjunction with avian imitation in Richard de Fournival's corpus. Starling researchers have in fact documented a tendency to fragment words and phrases among the birds, with one writer going so far as to describe the practice as a 'clear starling aesthetic'.[37] It is, in any case, no surprise that a bird should be less attentive to speech segmentation, privileging the material building blocks of language over lexemes. Marcabru's starling displays a keener interest in the *sound* of its composition, challenging the listener to reconstruct its sense by following a single word across a line break.

I want to suggest here that Marcabru's unusual solutions to the problem of finding six rhyme sounds in 'i' – solutions which involve systole and *rim trencat* – are intended to draw our attention to this rhyme sound in particular and by extension to all rhyme sounds *as sounds* and not merely as constitutive phonemes in banausic, denotative language. As I have already mentioned, this invitation to rematerialize them sonically is reinforced by two other features: first, that *only* the 'c' rhyme is *singulars* or non-repeating across stanzas, and, second, by the metrical structure of the poem, which places each 'c' rhyme in the shortest (trisyllabic) lines, where it is rapidly repeated. In sum, Marcabru's starling makes us hear the succession of /i/, /i/, /i/, /i/, /i/, /i/ as *noise* – noise encapsulated in semantic language, significantly, but also as non-referential noise. The more of Marcabru's starling we hear in these lines, the less we hear the semantic dimension of language.[38] All of these poetic devices, I would argue, are intended to evoke the starling's natural vocalization *without* framing it as linguistically alien to Occitan. Instead, the piece invites a kind of double-listening. In its apparently

37   West and King, 'Mozart's Starling', 108; David Rothenberg, *Why Birds Sing: A Journey into the Mystery of Birdsong* (New York, 2006), 103.
38   I am indebted here to Mutlu Blasing's remark, quoted by Jonathan Culler, that a lyric 'far from being a text where sound and sense, form and meaning, are indissolubly one, is a text where we witness the *distinct* operation of the two systems. We can always yield to the seductive call to "to stop making sense" and attend to the patterning of the non-sense. Or we can choose to switch to the symbolic and make sense. We cannot do both at once.' See Jonathan D. Culler, *Theory of the Lyric* (Cambridge, MA, 2015), 168. In Culler's reading of Blasing, 'the more a poem foregrounds vocal effects [...], the more powerful the image of voicing, oral articulation, but the less we find ourselves dealing with the voice of a person' (*Theory of the Lyric*, 168).

conventional Occitan lies latent starling song, waiting to be activated by a singer who, by singing the piece, must in turn imitate the starling, bringing the mimetic cycle full circle.

Richard de Fournival's Psittacine Poetics

A piece by the thirteenth-century poet Richard de Fournival, 'Quant jou voi' (RS 1677a), conjures up bird song similarly, using broken rhyme, short lines, and figures of repetition.[39] As far as I can tell, Richard's psittacine poetics do not extend beyond the acoustic dimension of language to the melody of the song.[40] Here is a translation of the piece, which evokes, in its exordium, the incipient birdsong of warmer seasons:

1	Quant jou voi	When I see
	La douce saison d'esté,	The sweet season of summer,
	Que cist oi-	And that those bi-
	seillon qi trop ont esté	rds who have been too long
5	mu et coi	Silent and calm,
	Se sont reconforté.	Have revived themselves,
	Et quant je les oi,	And when I hear them,
	Si m'ont tel atourné	They have affected me so much
	Qu'en la folie	That into the folly
10	Qu'avoie laissie	Which I had left behind
	M'ont retourné.	They send me back.
	Pas ne di	I am not saying
	Que folie soit d'amer,	That it would be folly to love,
	Mais ainsi	But as
15	Con j'en pens fais fol penser	I see it, I have crazy thoughts
	Quant celi	When she to whom
	M'estuet mon cuer douner	I must give my heart
	Qi moi a gerpi	– [She] who has abandoned me

39 RS numbers refer to Hans Spanke, G. Raynauds Bibliographie des altfranzö-sischen Liedes. Neu bearbeitet und ergänzt von Hans Spanke (Leiden, 1955).
40 The piece is song XI in Yvan Lepage's edition. I have provided a translation here because the piece is, to my knowledge, thus far untranslated. It is a *unicum* in *trouvère* songbook *a* (Vatican City, Biblioteca Apostolica Vaticana, MS Reg. lat. 1490, fols. 41v–42r). For an edition of the music, see *Trouvère Lyrics with Melodies: Complete Comparative Edition*, ed. Hans Tischler (Neuhausen, 1997), 9:972.

	Pour pïeur acoster,	To become close to a lesser man –
20	Se n'i pert mie	Loses nothing
	Tant con sa boidie	As much as her treachery
	Li peut grever.	Can hurt her.

	Car qi laist	For whoever leaves
	Son bon ami pour felon	His good friend for a traitor
25	Vers lui fait	Towards him commits
	En tel guise traïson	Treachery in such a way
	Qu'il mesfait	That he does wrong
	Meïsme a vengison,	Even against vengeance,
	Et se honte en fait,	And if he brings shame on himself,
30	Ja ne grouchera on;	One will never grumble as a result;
	Mais en ma vie	But in my life
	De sa felounie	Of this misdeed
	N'avrai renon.	I will not have the reputation.

	Si m'est vis	It seems to me
35	Que bien m'en deliverrai,	That I would happily be rid of her,
	Car toudis	For constantly now
	Desdaigneus cuer or avrai:	I will have a disdainful heart:
	Por c'envis	For with difficulty
	Son dangier souferrai,	I will suffer her power,
40	Puis qu'ele m'a mis	Since she makes me
	Muser au papegai;	Think of the parrot;
	Mout le fornie,	She contests it,
	Mais, que qu'ele en die,	But, whatever she says,
	Maugré l'en sai.	I hold it against her.

	Neporqant,	Nevertheless,
45	S'ele m'amer me revoloit	If she wanted to love me again,
	Et samblant	And if she showed me a semblance
	De loiauté me moustroit,	Of loyalty,
	Je dout tant,	I strongly fear that,
50	S'ele m'i renbatoit,	If she rejected me,
	Que che que j'en chant	She would make me atone for
	Conperer me feroit,	What I am singing about her,
	Si que vengie	Such that she would have vengeance
	Par sa tricherie	Through her treachery
55	De moi seroit.	On me.

Because it is composed of stanzas with lines as short as three and four syllables (lines 1, 3 and 5 and lines 9 and 11 respectively), the song already, by virtue of its form, foregrounds the sonic dimension of language: as was the case in Marcabru's starling songs, its naturally occurring repetition of rhyme sounds occurs much more frequently due to the lower number of syllables in the text as a whole. This lays the groundwork for what is, I would argue, a broader exploration of the sonic dimension of language in the piece. This begins with an allusion to birdsong that is more than an allusion. Richard's language in this particular passage actually *performs* the birdsong (and perhaps also the insanity) it describes. The third line of the poem splits the word 'oiseillon' in two, as if to find the music within the bird, thereby transforming its first syllable, 'oi', into a rhyme sound. We have already seen this procedure of *rim trencat* in Marcabru's second starling song, and it is even more unusual in medieval *langue d'oïl* lyric than in the *langue d'oc* corpus. Via *rim trencat*, Richard invites us to listen to lyric as sound disassociated from semantic meaning, calling attention to the recursive sonic structure that *is* poetic song. The initial 'oi' of line 3's 'oiseillon' finds an echo in line 7's 'oi' ('I hear'), a lexical choice that further encourages a kind of close listening that goes beyond language's denotative function. That Richard's lyric flags this feature of song *within* the word 'oiseillon' also acknowledges the deep kinship between human recursive sonic structures and avian ones. Through his acoustic reduplication he *becomes* – or at least comes to resemble – the birds he describes. Other figures of acoustic reduplication proliferate in the song, which deploys identical rhyme ('fait' in lines 25 and 29), a *rime léonine* (involving homonyms) with similar alveolar onset consonants ('d'esté' and 'ont esté' in lines 2 and 4), *rime paronyme* ('vis' and 'envis' in lines 34 and 38), *rimes dérivées* ('atourné' and 'retourné' in lines 8 and 11; 'fait' and 'mesfait' in lines 25, 27, and 29), and a *figura etymologica* ('felon' and 'felounie' in lines 24 and 32).[41] All of these poetic figures amplify the acoustic reduplication that is constitutive of most *trouvère* song beyond the requisite final vowel, thereby forging a psittacine language in which the same sounds constantly surface.

As if to hammer home the affinity between avian and human poesis, the speaker of this lyric regrets that his beloved turns his thoughts towards the parrot: '[…] ele m'a mis / muser au papegai' ('she made me think of the parrot', lines 40–1). Lepage suggests, following Jeanroy and Långfors,

---

41 All of these rhymes are noted by Lepage, who does not link them to the avian turn in the poem. See Richard de Fournival, *L'Œuvre lyrique de Richard de Fournival*, ed. Yves G. Lepage (Ottawa, 1981), 80.

that these lines be translated as 'since she condemned me to waiting in vain'.[42] While these lines are certainly startling, I see no need to resort to a figurative interpretation. We should, I think, take the lyric voice literally, that is, both non-figuratively and with attention to its *litterae* or letters. His beloved, Richard tells us here, makes him think of a parrot (and the verb used to describe this thinking – *muser* – suggests not just a fleeting thought, but a more profound type of mental reflection). Once again, Richard's language takes a performative turn via alliteration, with its insistent 'm's ('*m*'a *m*is / *m*user'), each followed by a different vowel, in a bird-like vocalization. And, indeed, the speaker's parrotese continues in the following lines, each of which begins with /m/: '*M*out le fornie, / *M*ais, que qu'ele en die, / *M*augré l'en sai' ('She contests it, / But whatever she says, / I hold it against her', lines 42–4). These four consecutive lines are, except for the repeated 'q' at the start of lines 9 and 10 (a repetition likely triggered by the poem's evocation of insanity at precisely that moment), the only instance of a recurring initial consonant in the song, and they arguably constitute an imitation of avian repetition.[43]

Moreover, Richard's parrot allusion does not just spark a series of sonic reduplications. It also retrospectively explains a sonic reduplication that has taken place throughout the entire song as avian in origin: the piece is *almost* composed of *coblas singulars* (that is, stanzas that preserve a rhyme scheme but do not reuse rhyme sounds). I have qualified my statement because the *c* rhyme of the song ('-*ie*') stays the same throughout. In the case of the fourth stanza, where the parrot allusion appears, this *c* rhyme, which has echoed throughout the song, makes an appearance directly after Richard mentions a 'papegai' (line 41). The placement of this structural echo in the song immediately after Richard's mention of the bird suggestively links the two ideas – parrot and repeated sound. That the speaker's rather cryptic allusion should be followed so soon by the reappearance of the single rhyme sound that has echoed throughout the song invites us to hear this repeated rhyme sound as yet another indication of Richard's psittacine qualities. And this allusion to the 'papegai' is itself located at the rhyme, a location

42   Richard de Fournival, *L'Œuvre lyrique*, 80; *Chansons satiriques et bachiques du XIIIe siècle*, ed. Alfred Jeanroy and Arthur Långfors (Paris, 1921), 137.
43   On the way in which medieval representations of madness also play with the sonic quality of language, 'excavat[ing] from words their sound', see Chapter 4, 'Madness and the Eloquence of Nonsense', in Emma Dillon, *The Sense of Sound: Musical Meaning in France, 1260–1330* (New York, 2012), 168.

that transforms the name into a local sonic echo, the rhyme sound -*ai* having already appeared three times in this stanza. The mention of the parrot thus explains various acoustic repetitions as psittacine in origin, both on the level of the stanza (in which the rhyme in *papegai* rings for the fourth time), and on the level of the whole composition (by having the sole repeated rhyme sound in the song follow directly the evocation of the bird). I want to emphasize here that Richard's parrotese, like Marcabru's sturnine experimentation, does *not* involve code-switching into an avian language that is separate from human language, but rather involves the increased and strategic use of formal and poetic devices that draw attention to language as sound. This suggests, I think, that Richard's lyric metamorphosis into a parrot should not be read exclusively as local and transitory. His sound effects here are nothing but an exaggeration of the repetitive sounds any lyricist must produce in the making of song. All poets, he suggests, are already parrots. And a poet who is obliged to repeat his songs endlessly, as he tells us that he himself must, in an ongoing attempt to secure his beloved's affections, is the parrot of a parrot.[44]

While the examples discussed here might seem like nothing more than parlour tricks, I think it is no coincidence that Marcabru's and Richard de Fournival's works display a keen interest in the relationship between human and non-human animals. The reiterated clicks and imitative practices of Marcabru's starling, and Richard de Fournival's psittacine and strategic micro- and-macro repetitions draw attention to the fact that all rhymed poetry is fundamentally nothing more than

---

44 The narrator's comparison of himself in the *Bestiaire* to a dog who returns to his vomit also associates a kind of repetition compulsion with love lyric (the *Bestiaire* makes clear that the vomit in question represents Richard's earlier lyric pleas): 'Car se jou puisse faire ausi come li chiens, ki est de tel nature ke quant il a vomi, k'i repaire a son vomite et le remangüe, jou eüse volentiers me proiere rengloutie cent fois, puis k'ele me fu volee des dens' ('if I could do as the dog, which is of such a nature that when it has vomited, he returns to his vomit and eats it, I would gladly eat my prayer a hundred times, since it flew from my teeth'. See Richard de Fournival, *Li Bestiaires d'amours di Maistre Richart de Fornival e Li Response du Bestiaire*, ed. Cesare Segre (Milan, 1957), 14–15. Regarding the poet as parrot, Sarah Kay suggests that all troubadours are parrots in another sense – that they must learn literary Occitan and compose in a language that is not strictly native to them. See Sarah Kay, 'The Monolingualism of the Parrot, or the Prosthesis of Origins', in *Las Novas del Papagay*, *Romanic Review* 101.1/2 (2010), 23–35 (25).

a recursive sonic structure – and one in which sound and sense are in constant tension.[45] Moreover, both poets implicitly theorize a radical kinship between human and avian *voces* as transmitted in song – a medium in which species boundaries are highly permeable and the distinction between 'meaningful' and 'meaningless' language, prized by medieval grammarians, threatens to collapse. An engagement with birdsong leads both poets not to use an imagined linguistic boundary to buttress species difference, but instead to foreground the noise at the heart of all language, and most especially poetic language.

I would note, further, that this shift towards the sense-perceptible dimension of language over and above content, and the associated failure to circumscribe avian speech in a way that might suggest its radical alterity, engenders a potential bestial metamorphosis not just in the performer of these songs, but also in their audience. According to Augustine's *De musica*, those who listen to song without intellectual understanding are like beasts. The master in this dialogue explains: 'we see elephants, bears, and many other kinds of beasts are moved by singing, and birds themselves are charmed by their own voices.'[46] As Leach remarks, it is only by listening actively that 'the medieval hearer can avoid being reduced to such a bestial status'.[47] Marcabru and Richard turn this dichotomy between attentiveness and bestiality on its head, however, in the sense that active listening to *their* poesis reveals the starling and the parrot songs respectively underlying each piece. And this revelation comes at the expense of the referential. As soon as one has registered Marcabru and Richard's zoopoetics, one begins to attend to the sonic over the semantic, thereby falling headfirst into, instead of eschewing, Augustine's bestial trap.

---

45   Emma Gorst also notes the association of bird language with formal complexity, and especially with verse. See her 'Interspecies Mimicry: Birdsong in Chaucer's "Maniciple"s Tale" and *The Parlement of Fowles*', *New Medieval Literatures* 12 (2010), 147–54.
46   Augustine, *De musica*, ed. and trans. R. Catesby Taliaferro (Annapolis, MD, 1939), quoted in Leach, *Sung Birds*, 2.
47   Leach, *Sung Birds*, 2.

4

Performing Friendship in Richard Rolle's *Incendium amoris**

R. JACOB MCDONIE

Rolle, Friendship, and Performance

The hermit-mystic Richard Rolle (c.1300–1349), one of the most prolific authors of the fourteenth century in England, seems initially an odd figure for a treatment of friendship.[1] The facts of Rolle's life suggest one for whom literal solitude was the *sine qua non* of contemplation, one who did not get along with others, and one who considered people at

---

* I am grateful, above all, to Andrew Albin for reading several drafts of this essay and providing invaluable insight and correction. Elizabeth Allen, Marsha Dutton, and Linda Georgianna read and commented on an earlier draft of this essay; I am grateful for their intervention. Nicholas Watson commented on the general scope of my argument by e-mail. Ralph Hanna referred me to a more accurate manuscript reading of the text than is available in print, and Andrew Kraebel, who has served as a generous interlocutor on Rolle, furnished me with a digital facsimile of it. Andrew Kraebel also assisted me with the transcription of some of the more difficult passages in the manuscript. I am finally grateful for the helpful comments of the two anonymous readers for *New Medieval Literatures*. Unless otherwise indicated, all translations of the Latin are my own, though Andrew Albin and Steve Barney helped with some of the more tortuous Latin syntax of *Incendium*.

1 Several studies mention Rolle's desire in *Incendium amoris* for a friend only in passing and without development. Malcolm Robert Moyes was the first to put Rolle and friendship in the same sentence; strangely, however, in the introduction to an obscure edition of a work that deals not at all with friendship: *Richard Rolle's Expositio super novem lectiones mortuorum*, ed. Moyes (Salzburg, 1988), 53–8. Claire Elizabeth McIlroy discusses friendship as a structuring technique in Rolle's English epistle, *The Form of Living*, in *The English Prose Treatises of Richard Rolle* (Cambridge, 2004), 140–86. No substantial work on friendship in Rolle's large corpus of Latin works has been written.

best impediments to the spiritual life (*Incendium amoris*, p. 257, lines 8–10), at worst carnal temptations (p. 172, lines 18–19).[2] Rolle fears the pleasure that derives from sociability but can sometimes be disenchanted by friendship *tout court*; he writes that his worst detractors were once his most trusted friends.[3] Problematizing thirty years of scholarship on medieval solitaries' busy social lives, Rolle pointedly affirms his rationale for solitude: 'Ego enim in solitudinem fugi quia cum hominibus concordare non potui' ('I fled into solitude because I could not get along with people', p. 220, lines 34–5).[4]

Nonetheless, Rolle is deeply interested in friendship and community, even in his most self-concerned writing. Rolle lived during a time when many hermit-mystics would have been inveterately social. Bernard McGinn argues for the communal, ecclesiological nature of mysticism, even if Rolle does not always conform to this model.[5] And Jonathan Hughes demonstrates that fourteenth-century hermits in Yorkshire like Rolle had intimate connections, however problematic, with their lay

2   All citations of *Incendium amoris* are by page and line number from *Incendium amoris*, ed. Margaret Deanesly (Manchester, 1915). Deanesly's edition is notoriously old and sometimes riddled with errors. I have checked her edition against Oxford, Bodleian Library, MS Bodley 861, fols 103vb–122rb, one of the most reliable readings of *Incendium*, and have indicated variants.

3   'Nam eos pessimos detractores habui, quos prius amicos fidos putaui' ('For I have as my worst detractors those whom I once thought were faithful friends', p. 188, lines 17–18). Later readers evidently sensed this inhospitableness in Rolle's Latin œuvre. Anne Clark Bartlett reports an instance in which a fifteenth-century Carthusian brother's reading of Rolle's warnings on temptation in the form of love of friends apparently provoked the brother to renounce his own friend (Bartlett, *Male Authors, Female Readers* (Ithaca, NY, 1995), 86–8).

4   Among others, Linda Georgianna, *The Solitary Self: Individuality in the Ancrene Wisse* (Cambridge, MA, 1981), 32–78; Christopher Cannon, 'Enclosure', in *The Cambridge Companion to Medieval Women's Writing*, ed. Carolyn Dinshaw and David Wallace (Cambridge, 2003), 109–23; Mari Hughes-Edwards, '"How good it is to be alone"? Solitude, Sociability, and Medieval English Anchoritism', *Mystics Quarterly* 3/4 (2009), 31–61.

5   Bernard McGinn, *The Foundations of Mysticism: Origins to the Fifth Century* (New York, 1997), xi–xx, 3–4. McGinn writes to broaden our understanding of mysticism, meaning not strictly union with the Godhead but the sensation of the presence of Christ more generally. In this view all human beings, especially when in a Christian community, contain the potential for mysticism, so different from Rolle's tendentious elitism.

patrons, often influencing lay piety, devotion, and readership.[6] Rolle wrote endearing English treatises of spiritual guidance for religious women, and in his role of mentor developed a spiritual friendship with one of them, an anchoress named Margaret Kirkeby.[7] But I do not wish to argue (as have some valuable studies of friendship for medieval coenobites and solitaries)[8] that Rolle 'had' a friend; this essay examines, more broadly, Rolle's rhetoric of friendship and, specifically, his textual construction of friendship as a spiritual phantasm that enables contemplation to proceed to fruition.

In Rolle's *Incendium amoris* (*The Fire of Love*), an early work pivotal to the development of his authorial career, ideas of performed friendship and community structure his mysticism.[9] I first demonstrate that solitude is communal for Rolle; he requires the strictest solitude only to imagine his liturgically oriented participation in a celestial, canorous community, enabled through affect. I then turn to Rolle's construction of the microcosm of this community, a phantasmal friend proficient in composing and performing mystical song when Rolle himself fails. This hypothetical friend takes Rolle through the mystical process that otherwise eludes him, as friendship becomes a model for mystical union and an affective experience. I then observe the ways in which Rolle opens up friendship, described with the highest approbation, to all Christians, even reframing his otherwise problematic relationship with women in terms of shared mystical endeavour and pastoral care. If friendship is conceived at the metaphysical level, Rolle quickly renders it palpable; it is a pleasure to be enjoyed even in this life, and keeps one on

6   Jonathan Hughes, *Pastors and Visionaries: Religion and Secular Life in Late Medieval Yorkshire* (Woodbridge, 1988), 78–113.

7   Hope Emily Allen was the first to establish Margaret's identity, in *Writings Ascribed to Richard Rolle Hermit of Hampole and Materials for his Biography* (New York, 1927), 35, 265–8.

8   In particular, this is the approach of the still standard account of medieval friendship, Brian Patrick McGuire, *Friendship and Community: The Monastic Experience, 350–1250* (Kalamazoo, MI, 1988; repr. Ithaca, NY, 2010).

9   I subscribe to Nicholas Watson's chronology of Rolle's textual production in *Richard Rolle and the Invention of Authority* (Cambridge, 1991), 273–94; on *Incendium* as an early work, see pp. 277–8. H. E. Allen, who established Rolle's canon in 1927, insisted that *Incendium* was written much later in Rolle's life (pp. 228–9, 255–6); but Watson convincingly argues that it was completed before 1343. The dating of some of the texts in Watson's chronology has been cogently challenged, but to my knowledge no one after Watson has argued in print that *Incendium* was written any time after 1343.

the mystical path. Moreover, Rolle's desire for spiritual friendship with others prepares him both intellectually and affectively for friendship with God.

I unpack the idea of performing friendship in several ways.[10] Jessica Brantley argues that performance underwent an important conceptual shift in fourteenth-century England, moving from signifying a process that was completed to one that was ongoing, like our modern sense of playing an instrument, singing, or acting.[11] Mysticism itself is thus often performance: it is constantly subject to interruption or failure and must repeatedly be begun anew, so much so that the goal of union is frequently substituted by the process that leads there. Often in *Incendium* the means, or process that leads to a putative mystical goal, becomes an end in itself: for Rolle, God as the end goal is often partially displaced by mystical song, the state of union one reaches not with God alone, but also with mediating angelic song inflected by the communally performed monastic liturgy. Moreover, textual affectivity, one of the defining means by which Rolle enters into community and friendship, has also recently been understood in performative terms. Sarah McNamer argues that affective texts are 'scripts for the performance of feeling';[12] and Mary Carruthers's work on memory and thought situates thinking as mental construction performed (or created and recalled) through emotional association. Affective *intentio* shapes useful images or phantasms to be stored for inventional recollection under similar emotional states.[13] Furthermore, Carruthers argues, the primary objective of monastic, like classical, rhetoric is community-building

10   Rolle's later works are often read as performative. Denis Renevey argues for a 'textual space' for a divinely inspired narrative voice to perform the script of experiential, exegetical texts to lead to self-discovery: *Language, Self, and Love: Hermeneutics in the Writings of Richard Rolle and the Commentaries on the Song of Songs* (Cardiff, 2001), 35. But to my knowledge no one has yet approached *Incendium* performatively.

11   Jessica Brantley, *Reading in the Wilderness: Private Devotion and Public Performance in Late Medieval England* (Chicago, 2007), 16–21.

12   Sarah McNamer, 'Feeling', in *Middle English: Oxford Twenty-First Century Approaches to Literature*, ed. Paul Strohm (Oxford, 2007), 241–57 (246). See also McNamer's *Affective Meditation and the Invention of Medieval Compassion* (Philadelphia, 2010).

13   Mary Carruthers, *The Craft of Thought: Meditation, Rhetoric, and the Making of Images, 400–1200* (Cambridge, 1998), 16, 113; Carruthers, *The Book of Memory: A Study of Memory in Medieval Culture*, 2nd edn (Cambridge, 2008), 76, 85–6, 103–4, 337.

through the arousal of emotions in one's audience and oneself.[14] Rolle's rhetoric of friendship likewise buttresses his solitary spiritual communal life through the performative, affective *inventio* of phantasmal friendship and community.

Because of Rolle's attainment of mystical song through a liturgical, quasi-textual experience created by friendship and community, Katherine Zieman's recent work on liturgy and literacy as modes of performance is especially engaging. Zieman argues in both a book and an important article that the performance and ritualization of sacralized language in liturgy yields what she dubs 'extragrammatical discourse': 'the various textual and linguistic practices [...] that are derived from yet in some way situated outside of the apparatus of Latinate textual authority'.[15] For a lay audience largely unlearned in Latin, participation in the liturgy functioned as an illocutionary force much akin to American children's recitation of the Pledge of Allegiance: they may not yet know what 'indivisible' means, but still understand the intention and cultural power of their performance.[16] For Rolle, however, a *bene litteratus*, the Latin liturgy may not have been extragrammatical *per se*; but Rolle's *canor* – liturgically inspired and mystical angelic song – created 'excess meaning generated in the performance of sacralized language', Zieman argues, and is thus extragrammatical performance with its own illocutionary force.[17]

Understanding of friendship took a similar performative turn in the Middle Ages.[18] Medieval authors inherited from Cicero and Augustine static, backward-looking friendship. In Cicero's *De amicitia*, the most

14   Carruthers, *The Craft of Thought*, 106–7, 132–3.

15   Katherine Zieman, 'The Perils of *Canor*: Mystical Authority, Alliteration, and Extragrammatical Meaning in Rolle, the *Cloud*-Author, and Hilton', *Yearbook of Langland Studies* 22 (2008), 131–63 (137). On the performativity of reading, so frequently collocated with 'singing' in elementary medieval education, Zieman notes that the term 'reading' rarely appears by itself in medieval documents but is almost always connected with literacy of a particular ritualized text – prayers, creeds, the Psalter – that would be repeatedly performed by the faithful: 'one does not simply learn to "read"; one learns to "read the Psalter"' (Zieman, *Singing the New Song: Literacy and Liturgy in Late Medieval England* (Philadelphia, 2008), 36). On liturgical singing as a mode of performance, see especially, in *Singing the New Song*, 40–9.

16   Zieman, *Singing the New Song*, 129–30.

17   Zieman, 'Perils of *Canor*', 137.

18   Chapter 39 of *Incendium*, in which friendship is described as a process leading to God, implicitly recognizes this.

influential secular text of the Middle Ages, the only good friend is a dead one, the memory of whose virtue guides our own moral activity and lends itself toward memorial.[19] For Augustine, in the *Confessions*, friends were or would soon be in the past; even the best of friends are to be enjoyed and then transcended by love of God, to say nothing of the many friends who seduced Augustine away from God to worldly pleasure.[20] But the trajectory of friendship shifted in the twelfth century when the Cistercian abbot Aelred of Rievaulx penned *De spirituali amicitia*, one of the greatest contributions to European humanistic thought, which has been argued to have influenced Rolle.[21] For Aelred, friendship anticipates beatitude, when friendship with one's monastic brethren will be fully realized.[22] Earthly friendship is a foretaste of and pilgrimage towards heavenly friendship.[23] Aelred sanctifies friendship. Monastic friendship becomes a daily, internally ritualized performance of the divine.

It is against these backdrops that *Incendium* concerns itself not only with communal participation in *canor*, mystical song, but also with Rolle's confident manifesto that *canor* constitutes the authoritative height of the contemplative life. However, Rolle's own description of *canor*'s performance falls flat. He thus desires a phantasmal friend who might notate this rapturous song so that he himself might perform it. Rolle also experiments with more formal, textual performances of friendship by self-consciously creating textual space for friendship. And Rolle performs friendship with God in Ciceronian and Christian

19   Cicero, *De amicitia*, in *De re publica, De legibus, Cato Maior de Senectute, and Laelius de Amicitia*, ed. J. G. F. Powell (Oxford, 2006), 4.15, 7.23, 27.102. On the influence of this sacrosanct treatise to the Middle Ages, see Jan M. Ziolkowski, 'Twelfth-Century Understandings and Adaptations of Ancient Friendship', in *Mediaeval Antiquity*, ed. Andries Welkenhuysen, Herman Braet, and Werner Verbeke (Leuven, 1995), 59–81 (63–4); and Colin Morris, *The Discovery of the Individual, 1050–1200* (London, 1972; repr. Toronto, 1987), 98.

20   On Augustine's need to transcend friendship see especially Book Four of *The Confessions*, in which he worries that he has let affection for an ephemeral friend replace love for God: Augustine, *Confessiones*, ed. James J. O'Donnell (Oxford, 1992), 4.8.13; 4.9.14.

21   *Richard Rolle's Expositio*, ed. Moyes, 53–8.

22   Aelred of Rievaulx, *De spirituali amicitia*, in *Aelredi Rievallensis opera omnia*, ed. A. Hoste, and C. H. Talbot (Turnhout, 1971), 3.134.

23   Marsha L. Dutton, 'Friendship and the Love of God: Augustine's Teaching in the *Confessions* and Aelred of Rievaulx's Response in *Spiritual Friendship*', *American Benedictine Review* 56 (2005), 3–40 (31–40).

terms by conforming his will with God's in dramatically staged divine recreations of friendship. Friendship with God, which is itself figured as mystical union, is possible only because the discourse of friendship permeates *Incendium*, a text commonly thought to be the product of a spiritual loner.[24]

Canorous Communities

Incendium amoris is a long Latin treatise consisting of a prologue and forty-two chapters of varying length, and containing a curious blend of apologetic autobiography, evangelical didacticism, and mystical sensation. It represents Rolle's first authorial attempt to expound the components of mysticism, structured around narratives of how the gifts of contemplation – *fervor*, *dulcor*, and *canor* (heat, sweetness, and song) – were bestowed upon him. Given the great popularity of *Incendium* in medieval and modern times, evident from its many translations and citations, it is surprising how little scholarship is written on it.[25] Nicholas Watson's ground-breaking treatment, published in 1991 and still the prevailing scholarly view, examines the many difficulties Rolle faced in his self-presentation while constructing himself as an *auctor*. Watson argues that Rolle successfully lays claim to his ability to practise *canor*, authorizing himself as one of God's chosen few and his book as the product of a saint-like figure who must be listened to:

> The apologetic structure of the work, it now appears, is self-supporting. Rolle's experience of *canor* is what makes his whole account of the spiritual life plausible [...] *Experientia* can become the basis for *auctoritas* because of Rolle's increasing ability to defend and to explain that experience, but above all because of his ability to recreate it verbally.[26]

While Watson (whose contributions to our understanding of Rolle's construction of authority are numerous and valuable) posits for Rolle

---

24 The three thematic threads of Watson's *Invention of Authority* reinforce this perception: Rolle's frequent preference for apology over didacticism, his articulation of spiritual elitism, and his vigilant self-presentation, 75.

25 *Incendium amoris* survives in over forty manuscripts, on which see Allen, *Writings Ascribed to Richard Rolle*, 209–25; also *Incendium*, ed. Deansley, 1–37.

26 Watson, *Invention of Authority*, 140.

a certain fluency in *canor*, Rolle in fact has a much more problematic relationship to *canor* as he tries to stake his authority as a solitary on it, for *canor* is not a self-contained experience (nor can it be recreated verbally). Desire for God is mediated through the allure of choral (and necessarily communal) angelic song. The goal of solitary *canor*, as Watson concedes in a later piece, is not neoplatonic ascent to the Godhead but worship of God within an imagined community of song, the roots of which are grounded not in eremitic habitude, but in the monastic liturgy.[27] Thus Rolle, as a solitary, stages his communally inspired conversion to *canor* as he recites the Mass in Chapter 15 of *Incendium*:

> Dum enim in eadem capella sederem, et in nocte ante cenam psalmos prout potui decantarem, quasi tinnitum psallencium uel pocius canencium supra me ascultaui. Cumque celestibus eciam orando toto desiderio intenderem, nescio quomodo mox in me concentum canorum sensi, et delectabilissimam armoniam celicus excepi, mecum manentem in mente. Nam cogitacio mea continuo in carmen [canoris] commutabatur, et quasi odas habui meditando, et eciam oracionibus ipsis et psalmodia eundem sonum edidi.
>
> (p. 189, line 19–p. 190, line 1)[28]

> (While I was sitting in the chapel and singing the psalms at night before dinner as best I could, I discerned above me something like the sound of those giving praise, or, rather, of singers. And, indeed, as I stretched forth with all my longing in prayer toward heaven, I soon sensed in me (I know not how) a choir overflowing with melodies, and received that most delectable harmony by divine inspiration, which remained with me in my mind. For my thoughts were immediately turned into a song of melody, like odes received through meditation, and I gave forth the same sound even in my very prayers and psalms.)

While Rolle performs the liturgy, underwritten by communal practice, he hears the ringing ('tinnitum') not of song, technically, but of the throng of celestial singers ('psallencium', 'canencium', 'concentum'), who, in turn, inspire his melodic outpouring. The two communal

---

27   Watson, 'The Middle English Mystics', in *The Cambridge History of Medieval English Literature*, ed. David Wallace (Cambridge, 1999), 539–65 (549).
28   Corrected from Bod. 861, fol. 109rb (reading *canoris* for Deanesly's *canorum*).

performances, those of the earthly and angelic choirs, are linked. While *fervor* and *dulcor* are largely self-contained psychosomatic excitations, *canor*, by contrast, Zieman observes, 'is modelled on the experience of mediated divinity in the form of the angelic choir and necessarily entails a relationship to that mediating presence'.[29] Rolle's invocation of angelic choral singing in this scene bespeaks its institutional nature, anchored in Latin monastic and liturgical communities, which, Zieman writes, allows him 'to situate "private", unsanctioned mystical experience in relation to "public" ecclesiastical institutions'.[30] Zieman offers extensive evidence that liturgy was associated with letteredness: it created textual communities, and metonymically functioned for clerical, literate knowledge even when performed from memory.[31] By extension, Zieman argues that the ritualized liturgical Latin of communal song enhances Rolle's authority in his performance of *canor* in the heavenly choir and thus legitimizes an otherwise unorthodox contemplative experience on which Rolle must work to ground much of his personal authority.

But whereas Watson tends to overlook somewhat the role of canorous communal mediation in the construction of Rolle's authority, Zieman's heavy emphasis on the liturgical underpinning of authorization (while valuable to my argument) nonetheless elides *canor*'s other effects. *Canor* not only confirms Rolle's authority but also enables both the pleasure that Rolle derives from this angelic community of singers, constructed in the passage just quoted, and, as we shall later see, the microcosm of this community, an invented canorous companion in Chapter 34 of *Incendium* without whom Rolle is unable to sing. Rolle turns first to his affective entrance into celestial and pleasurable canorous community, which is more than a self-authorizing ploy or means to an end, then engages with canorous companionship in Chapter 34.

For Rolle the community of song once realized in heaven may certainly include mystical union with God *per se*, but is not limited to it; indeed, it tends to be an end in itself, achieved through affective meditation. While some medieval thinkers, like Aquinas, viewed heaven as abstract, cerebral, and theocentric – disembodied contemplation of the Godhead – by the fourteenth century heaven began to be seen in more affective and social terms as a paradise where lovers and friends

29   Zieman, 'Perils of *Canor*', 139.
30   Ibid., 139.
31   Zieman, *Singing the New Song*, 3–4, 31–7, 40–9.

gathered, and a city in which each citizen had his or her social role.[32] Denis Renevey explores the tendency in Rolle's œuvre for the goal of union with God, or of the understanding of Scripture, to be displaced by the desire inherent in the mystical and exegetical processes themselves, processes which would otherwise be means to an end, leading one to their putative goals.[33] Similarly, in *Incendium*, punishment for the wicked is separation not from God *per se*, but from the fellowship of singers: 'Sequestrabuntur eciam *a consorcio canencium* in caritate Creatoris et gemebunt iugiter eiecti *a iocunditate iubilancium* in Ihesum' ('Indeed, they will be removed from the community of singers in love of the Creator and will wail constantly as they are ejected from the joy of those making jubilation in Jesus', p. 158, lines 6–8). Paradise is described as a *locus amoenus* for melodious friends: '[C]oncurrunt in canticum clari concentus, et armonie amorose, atque in amenitate amicabili obumbra-cionem habent celicus infusam' ('They run together in the song of bright singing and harmony full of love, and they have a shadow poured over from heaven in friendly pleasantness', p. 158, line 30–p. 159, line 1). The communal harmony and ritualized social relations of Rolle's angelic choir (described here elliptically as friendship) derive from what Zieman calls the 'ideal social body' of the harmonious, egalitarian, earthly liturgical choir; textual ignorance (not learning one's lines) was understood as a crime against not only God's word, but also peaceful choral communal relations.[34] But the pleasure of angelic liturgical community (unlike the terms of earthly liturgical community, which Zieman has so cogently traced) seems an end in itself in *Incendium*, rather than only a further means of authorization.

Meditation on the unified choir of Paradise, however, is not always the anticipation of a future event for Rolle; present and future merge so that it is no longer clear if Rolle rejoices with the angelic choir proleptically

---

32   Colleen McDannell and Bernhard Lang, *Heaven: A History* (New Haven, 1988), 69–110.

33   Renevey, *Language, Self, and Love*, 118–25, 145–6.

34   Zieman, *Singing the New Song*, 40, 62–70. Ambrose writes: 'Psalmus dissi-dentes copulat, discordes sociat, offensos reconciliat; quis enim non remittat ei, cum quo unam ad deum vocem emiserit?' ('A Psalm joins those with differences, unites those at odds, and reconciles those who have been offended, for who will not concede to him with whom one sings to God in one voice?'), *Explanatio psalmorum* 1.9, 8. Quoted and translated in Bruce Holsinger, *Music, Body, and Desire in Medieval Culture: Hildegard of Bingen to Chaucer* (Stanford, CA, 2001), 259 n. 1; requoted in Zieman, *Singing the New Song*, 42–3.

in the mind or presently in his cell. He imagines the elect one day (in the future) 'assistens inter celicolas in sede beata' ('taking his place among the heaven-dwellers in a blessed seat', p. 192, lines 28–9), and shortly thereafter writes: 'Quia mors, quam multi metuunt, mihi esset ut melos musice, quanquam iam, tanquam in paradiso positus, subsistam, sedens in solitudine, illic suauiter sonans amorosum canticum, in deliciis quas dedit mihi dilectus' ('For death, which many fear, might be to me as a melody of music, *although I already subsist as if placed in paradise, sitting in solitude*, sweetly resounding *there* a song of love, in the delights which my Beloved has given to me', p. 193, lines 11–15). The play on words, 'sede [...] sedens', Rolle's communal heavenly seat and his solitary earthly one, associates two different times and places. R. Hanna writes that for Rolle sitting is a 'powerfully inactive verb' that 'functions as an emblem for the acts of eternity'.[35] While seated in his cell Rolle, as a solitary, perceives communal and melodious joy, but also suggests that he will one day live *as* a solitary in communal and melodious heaven ('illic'). '[S]edens in solitudine' (placed ambiguously between the *tanquam* ('as if') clause and a prepositional phrase describing the joys of heaven) can refer both to his present state in which he imagines the future, and to that imagined future state itself. Solitude on earth and in heaven is curiously communal, and the two devotional arenas of song (earth and heaven) become mirror images of each other. Desire for one's earthly seat is desire for one's heavenly one. Rolle fashions communal *canor* in the earthly seat as preparation not explicitly for God, but for communal *canor* in the heavenly one.[36]

God's partial displacement slightly problematizes the critical argument that Rolle's various liturgical communities serve only to authorize him, for it makes the connection between community and God somewhat tenuous. Celestial canorous community, which may include the presence and enjoyment of God, is also something to be enjoyed on its own pleasurable terms – it is notable that earthly and angelic liturgical communities are almost never explicitly cited in

35   R. Hanna, 'Rolle and Related Works', in *A Companion to Middle English Prose*, ed. A. S. G. Edwards (Cambridge, 2004), 19–31 (23).

36   Rolle elsewhere in *Incendium* writes of such spiritual preparation for heavenly joy, contrasting the solitary's body, which sits in solitude, and his spirit, which walks with the angels, explicitly including God in the process in this instance: 'Quorum corpora solitarie sedebant, et mentes inter angelos ambulantes ad dilectum anhelebant' ('Their bodies were sitting in solitude while their spirits walked among angels and panted to their beloved', p. 152, lines 11–12).

Incendium as constituting the path toward God alone. The angelic choir is the site of affective performance as Rolle fervently acts out canorous collegiality in his mind, '*sweetly* resounding a *song of love* in the *delights*' of the '*friendly pleasantness* of heaven' ('suauiter sonans amorosum canticum, in deliciis'; 'amenitate amicabili').[37] For Rolle, as for later Carthusian solitaries, as Brantley's work has shown, to be alone is not only to prepare for one's entrance into a celestial community, but also to participate in that community itself.[38]

Phantasmal Friendship

Rolle amply demonstrates his wish to partake in canorous communities through affect. In Chapter 34 of *Incendium*, Rolle desires a more localized canorous companion, the microcosm of the angelic choir, calling into further doubt his reputation as a spiritual loner. When *canor* fails him, Rolle invents a phantasmal friend accomplished in composing and performing spiritual song. In vivid, concrete terms, friendship is structured as a desirable and even integral part of mystical experience. Friendship becomes an affective event that enables mysticism. Friendship, the joint perception and sharing of hidden knowledge, ultimately provides a model for mystical union in all its stages. Rolle is united not with God alone, but also with the idea of a mystical Other, defined as a friend, circulating mystical desire, and standing in metonymically for both the angelic choir and God. Contemplation in *Incendium* is framed in terms of social solitude.

In the last third of *Incendium*, Chapters 31–42 (demarcated as 'Book Two' in some manuscripts), Rolle makes his apologia for *canor*.[39] Here

37 My thinking here is influenced by McNamer, 'Feeling', especially 245–6, which suggests that medieval affect, aroused by textual scripts, is inherently performative. See also, more generally, McNamer, *Affective Meditation*.
38 Brantley argues that late medieval Carthusian reading communities acted out a spiritual community that would exist in heaven by means of solitary devotional practices. See especially *Reading in the Wilderness*, 76, 109.
39 Deanesly's and H. E. Allen's surveys of the manuscripts of *Incendium* report that Cambridge, Cambridge University Library, MS Dd.v.64 divides the text into two books, the second book beginning at Chapter 31. Richard Misyn's fifteenth-century Middle English translation also begins a second book at Chapter 31, a system alluded to in what Deanesly calls the 'Short Text' manuscript tradition

Rolle desires a phantasmal friend to communicate *canor* and comfort him. Chapters 31–4, the continuity of which Rolle takes pains to establish, are a publicly delivered manifesto.[40] A justification of *canor* delivered to all of his nay-sayers, this is Rolle's chance to prove to the world that he has not been misguided in his unconventional eremitic life.[41] Rolle opens Chapter 31 by addressing complaints that he does not sing 'corporaliter' (p. 232, line 17) in the church choir. He has remained silent in the past because he thought it impossible to convince the 'inferiores' (p. 233, line 18) of the merits of his own song compared to their earthly noise. But he begins to change course in Chapter 31, with the pointed proclamation 'Propalabo' ('I shall make this public', p. 234, line 3). This is an echo of 'si propalare uolo' in Chapter 15's introduction to *canor* (the only other time in *Incendium* that this verb is used (p. 187, line 17)), a point at which Rolle attempts to authenticate his past mystical experience, even supplying us with the dates of various experiences. Here, in Chapter 34, however, Rolle is focused on authentication through his present state, not his past one. No longer reserved, he proceeds to prove himself through a description of his performance of *canor*.

Numerous scholars have argued for Rolle' ability to recreate and perform *canor* in his literary outpouring.[42] But here in Chapter 34 Rolle cannot even manage to describe it:

of *Incendium*, represented in Oxford, Bodleian Library, MS Laud 528. See Allen, *Writings Ascribed to Richard Rolle*, 214; and *Incendium*, ed. Deanesly, 7, 83–90. See also Watson, *Invention of Authority*, 313 n. 5 for a synopsis, and Misyn's 1435 Middle English translation *The Fire of Love and The Mending of Life; or, The Rule of Living [...] by Richard Misyn*, ed. Ralph Harvey, EETS o.s. 106 (London, 1896).

40 Watson, *Invention of Authority*, 120.

41 Rolle's eccentric eremiticism is best contextualized and analysed by Watson, *Invention of Authority*, 40–53.

42 Watson, *Invention of Authority*, is the chief example; see especially pp. 132–41 on the self-supporting structure of *canor* in *Incendium* itself, and his chapter on Rolle's English works as expressions of *canor* crafted to be both seductive and imitable (pp. 222–56). See also Vincent Gillespie, 'Mystic's Foot: Rolle and Affectivity', in *The Medieval Mystical Tradition in England II*, ed. Marion Glasscoe (Exeter, 1982), 199–230 (especially 209-16); Zieman, 'Perils of *Canor*', 144–45; Rosamund Allen, '"Singuler lufe": Richard Rolle and the Grammar of Spiritual Ascent', and Rita Copeland, 'Richard Rolle and the Rhetorical Theory of the Levels of Style', both in *The Medieval Mystical Tradition in England III*, ed. Marion Glasscoe (Cambridge, 1984), respectively 28–53 (especially 37–47), and 55–80 (especially 65, 66, 72).

Amator itaque estuans in ipsos incorporeos amplexus, et oculo intel-
lectuali amatum suum intueri, (purgatis spurciciis et euanescentibus
cogitacionibus omnibus, que non ad unum tendunt), anhelans: habet
utique clamorem ad Conditorem suum, ex intimis medullis amoris
affectuosi excitatum et erumpentem, quasi a longe clamaret. Uocem
eleuat interiorem, que non nisi in amante ardentissimo, (ut in uia fas
est) inuenitur. Hic deficio pre insipiencia et hebetudine ingenii: quia
non sufficio hunc clamorem describere, nec eciam quantus sit uel quasi
iocundus cogitare, sentire, et efferre pro modulo meo potui. Sed uobis
enarrare nec potui nec potero.

                                                        (p. 243, lines 21–32)

(And so after he has purged all inner filth, and all of his thoughts which
do not tend toward the one have vanished, the lover burning in those
bodiless embraces and exhaling to consider his beloved with his mind's
eye by all means makes a cry to his Creator, stirred up and breaking forth
from the inmost marrow of affectionate love, as if he were crying out
from afar. He raises his interior voice which cannot be found except in
the most ardent lover, as is permitted in one's earthly journey. Here I fail
on account of the senselessness and dimness of wit: for I am incapable
of describing that cry, nor in the smallest measure have I been able to
consider, experience, or describe even how great or how much like a joy
it is. But I have not been nor will I be able to explain it in any detail for
you.)

Rolle often states that *canor* is ineffable, but never frames the impossibility of its description quite so dramatically as he does here, with the
lover's ardent longing described in seven highly active verbal forms all
of which terminate anticlimactically in ineptitude ('insipiencia'). Several
times here Rolle repeats his failure to describe the performance of *canor*
fully ('deficio', 'non sufficio', 'nec potui nec potero'), failure which he has
previously attributed to the demands of the world that will not stop
bothering him. Rolle publicly stages his vulnerability as a mystic and the
vulnerability of his authority derived from *canor*.

But because so much depends on Rolle's asserted ability to sing, he is
no longer content with resignation and uses personal failure to seek help
from an unexpected source:

Quis ergo mihi modularetur carmina cantuum meorum, et gaudia
affectuum cum ardoribus amoris, et amorose adolescencie mee uscionem,

ut saltem ex canticis caritatis sodalis subtiliter indagarem substanciam meam, et [mensura][43] modulacionum, in quibus prestabilis putarer, mihi innotesceret, si forte ab infelicitate exemptum me inuenirem, et quod per me predicare non presumo, quia nondum reperi quod exopto, in solaciis socii mei requiescerem cum dulcore. Siquidem si clamorem illum canorem ab extrinsecis auribus omnino absconditum arbitrer, (quod et uere esse audeo annunciare,) utinam et illius modulaminis inueniam auctorem hominem, qui etsi non dictis, tamen scriptis mihi gloriam meam decantaret, et [neupmata][44] que nexus in nomine nobilissimo coram amato meo edere non erubui, canendo ac [neupmatizando][45] depromeret. Hic etenim esset mihi amabilis super aurum: et omnia preciosa non adequarem ei que habentur in hoc exilio. Uenustas namque uirtutis cum ipso habitat, et amoris arc[h]ana[46] perfeccius inuestigat. Diligerem denique illum sicut cor meum nec esset aliquid quod ab ipso occultare intenderem, quia canorem quod [*sic*] cupio intelligere mihi exprimeret, et iubilum iocunditatis mee clarius enodaret. In hac equidem apercione exultarem amplius, aut certe uberius emularem; quoniam mihi ostenderetur incendium amoris et sonora iubilacio euidenter effulgeret. Clamosa quoque cogitacio sine laudatore non laberetur, neque [sic][47] in ambiguis laborarem. Nunc uero me deprimunt [langores][48] erumpuosi exilii et molescie aggrauantes uix [me][49] subsistere permittunt, et cum intus inardescam calore increato, foris quasi fuscus et infelix sine luce delitesco.

Ergo ne, Deus meus, cui deuocionem offero absque ficcione, recordaberis mei in miseracione? Quia miser sum, misericordia indigeo; et nonne [langorem][50] qui me ligat subleuabis in lucem, ut opportune habeam quod concupisco?

(p. 243, line 34–p. 244, line 32)

(Therefore, who might sing to me the songs of my singing, the joys of affection with flames of love, and the burning of my loving youth so

---

43 Corrected from Bod. 861 fol. 117ra. (reading *mensura* for Deanesly's *mensuram*).
44 Ibid., reading *neupmata* for Deanesly's *pneumata*.
45 Ibid., reading *neupmatizando* for Deanesly's *pneumatizando*.
46 Ibid., reading *archana* for Deanesly's *arcana*.
47 Ibid., reading *sic* for Deanesly's *si*.
48 Ibid., reading *langores* for Deanesly's *languores*.
49 Ibid., reading *me* for Deanesly's *ne*.
50 Ibid., reading *langorem* for Deanesly's *languorem*.

that at least from a companion's songs of love I might subtly seek out my essence, and so that the measure of melodies in which I might be thought pre-eminent might become known to me, if by chance I might find myself exempt from unhappiness to rest with sweetness in the comforts of my companion – something that I do not presume to preach on my own authority, because I have not yet found what I desire. Since indeed if I should judge that cry to be that song hidden completely from external ears (which, in truth, I dare proclaim it to be) would that I might find one who originates that song, who even if not in spoken things, nonetheless in written ones might recite in song my glory to [for] me and utter in song and the singing of the descant the song which I, bound to the most noble name, have not blushed to utter in the presence of my beloved. And indeed, this man would be amiable above gold to me. To him I could not begin to compare all things held precious in this exile. For the charm of virtue dwells with him and he more perfectly seeks out the mysteries of love. Finally I would love him as my own heart and there would be nothing that I would intend to hide from him, for he would express the song to [for] me that I desire to know and make clear to [for] me the cry of my joyfulness. Being thus stirred up, I would rejoice more fully, or rather emulate more abundantly; since he might reveal to [for] me the fire of love and shine forth clearly with sonorous jubilation. The clamour of thought would not glide away without a praiser, nor would I labour thus in uncertainty. Now, however, the languor of this exile that breaks forth is weighing me down and oppressive troubles scarcely allow me to subsist, and when I would kindle myself within with uncreated heat, I withdraw on the outside like a dark and unhappy man without light.

Therefore, my God, to whom I offer unfeigned devotion, you will not forget me in my misery, will you? Because I am a wretch I require mercy; and you will lift up into light the languor that binds me so that I might favourably have that which I desire, won't you?)

Rolle arrives at the surprising but forceful conclusion that he needs a musical companion ('sodalis', 'socii') to notate his song for him so that he might better understand not only the song but also his very self. *Sodalis* and *socius* more often mean 'companion' than 'friend', especially given Rolle's reservation of the prestigious language of spiritual *amicitia* for a later chapter (39); but, as we shall see, this phantasmal companion assumes attributes of a friend (*amicus*) as defined by Rolle in Chapter 39, so *sodalis* and *socius* will be interpreted as both 'companion' and 'friend' interchangeably. Perhaps because the idea of a canorous phantasmal companion is so novel to his thought, Rolle seems not to have worked out in his mind what the exact differences between a *sodalis/socius* and an *amicus* were; he explores such paradigms rather hesitantly at first, with the more neutral *sodalis socius*, until in Chapter 39 he begins to understand the role that an *amicus* might play in the spiritual life and there more boldly asserts the language of *amicitia*.

The very novelty of Rolle's thought is borne out by comparison to other mystical authors. Augustine often writes that failure to achieve contemplation should prompt us to further self-examination, but never advocates the help of a phantasmal companion.[51] So too, though the literary accounts of Christian mysticism with which Rolle would have been familiar may be initiated through fraternal support in charity (as in Bernard of Clairvaux's sermons), or may result in communal harmony (as in *The Life of Saint Antony*) or salvation (as in the rapture of St Paul), the mystical experience itself is almost never a social event.[52] This is one reason why Augustine's ascent with his mother in *The Confessions* is so exceptional. It is unusual, to say the least, for a medieval author to measure his spiritual progress by reference to a companion who does not even exist. If Rolle could be said to be working with any model of friendship, it may in fact be Augustine's in *The Confessions*. In Book 5 Ambrose in effect shows Augustine a text to be pondered, expounding the writings of the Old Testament in a more abstract, spiritual sense ('spiritaliter') than Augustine was accustomed to, and thus laying the groundwork for his conversion.[53] Rolle's wish is that his phantasmal friend might somehow also show him written things ('scriptis') in which he might communicate spiritual *canor* for him.

We must be clear about what this canorous companion is *doing* here. It would be false to say that his intervention inspires Rolle to compose *canor* on the page before us. Contrary to what many readers have posited, Rolle insists that *canor* cannot be reproduced in language, no matter how eloquent the frequent alliteration, elevated diction, and

51   In his fifty-second sermon, Augustine addresses the consequences of failed mystical endeavour, 52.6.16; PL 38:361.

52   Bernard of Clairvaux, *Sermones super Canticum Canticorum* in *Sancti Bernardi opera*, ed. Jean Leclercq, C. H. Talbot, and Henri Rochais, vols 1 and 2 (Rome, 1957–98), 23.1–2. Athanasius, *The Life of Antony and the Letter to Marcellinus*, trans. Robert C. Gregg (Mahwah, NJ, 1980), 42; on Paul's rapture, whose revelation is designed to be evangelical, see 2 Corinthians 12.

53   Augustine, *Confessiones*, 5.14.24.

sonorous style in Chapters 31–4.[54] Wolfgang Riehle correctly notes, '[C]*anor* cannot take concrete shape in natural language, but can only be alluded to'.[55] *Canor* is a spiritual gift that is received by a select few through grace, and Rolle, so far as we can tell, is the only member of this club.[56] The phantasmal companion instead embodies Rolle's desire for a means of voiced or textual communication of *canor* in the face of his own inability, even if this is impossible: 'utinam et illius modulaminis inueniam auctorem hominem, qui etsi non dictis, tamen scriptis mihi gloriam meam decantaret' ('would that I might find one who originates that song, who even if not in spoken things, nonetheless in written ones might recite in song my glory to [for] me'). The key word upon which this passage rests is the Latin *utinam*, indicating a wish or desire (for a companion) that cannot, and will never, be fulfilled. So, we might ask, why bother?

Engaging with Michel de Certeau's theoretical mysticism, Karma Lochrie frames the medieval mystical text as one in which desire for God cannot be satisfied by means of either the author or his text alone. Lochrie argues that the medieval mystic voids himself of himself, leaving a lack, the 'empty space from which the Other [i.e. the divinity] speaks', a space which can only be filled by meditation on Christ.[57] For Lochrie, Christ becomes compensatory, filling in the gaps of the mystic's bodily and spiritual identity and also of his text: 'While mystical texts fail in their utterance, they do provide passage through utterance to *something else* – through the Name or experience of immersion in the body of

---

54 'Mundi quippe amatores scire possunt uerba uel carmina nostrarum cancionum, non autem cantica nostrorum carminum; quia uerba legunt, sed notam et tonum ac suauitatem odarum addiscere non possunt' ('Lovers of the world can know the words or incantations of our songs, but not the music of our songs; because they read the words, but they cannot learn the notes, tones, and sweetness of the odes', p. 278, lines 11–15). Even if Rolle technically leaves the door open to the legibility of verbal *canor* for those who are not lovers of the world ('mundi amatores'), his system of inclusion is not a democratic one. Watson ably argues that Rolle is an elitist who can see no one but himself as capable of *canor*: *Invention of Authority*, 58–60, 70–2, 165–6, 189–90.
55 Wolfgang Riehle, *The Secret Within: Hermits, Recluses and Spiritual Outsiders in Medieval England*, trans. Charity Scott-Stokes (Ithaca, NY, 2014), 94.
56 Watson, *Invention of Authority*, 165–6.
57 Karma Lochrie, *Margery Kempe and Translations of the Flesh* (Philadelphia, 1991), 62–4 (62). Lochrie draws upon Michel de Certeau's *Heterologies: Discourse on the Other*, trans. Brian Massumi (Minneapolis, 1986).

Christ – *which is elsewhere than the utterance* [my emphasis].'[58] In a work that deals very little with the function of Christ, the key figure for Lochrie, Rolle substitutes this phantasmal companion for Christ in his mediating function; Rolle's companion is this 'something else [...] elsewhere than the utterance', who circulates and stages Rolle's desire. Moreover, the same outpouring of affect that many mystics reserve for the name of Christ is here transferred to the companion who assuages Rolle's desire for mystical fruition and communicates with Rolle dialogically in the empty space that Rolle has created in himself (the locus of his failure to describe *canor*). The companion becomes Rolle's hypothetical mystical text, desire for whom opens up *canor* even if he does not allow Rolle to generate *canor* directly in language.

Rolle's companion assists him in all stages of the traditional mystical process that scholars commonly identify (preparation, experience, and response), and in doing so bridges the semantic and conceptual gap between the companion (*sodalis*, used in Chapter 34) and the friend (*amicus*, used elsewhere in *Incendium*).[59] Rolle's relation with others, a persistent problem throughout *Incendium*, now becomes the solution: meditation on his companion allows the distracting thoughts of the world ('clamosa quoque cogitacio') that are always impeding *canor* to glide away ('laberetur'), preparing him for rapture. This hypothetical companionship additionally enables mystical experience itself. In his rapture described in 2 Corinthians, Paul, Rolle's favourite mystic, famously hears 'arcana verba' (mysterious words), which it is not permitted for one to speak ('quae non licet homini loqui', 2 Cor. 12:4). In Rolle's case, though, his companion transposes occulted mystical knowledge; he will help Rolle to seek out ('inuestigat') the very mysteries of love ('amoris arc[h]ana'), now performed for him as the subject matter of *canor*. Throughout several earlier chapters in *Incendium* which treat Rolle's relationship to the angelic choir, the mystical event, defined in particular as the canorous *arcana*, is enabled by the communal, choral sharing of secret knowledge modelled on notions of reciprocity that inform classical and medieval ideas of friendship (p. 151, line 28–p. 152, line 2; p. 200, line 12). Here, in Chapter 34, companionship is replete

58   Lochrie, *Margery Kempe*, 69.
59   McGinn argues for a capacious understanding of mysticism whose actual event includes 'the preparation for, the consciousness of, and the reaction to what can be described as the immediate or direct presence of God', *The Foundations of Mysticism*, xvii.

with similar language of shared penetration and opening ('apercione') of mystical knowledge. Thus begins the shift from *sodalis*, the explicit, more neutral appellation of Chapter 34, to *amicus*, the prestigious spiritual role that he later assumes.

For Rolle mysticism is not a solitary experience, though he does prefer to be in physical solitude to contemplate God. Rolle yearns to share the mystical experience not just with an audience, but also with this phantasmal friend, through love, because the friend might share mystical experience with him: 'Diligerem denique illum sicut cor meum nec esset aliquid quod ab ipso occultare intenderem, quia canorem quod [*sic*] cupio intelligere mihi exprimeret, et iubilum iocunditatis mee clarius enodaret' ('Finally I would love him as my own heart and there would be nothing that I would intend to hide from him, for he would express the song for me that I desire to know and make clear for me the cry of my joyfulness'). Rolle seeks perfect parity and transparency between himself and the friend so that friendship becomes a model for the joint enterprise of receiving and sharing illuminated mystical union. This anticipates the Ciceronian language in Rolle's effusive treatment of *amicitia* in Chapter 39, describing friends' shared wills ('[a]micicia est connexio uoluntatum', p. 261, line 1), merging of selves ('amancium consolidacio', p. 264, line 29), and mutual consolation ('mencium consolacio', p. 264, lines 29–30). The *sodalis* now shares the prestigious rank of spiritual *amicus*. The friend becomes sacralized not only as the joint recipient and propagator of mystical experience, but also perhaps even as an end of mystical contemplation itself, much like the angelic choir does elsewhere. Indeed, Rolle equates the friend with God several times by using nearly identical adjectival language to describe both of them in Chapter 34 and elsewhere in *Incendium*.[60] The presence of God is realized largely through the idea of a canorous friend.

Finally, the idea of the friend brings Rolle closer to melodious enunciation of both mystical *canor* and friendship, even if neither can be fully realized. Rolle's ostensible speechlessness is not necessarily an

---

60   To cite just one example, the 'uenusta uirtus' ('graceful virtue') is present ('aderit') in God, (p. 180, line 7), and in Chapter 34, 'uenustas namque uirtutis cum ipso habitat' ('for the grace of virtue dwells with the friend', p. 244, lines 15–16). At the end of Chapter 34 we are also reminded of the association when Rolle longs to see God 'in uenustate sui decoris', ('in the grace of his beauty', p. 244, line 35). I believe these are the only three times that 'uenustas' is used in *Incendium*, which makes the link between God and the numinous friend all the more pronounced.

ineffability topos. Watson writes that Rolle is of all medieval mystics '*least* interested in the fact that mystical experience is ineffable'.[61] Rolle approaches *canor* thus: 'In hac equidem apercione exultarem amplius, aut certe uberius emularem; quoniam mihi ostenderetur incendium amoris et sonora iubilacio euidenter effulgeret' ('Being thus stirred up, I would rejoice more fully, or rather emulate more abundantly; since he might reveal to me the fire of love and shine forth with sonorous jubilation'). Zieman notes that in Chapter 15 of *Incendium* Rolle's initial experience of *canor* may be contrasted to other conversion or hailing narratives (that of Augustine, for example) insofar as Rolle is called not towards but away from sacred language: 'the text that the choir performs is largely irrelevant, subordinated to the ideal of communal singing'.[62] Likewise, Rolle's friend, a similarly extragrammatical phenomenon, calls Rolle away from language as registered in Rolle's failure to describe *canor*, which, however, is then transformed into the call-and-response trope of the numinous liturgy between Rolle and his desired friend. Here, in Chapter 34, Rolle responds antiphonally to the friend to circulate desire for utterance of God, in Lochrie's terms. What began in Chapter 31 as a promised triumph of independently self-sustained *canor* has become a jubilant celebration of its being motivated by a friend, perorating in an abject prayer meekly requesting that either *canor* or the friend be given to him. In these closing lines, it seems no longer to matter which of the two is the object of Rolle's unfulfilled desire, as both become a single metonym for all stages of the mystical process.[63]

For Rolle, contemplation in all of its stages is also permeated with affect, and Rolle's desired friend is the locus of affect. In Chapter 31, Rolle's complaint against his stupid detractors ('stultis hominibus', p. 233, line 32), the *inferiores* who complain that he does not sing in church with them, is that they have never experienced *canor* and cannot know how superior his version is to theirs: they cannot *feel with him* ('me [...]

---

61 Watson, 'Translation and Self-Canonization in Richard Rolle's *Melos Amoris*', in *The Medieval Translator: The Theory and Practice of Translation in the Middle Ages*, ed. Roger Ellis (Cambridge, 1989), 167–81 (179). Bernard McGinn concurs, *The Varieties of Vernacular Mysticism, 1350–1550* (New York, 2012), 346.
62 Zieman, 'Perils of *Canor*', 140.
63 Renevey contends that in the exegetical tradition of the Song of Songs, of which Rolle forms a crucial part, the narrative voice enters not to interpret or explain the text, but to serve as a conduit for the mystical experience itself (*Language, Self, and Love*, 4). The friend likewise does not explain mysticism, but enables it.

non cognouerunt consentire', p. 233, line 32–p. 234, line 1). Chapter 34 responds to the lack created in Chapter 31 by offering a potential friend, someone to feel with (con-sentire). In Bonaventuran and Franciscan terms, affective piety is a reordering of the *affectus*, and hence of the *intellectus*, often through the formal structures of literature, usually by shifting one's attention from worldly desires to emotionally tinged aspects of desire for Christ.[64] Though thirteenth-century commentators first began to discuss affectivity formally as heightened emotional responses to a reading of sacred Scripture, by Rolle's time the 'text' to prompt affective response was often the suffering Christ for whom one burns with love.[65] Yet in *Incendium* the phantasmal friend becomes what McNamer would call the 'script' for affect.[66] The performativity of this 'script' is further suggested by Carruthers's commentary on Quintilian's ancient advice for orators performing to elicit affective response from their audience so that they might then be persuaded: orators must first use carefully crafted *visiones* (Latin) or *phantasias* (Greek) to experience the emotion *themselves*, and even act out their response to these *visiones/phantasias* in very dramatic ways, if they hope to move the audience.[67] Rolle's vision or phantasm, in the form of a friend, is likewise intended to generate affective response, which Rolle consistently associates with progress towards contemplative fruition, *canor*.

The ordering process implicit in spiritual affectivity threatens to break down when Rolle confesses his inability to recount his performance of *canor* – until he introduces the phantasmal friend with and by whom he might approach *canor*. The friend lacks the cachet of the angelic choir, Rolle's supreme structuring principle of melodious order, which we might think the best remedy for the affective impotence contained in Rolle's failure to describe *canor*. But throughout the passage quoted above Rolle seeks in the friend what he typically seeks in solitary contemplation:

64   The background to the medieval discussion of literature as a means of engaging the affect to reform the intellect is discussed in Chapter 12 of Ernst Robert Curtius, *European Literature and the Latin Middle Ages*, trans. Willard R. Trask (Princeton, 1953); see also Alastair Minnis, *Medieval Theory of Authorship: Scholastic Literary Attitudes in the Later Middle Ages*, 2nd edn (Philadelphia, 1988), 49–52, 119–22; and Gillespie's incisive summary and notes, in 'Mystic's Foot', 209–12.
65   Gillespie, 'Mystic's Foot', 199–207.
66   McNamer, 'Feeling', 246; McNamer, *Affective Meditation*, 11–14.
67   Carruthers, *The Craft of Thought*, 132–3, comments on Quintilian, *De institutione oratoria* VI.xxx–xxxii.

'gaudia affectuum cum ardoribus amoris' ('the joys of affection with flames of love'); he hopes that 'in solaciis socii mei requiescerem cum dulcore' ('I might rest with sweetness in the comforts of my companion'), since 'mihi ostenderetur incendium amoris et sonora iubilacio euidenter effulgeret' ('he might reveal to me the fire of love and shine forth with sonorous jubilation'). The language of contemplation in *Incendium* becomes the language of friendship; contemplation becomes social and is structured through hypothetical friendship. Rolle presents a model of solitary sociability that would later appear more concretely in the work of mystical writers like Walter Hilton.[68] Structuring affect to achieve rapprochement with God requires a receptive object on whom affect might be realized, one who, in this instance, is not Christ. Yet for Rolle affect is not 'self-expressive', but performative (substituting for a failure to recount his performance of *canor*), and therein constitutive of identity via the friend.[69]

Philosophy of Friendship

After ending Chapter 34, Rolle begins Chapter 35 with an impassioned prayer to Christ:

> O Ihesu in te cum iubilacione ardeo, et iugiter ingeret se estus amoris, ut te, o amantissime, plene amplexarer, et differor dilectissime ab hoc ad quod anhelo. Insuper et anguscie accidunt, ac uasta solitudo uiam intercludit, amanciumque habitaciones in unum adhuc non sinit edificari.
>
> (p. 245, lines 1–6)

> (O Jesus I burn in you with jubilation, and continually the fire of love pours itself out, most loving one, so that I might embrace you fully, most beloved, and be carried from here to that which I long for. But hardships befall me, and vast solitude closes the way to me, hitherto not permitting a dwelling place of lovers to be established in one place.)

It is nothing short of remarkable for Rolle to suggest that solitude ('solitudo') hinders devotion to God while wishing instead for a home

---

68 Hughes-Edwards, 'How good it is to be alone?', 43–7.
69 McNamer makes a similar point about affective authors who are too rashly labelled 'self-expressive', when they are in fact opening up performative opportunities for themselves and their audiences, *Affective Meditation*, 12–13, 65–7.

('habitaciones') where lovers of God might dwell together, however metaphysical that place may be. Rolle's ostensible renunciation of *solitudo* has confused translators of *Incendium*. In his 1435 Middle English translation, Richard Misyn translates *solitudo* as an impeding 'wilderness', as does Clifton Wolters in his 1972 Modern English translation, though M. L. del Mastro renders it as 'solitude' in his 1981 translation.[70] Any medieval Latin lexicon will show that *solitudo* can in theory mean 'wilderness', which would suggest in this passage, as Misyn and Wolters surmise, that the vast wilderness of the world keeps tripping Rolle up. But to the best of my knowledge Rolle, in his corpus, never intends for *solitudo* to mean 'wilderness'. For Rolle, *solitudo* is solitude.[71] There is no good reason to translate *solitudo* as 'wilderness' in this passage other than the fact that scholars are not used to thinking of Rolle as suspicious of solitude, as is evident from translators' misapprehensions. For in this passage Rolle favours community, however metaphysical, to solitude; living life only as a traditional solitary may cut off ('intercludit') the spiritual benefits of community, that *habitacio* of lovers.

The *habitacio* that Rolle seeks, the asylum for a community of lovers and friends in God, is the textual space of Chapter 34 and, especially, Chapter 39, in which Rolle expounds a generous philosophy of friendship. Chapter 39 is Rolle's textual performance of friendship, the creation of textual space in which friendship (now, among all Christians) might dwell peacefully and more assuredly than in Chapter 34, protected from the many strains of thought in *Incendium* which seem hostile to human relations. It is also Rolle's performance of friendship as an author; after experimenting tentatively with ideas of otherness earlier in *Incendium*, he is now ready to pronounce confidently on the fitness of human relations.

In Chapter 39, the longest chapter of *Incendium*, Rolle treats friendship more explicitly than anywhere else in his œuvre, and in doing so treats friendship so that it no longer centres around him, but is open to all

---

70   Misyn, *The Fire of Love*, ed. Harvey, 78; Richard Rolle, *The Fire of Love*, trans. Clifton Wolters (New York, 1972), 154; Richard Rolle, *The Fire of Love and the Mending of Life*, trans. M. L. del Mastro (New York, 1981), 223.
71   For example, in his English Psalter commentary on Psalms 54:7, Rolle translates the kind of *solitudo* that he has entered as 'anly stede', which means, simply, 'solitude': *The Psalter of the Psalms of David and Certain Canticles, with a Translation and Exposition in English*, ed. H. R. Bramley (Oxford, 1884), 195.

Christians. Rolle pens a capacious philosophy of friendship, the subject matter of the entire chapter, beginning with a Ciceronian commonplace that nonetheless refigures one's relation to God:

> Amicicia est connexio uoluntatum, eisdem consenciencium et eisdem dissencium [...] et maxime deberet esse inter Deum et animam que diuine uoluntati uoluntatem suam tenetur conformare in omnibus; ut que Deus uelit, uelit et ipsa; que Deus nolit, nolit et ipsa; sic quidem plena erit inter eos amicicia [...] Est enim uere amicicia: cum amicus se habet ad amicum sicut ad seipsum, cum amicus sit alius ipse, et ipsum amat propter ipsum, non propter utile quod se sperat ab eo percepturum.
>
> (p. 261, lines 1–16)

> (Friendship is the joining of wills consenting to these things and dissenting from others [...] And chiefly friendship ought to be between God and the soul, which is held to conform its will to the divine will in all things; so that what God wills, the soul wills the same; and what God does not will, so the soul does not will the same; thus full friendship will certainly be between them [...] For this truly is friendship: when the friend holds himself toward the friend as toward himself, when the friend is another himself, and he loves the friend himself on account of the friend himself, and not for anything useful that he hopes to gain from him.)

The similarly constituted wills, self-love, and disinterestedness of friends in secular Ciceronian friendship reign supreme, expressed in language almost identical to Cicero's, making it difficult to discern if Rolle knew Cicero intimately or if the popularity of *De amicitia* in the Middle Ages had rendered such topoi conventional.[72] Human friendship in which both friends have the same Ciceronian will ('uoluntatum', p. 261, line 1)

---

72 *De amicitia*, 4.15, 9.31, 21.80. J. P. Schneider was the first to argue for Rolle's debt to Cicero in Chapter 39 of *Incendium*, in Schneider, *The Prose Style of Richard Rolle of Hampole, with Special Reference to its Euphuistic Tendencies* (Baltimore, 1906), 58–61. Schneider's argument is supported by Deanesly, the text's editor, at p. 261 n. 1. Moyes complicates this assumption suggesting that Rolle draws upon Aelred's adaptation of Cicero instead (*Richard Rolle's Expositio*, ed. Moyes, 55–8). Moyes's approach, however, is somewhat tendentious, drawing upon a few isolated examples, and dichotomous. In the passages that Moyes cites it is clear that Rolle's thinking is more closely aligned with Aelred's, but it could surely be the case that Rolle knew both Aelred and Cicero, the influence of

is greatly meritorious ('multum meritoria', p. 262, line 37), but only 'si gracia Dei [est][73] informata et tota in Deo fiat, et ad Deum referatur et tendat' ('if it is informed by the grace of God, and becomes complete in God, and is directed and extends toward God', p. 262, lines 35–6). Friends share communion in both Ciceronian and Christian terms, as they both have the same wilful love of God. Friends no longer mediate between one another and God; God mediates between them, insofar as he is an instrument of contact for them.

Surprisingly, Rolle also addresses friendship with women, who are usually absent from medieval discussions of friendship; in Chapter 39, Rolle opens up the possibility of virtuous opposite-sex friendship in a work that elsewhere closes it down. Readers of *Incendium* are familiar with its irritating misogyny: beautiful, flattering women cause men to sin, separating them from God and contemplation. Rolle renounces women in many works.[74] Repeatedly in Chapter 39 Rolle treats opposite-sex friendship only to highlight its deadly snares. But, he writes:

> Est et quedam naturalis dileccio uiri ad mulierem, et mulieris ad uirum, qua nullus caret nec eciam sanctus, secundum naturam a Deo primo institutam, per quam simul existentes et inuicem concordantes, naturali instinctu socialiter letantur. Que quidem dileccio eciam suas habet delectaciones ut in mutuis colloquiis et tactibus honestis, grataque cohabitacione.
>
> (p. 263, lines 28–34)

> (There is a certain natural delight of men for women, and of women for men, which no one lacks, not even a holy man, instituted originally according to nature by God, through which they simultaneously live in mutual concord, gladdened by their company through this natural

whose *De amicitia* on the Middle Ages is immeasurable. In short, Rolle's diction and thought are just as close to Cicero's as to Aelred's.

73   Supplied from Bod. 861, fol. 120vb.

74   The misogyny in *Incendium* is so pervasive that it is difficult to isolate in a single note. Chapter 12, told in narrative form, is the most extended account of Rolle's distaste for and renunciation of women. In his *Super Canticum Canticorum*, Rolle writes of a vision he had one night in which the devil disguised as a beautiful young woman tried to tempt him sexually, only to be vanquished by Rolle's invocation of the name of Jesus; see 'Richard Rolle's *Comment on the Canticles*', ed. Elizabeth Murray, PhD diss. (Fordham University, 1958), 48.

instinct. This delight pertains to mutual conversation, chaste touches, and their living together in grace.)

Much of the same language that Rolle uses for spiritual friendship with men (dwelling together, 'cohabitacione'; mutual interchange of discourse, 'mutuis colloquiis'; and spiritual harmony and gladness, 'concordantes', 'socialiter letantur') is here used for friendship with women. Despite the masculine pronouns that Rolle (and, consequently, I) use to discuss the metaphysical friend in Chapter 34, a woman could also be Rolle's canorous or spiritual friend.

Moreover, Rolle contradicts his earlier self: God does not wish women to be despised ('despici', p. 264, line 20) by men but taught ('erudiri', p. 264, line 22) by them. Rolle imagines friendship with women as not just metaphysical but didactic; it is plausible that women could follow Rolle's mystical programme as reliably as men can. Riehle argues that parts of *Incendium* make their way into Rolle's later English works that were written largely for women.[75] And, as Watson has demonstrated, in *Incendium* Rolle authorizes himself as a teacher of women, a role that comes to fruition as he writes in the persona of a friend to women in his didactic English epistles, and as he develops both textual and historical relationships with members of their audience (one of whom was his illustrious spiritual friend Margaret Kirkeby, about whom much is now being written).[76] Although *Incendium* is an early work, it nonetheless reveals a forward-thinking Rolle. For Rolle, women have the potential to be friends in nearly all the ways that men can, even if he pays so little positive attention to them in *Incendium*.

Rolle writes effusively of friendship in Chapter 39, but in doing so develops the thought of Aquinas, who wrote years before him that friendship figures not just as spontaneous affection but as a moral relationship subtended by God.[77] Friendship is a great good of life for any Christian to enjoy for its corporal and spiritual benefits:

75 Riehle, *The Secret Within*, 118.

76 Watson, *Invention of Authority*, 222–6; McIlroy, *The English Prose Treatises*, 140–86.

77 James McEvoy, 'The Theory of Friendship in the Latin Middle Ages: Hermeneutics, Contextualization and the Transmission and Reception of Ancient Texts and Ideas, from c. AD 350 to c.1500', in *Friendship in Medieval Europe*, ed. Julian Haseldine (Stroud, 1999), 3–44 (15); Daniel Schwartz, *Aquinas on Friendship* (Oxford, 2007), 6–21.

Est autem uera amicicia amancium consolidacio, mencium consolacio, anguscie releuacio,[78] tristicie secularis expulsio, reformacio [peccatoris][79], augmentacio sanctitatis, diminucio [scelerum],[80] multiplicacio bonorum meritorum.

(p. 264, lines 29–32)

(This is true friendship: the merging of lovers, the consolation of spirits, the lightening of hardship, the expulsion of secular sadness, the reformation of the sinner, the augmentation of sanctity, the diminution of wickedness, the multiplication of good rewards.)

Rolle spends some time here addressing attributes of friendship that apply largely to the metaphysical variety: the 'amancium consolidacio', a new name for the dwelling-place of lovers ('amancium habitaciones') to which Rolle alludes in Chapter 35; the 'mencium consolacio', much like the solace Rolle feels from the canorous friend in Chapter 34; the '[angustie] releuacio', the solution to the languor that a friendless Rolle feels in Chapter 34.

But then, in chiasmal structure, the word order changes in the middle of the list: in 'reformacio [peccatoris]' the nominative appears before the genitive, whereas previously the genitive came first. The change in grammar marks a more significant change from the metaphysical qualities of friendship to its pastoral and moral qualities, as it helps us to combat sin and increase our holiness. Friends draw us away from sin and 'inflame' ('inflammatur', p. 264, line 34) us towards good (metaphors of heat deriving from the friend, not now from the self-sufficient lover of God); friends provide an exemplum whose virtues we admire ('intuetur', p. 264, line 35), so that we may have them in ourselves ('in se habere', p. 264, line 35 – not unlike Rolle's canorous friend, whom he earlier wishes to emulate ('emularem', p. 244, line 21)); friends supply spiritual counsel ('consiliis', p. 265, line 2) and help ('auxiliis', p. 265, line 2); and friends anticipate that social fellowship of eternal quiet ('eterne quietis consorcium', p. 221, lines 222–3), for which God is figured as the means,

---

78   Bod. 861's *reuelacio* (fol. 120ra) seems to be an error for *releuacio*, the reading Deanesly here records.

79   Corrected from Bod. 861, fol. 120ra (reading *peccatoris* for Deanesly's *peccatorum*).

80   Ibid., reading *scelerum* for Deanesly's *sceleris*.

the end, and the co-requisite ('in quo et pro quo amicos habemus', p. 265, lines 4–5).

To those nay-sayers who believe friendship should be renounced along with the rest of the world, Rolle replies with the same argument that he uses against those who believe the eremitic life should be lived more ascetically than Rolle is wont to do: over-abstemiousness hinders devotion to God (p. 265, line 5–p. 266, line 9). Friends, like food and drink, are *necessary* ('necessariis', p. 265, line 30) and must not be renounced incautiously ('incaute', p. 265, line 30). And Rolle in this chapter explicitly retracts an earlier statement that things of the world both licit and illicit must be rejected (p. 257, lines 8–10); when friendship enters the picture, only the illicit must be rejected (p. 265, lines 21–3), a sure sign of progress.

But such progress is fleeting. Rolle brings friendship out of its self-serving, highly abstract state and highlights its potential for fully realized spiritual friendship within a community, only to abjure it all. Rolle must have sensed that he was running into a problem: even if such friends might be read metaphysically, Chapter 39's effusive treatment of the hypothetical friend's presence ('eius presencia', p. 265, line 16), conversation ('alloquio', p. 265, line 16), and even of living together ('cohabitacione', p. 265, line 17) were beginning to sound like a monastic treatise on communal living, something in the vein of Aelred or Bernard, while Rolle himself endeavours throughout *Incendium* to place the contemplative life far above the coenobitic (e.g. p. 179, line 18–p. 182, line 14). The kind of hypothetical friendship discussed in Chapter 39 is, moreover, almost completely removed from the discourse of communal *canor* enabled by friendship, and must simply be discarded as it has little utility for Rolle's authorial and literary agenda.

And thus Rolle ends Chapter 39, which has been exclusively on friendship, as abruptly as it began, complaining in a couple of hundred words of the inane ostentation of women's clothing before finally dismissing the digression that this long chapter has become: 'Sed nunc ad alia transeamus' ('But let us now move on to other things', p. 266, line 33). Rolle seems eager to dispense with tangible friendship, begun from his desire for social relations. The friends of Chapter 39 have come too close for comfort at this early stage of his literary career, where the best friend is still one who does not exist. Chapter 39, Rolle's *habitacio* for real, lived friendship, may or may not be compatible with Rolle's idea of the contemplative life.

Sacral Society

For Rolle, even if sociability encompassing the presence of God sometimes seems an end in itself, friendship is nonetheless an intellectual and affective exercise to prepare him for love of God. Chapter 39 began by invoking God as the greatest of friends, with whom we share a similar Ciceronian will (*voluntas*), though the idea is largely undeveloped in that chapter as the focus shifts to humankind. But evidence for God as a friend is dispersed throughout *Incendium*.[81] Rolle conforms his habit to the medieval philosophy underlying affective piety, in which the *affectus* now reformed by the imagined joys of spiritual friendship prepares the *intellectus* for new understanding of God – namely, God as a friend.[82] This was anticipated as early as Chapter 8, in which our relationship to God is figured in Chapter 39's terms of one's love for a disinterested friend in whom we seek no other reward than the friend himself ('propter seipsum, non propter utile uel delectabile', p. 261, line 23); thus we are in Chapter 8 asked to require no other reward in heaven except friendship with God, which is God himself ('amiciciam Dei que est ipse Deus', p. 165, lines 10–11). In Chapter 41, 'me et amibilem meum amor unit, et unum ex duobus facit' ('love unites my beloved and me, and makes one out of two', p. 275, lines 6–7), just as, in Chapter 39, friends bound by indissoluble bonds ('insolubile uinclum coherentis amicicie', p. 261, line 10) should never be separate in soul when they are separate in body ('absit ut distancia corporum separabilitatem faciat animorum', p. 261, lines 8–9).

Moreover, friendship serves as a model for mystical union with God. Rolle establishes the parity of the lover (his hypothetical self) and the beloved (God) several times in *Incendium*. In Chapter 4, love of God 'transformat nos ad suam similitudinem' ('transforms us to his likeness', p. 156, lines 1–2). In Chapter 17, 'Assimilatur autem omnis amans suo amato, et similem facit amor illum qui amat ei quod amatur'

---

81   Outside of *Incendium*, Rolle writes in *The Form of Living* that God 'is homelier to ham [lovers of God] þan [. . .] any frend þat þai most loued or most trusteth on' (*Richard Rolle: Prose and Verse*, ed. S. J. Ogilvie-Thomson (Oxford, 1988), 15).

82   Gillespie writes, 'The role of affective literature is to regain the attention of the *affectus*, by winning it away from the proximate things to which it has become attached and focusing it firmly on absolute good, to enable the intellect to penetrate more deeply into its understanding of absolute truth, which it knows to be desirable but from which it is constantly distracted by the dissipation of the will' (Gillespie, 'Mystic's Foot', 203).

('the entirety of the lover is assimilated to his beloved, and love makes him who loves similar to that which is loved', p. 195, lines 15–17). Rolle imagines himself to be so merged with Christ that if Rolle were to offend God, he would only be betraying himself (p. 209, lines 13–16). This very parity allows their Ciceronian wills (*voluntas*) to join, and allows mystical union, framed as friendship, to follow:

> Amor enim dulcis et deuotus cor in diuina dulcedine sic resoluit, quod uoluntas hominis cum uoluntate Dei mirabili amicicia unitur, in qua unione tanta suauitas feruoris dulcoris et canoris amanti animo infunditur quantam senciens non potest explanare.
>
> (p. 196, lines 13–17)

> (Sweet and devout love so melts the heart in divine sweetness that the will of man is united with the will of God in a marvellous friendship, in which union the charm of *fervor*, *dulcor*, and *canor* is poured into the loving soul so much so that he cannot explain it.)

Friendship *is* performed mystical union. Understood as parity of wills between God and humankind, friendship becomes the very basis for receiving the fruits of the mystical life, *fervor*, *dulcor*, and *canor*. In Chapter 33, Rolle writes that he fled earthly song to conform himself to ('conformaui') and perform ('perficerem') God's will ('uoluntatem', p. 239, lines 20–1), the prerequisite of divine friendship, so that he would not lose the mystical gifts which had been bestowed upon him (p. 239, lines 20–6). Performed friendship with God is the authority on whose basis mysticism can proceed. In *Incendium amoris* mystical endeavour requires a performed friend, whether an angelic choir of friends, a canorous phantasmal friend, or God himself.

But in *Incendium* friendship with God is not a one-sided exercise of conforming our will to his. Chapter 42, *Incendium*'s final chapter, shifts the agency of will-conforming to Christ and reminds us that he seeks the lover's friendship as much as the lover seeks his:

> Ipse enim habet amandi bonum inicium, qui lacrimas habet amatorias, cum dulci languore et desiderio eternorum. Ipse uero Christus quasi nostro amore languet, dum tanto ardore ut nos adquireret ad crucem festinauit: sed uerum dicitur quia amor preit in tripudio, et coream ducit. Quod Christum ita demissum posuit, nihil nisi amor fuit.
>
> (p. 276, lines 4–10)

(He [the lover of Christ] has a good beginning of loving who has the
tears of lovers with sweet languor and the desire of eternity. One might
say that Christ languished for our love while he made haste to the Cross
and acquired us with great ardour: but it is truly said that love precedes
the dance and takes the lead. That Christ was brought so low was nothing
if not love.)

Just under ninety words later, Rolle writes, referring to Christ, 'Gloria
enim mea amicicia est' ('Friendship is my glory' [or 'my friendship
is glory'], p. 276, lines 21–2); nearly 140 words after that the lover of
Christ is called an 'amicus' (p. 277, line 3). In this final performed act of
friendship in *Incendium* Christ, staged as he is, assumes the will of the
prototypical Rollean lover, overcome with affect, humble, and eagerly
languishing for the love of his beloved. Lover and beloved suffer together
(*consentire*), two friends bound by a common Ciceronian will.[83]

McNamer argues that medieval female audiences are enjoined to suffer
to prove their love to Christ, thereby legally enacting formal marriage to
him.[84] And Renevey has argued that the relationship between Christ and
the soul in Rolle's corpus overall is best expressed through paradigms
of courtship, spiritual marriage, and erotic consummation, drawn from
the Cistercian *Song of Songs* commentary tradition.[85] But in *Incendium*
Rolle, writing for a masculine audience and himself largely hostile in this
work to opposite-sex erotic love (however sublimated it may be), uses
friendship instead of marriage or erotic love as a paradigm for the soul's
relation to Christ. The specific language of friendship (*amicitia* and
amicus) contextualizes this passage, as we have seen. And, unlike erotic
courtship allegory, the focus is much less on consummation of passion
than on the parity of that passion, or the parity of wills (Ciceronian
voluntas). This abbreviated scene lacks the detail and intensity of erotic
passion found in many Passion meditations; Rolle is certainly capable of
writing such scenes, though he does so rarely in his Latin literature, but
here he pares all such language away to focus almost exclusively on the
equality of the performed wills of Christ and the lover, that enduring
Ciceronian element of friendship which guides Rolle's thought on

83   Christ is subject to what Richard of St Victor calls *caritas ligans*, binding
love, over which God himself has no power – a hallmark of late medieval
mystical texts. On Richard's *caritas ligans*, see Riehle, *The Secret Within*, 51.
84   NcNamer, *Affective Meditation*, 49–53.
85   The general argument of Renevey, *Language, Self, and Love.*

spiritual love. Gaining Christ's friendship involves merely loving him ('cum dulci languore et desiderio') in the same manner that Christ has wooed him ('languet', 'tanto ardore'). Rolle must perform friendship in return. Friendship with the angels, the canorous friend, and humankind has prepared Rolle to gain entrance affectively and performatively to the greatest friendship of all.

Conclusion

This essay began by challenging Rolle's status as a spiritual loner; but it could be argued that in seeking friends who are exactly like him (indeed, just extensions of himself), blessed with the gift of *canor*, and lacking the texture of real life, Rolle only confirms and congratulates his solipsism. We might well ask: didn't Rolle have any real friends? If Rolle does desire physical friendship, he channels that desire into more safely contained metaphysical friendship. As Carolinne White observes of fourth-century spiritual friendships maintained in absence through letter writing, 'Some writers of this period occasionally come close to expressing the view that since spiritual friendships are the strongest kind, and friendship in absence depends on spiritual unity, friendships in absence are actually superior to those where the friends are able to meet in person.'[86] Even in constructing hypothetical, metaphysical friends, Rolle is not unlike the many medieval friends from late antiquity through to the twelfth century who desire to communicate in absence through profuse Latin letter collections, and to express the desire that their addressees (absent friends) might behold their metaphysical presence.[87] Spiritual friendship is spiritual friendship, whether the friend is absent or simply unreal.

---

86   Carolinne White, 'Friendship in Absence – Some Patristic Views', in *Friendship in Medieval Europe*, ed. Julian Haseldine (Stroud, 1999), 69–88 (78).
87   Carolinne White writes on the friendship letters of Basil, Gregory of Nazianzus, Ambrose, Jerome, Paulinus of Nola, and Augustine in her *Christian Friendship in the Fourth Century* (Cambridge, 1992); R. W. Southern treats the friendship letters of Anselm in *Saint Anselm: A Portrait in a Landscape* (Cambridge, 1990), 138–65; Haseldine treats the friendship letters of Bernard of Clairvaux, Peter the Venerable, and Peter of Celle in 'Monastic Friendship in Theory and in Action in the Twelfth Century', in *Friendship in the Middle Ages and Early Modern Age*, ed. Albrecht Classen and Marilyn Sandidge (Berlin and New York, 2010), 349–93; McGuire treats these and most others throughout *Friendship and Community*.

Yet, despite Rolle's solipsism, beginning with Chapter 39 and culminating in *Incendium's* final chapter, Rolle's performance of friendship, previously understood largely in terms of self-aggrandizement, gives way to a more pastoral and evangelical performance to be imitated by readers of *Incendium*: Rolle creates a space in which friendship is to be desired for its moral qualities that allow one to draw close to God, even if such progress is couched in the same language as the phantasmal friendship of Chapter 34. And in Chapter 42, Rolle consummates his friendship with Christ by drawing on the traditions of affective piety, which he tries to teach to his audience in *Incendium* (p. 221, line 24–p. 222, line 8) so that they too might understand their love for Christ and his love for them in terms of friendship between two similarly constituted wills. Chapters 39 and 42 are the climactic end towards which experimental engagement with spiritual love and phantasmal friendship tend.

The structure of Rolle's desire for God is mediated by others. However much Rolle needs to claim that his is a necessarily lonely profession, he cannot fathom how to approach God without reference to others figured as friends, even if some of these friends only reinforce his loneliness. Rolle's public manifesto of *canor*, which we might expect to express the authority of an experience peculiar to him and earned by his own merits, is surprisingly social: Rolle openly exposes his deficiencies in the contemplative life, which cannot be helped unless by a friend in shared endeavour. Authority is not necessarily, as Watson suggests, something which Rolle makes up as he goes along on the strength of his own ingenuity, textuality, and constructed narrative experience, but rather something which inherently relies upon others for its strength, including a hypothetical friend who might function as an *auctor* by showing Rolle his canorous text. Friendship is performed in various spiritual ways. Rolle uses friendship to initiate himself affectively into heavenly community, to fill the gap within himself created by his momentary inability to recount *canor*, to provide a model for mysticism, to include others in the mystical life, and to reframe love for God. Above all, for Rolle, friendship is an impetus toward *canor*, and in being so legitimizes, inspires, melodizes, and sometimes simply overwhelms a figure no less than Richard Rolle himself, whose reputation as a spiritual loner is in need of serious revision.

5

Damaged Goods

Merchandise, Stories and Gender in Chaucer's *Man of Law's Tale*

DIANE CADY

Readings of the *Man of Law's Tale* frequently impugn its narrator for his mercantile attitude. In the tale's prologue, the Man of Law indulges both in an enthusiastic encomium dedicated to merchants and their wealth, and in a lengthy rant against poverty. Such speeches seem wildly inappropriate for a tale that is, ostensibly, about a woman's patient tolerance of penury. Scholars argue that, due to his preoc-cupation with wealth and commerce, the Man of Law fails to grasp the deeper spiritual significance of the story that he tells. Instead, he ends up converting everyone and everything in the world of the story into commodities, from Custance to Christ's providence.[1] Even stories become commodities for the Man of Law, commodities that are in limited supply and that possess a range of values. Those stories that are new (or at least appear new to a particular audience) have the most value in the literary marketplace. The Man of Law worries that these valuable stories are in short supply because Chaucer, albeit 'lewedly',

---

1   See, for example, Laurel Hendrix, '"Pennance profytable": The Currency of Custance in Chaucer's *Man of Law's Tale*', *Exemplaria* 6.1 (Spring 1994), 141–66. Hendrix contends that the Man of Law 'converts the enigmatic workings of God's providence into the logic of the marketplace' (154) and 'collapses the distinction between spiritual, verbal and monetary exchange, attempting to reduce Custance and Christ into signs which are freely traded and manipulated for profit, and the act of "enditing" into a form of merchandising' (141). Roger A. Ladd identifies the Man of Law as the first in a series of mercantile misreaders in the *Canterbury Tales* who are 'unable to pull fruyt from narrative chaf' due to their commercial self-interest. See Ladd's 'The Mercantile (Mis)Reader in *The Canterbury Tales*', *Studies in Philology* 99.1 (Winter 2002), 17–32 (19).

has told them all.[2] The idea of storytelling as a zero-sum game, in which valuable stories are instantly devalued because they are already-told stories, runs counter to most of our working assumptions about the production of medieval narrative, in which 'the important thing is not the originality of the basic story, but rather the artist's execution of it'.[3]

In contrast to his narrator, Chaucer often is viewed as a more sophisticated storyteller, one who understands the roles of intertextuality and influence in narrative production.[4] For such a reading to succeed, a certain philosophical distance between Chaucer and the Man of Law is required. One of the most effective ways to create such a distance, as A. C. Spearing has argued, is by reading the *Canterbury Tales* dramatically, through the lens of their narrators. The long tradition of dramatic reading produces much of the irony that scholars locate in the *Tales*. It

2   Geoffrey Chaucer, the *Man of Law's Tale*, in *The Riverside Chaucer*, ed. Larry Benson, 3rd edn (Boston, 1987), 87–104, line 47. All citations that follow are from this edition and are cited parenthetically by line number.

3   See Chauncey Woods, 'Chaucer's Man of Law as Interpreter', *Traditio* 23 (1967), 149–90 (156). R. A. Shoaf describes the Man of Law as a 'property master' who is 'obsessed with retention', causing him to want to possess, rather than circulate, the story of Custance. See '"Unwemmed Custance": Circulation, Property, and Incest in *The Man of Law's Tale*', *Exemplaria* 2.1 (1990), 287–302. Kathryn Lynch argues that due to his 'pinching commercial mentality' the Man of Law operates from an economy of possession, desiring to hoard the stories he possesses. See Lynch's 'Storytelling, Exchange, and Constancy: East and West in Chaucer's *Man of Law's Tale*', *The Chaucer Review* 33.4 (1999), 409–22. More recently, Lynch has argued that Chaucer may associate the Man of Law with merchants in order to make the reader question the narrator's values. See Lynch's '"Diversitee bitwene hir bothe lawes": Chaucer's Unlikely Alliance of a Lawyer and a Merchant', *The Chaucer Review* 46.1/2 (2011), 74–92 (83).

4   Shoaf views Chaucer as 'a better storyteller than this lawyer. For Chaucer, who is a poet, knows that the sign must circulate, the coin get dirty, the manuscript corrupted'. Shoaf, 'Unwemmed Custance', 288. Lynch makes a similar argument, noting that since Chaucer is the authorial presence behind the Man of Law, it would be absurd to imagine that the *Man of Law's Tale* is depleted by the collected works of Chaucer ('Storytelling, Exchange, and Constancy', 414). Marc Pelen argues that the Man of Law 'exposes himself to Chaucer's irony' and that Chaucer's condemnation of his narrator 'awards a clear, if unstated, victory to the poet's sovereign Muse'. See Pelen's 'Providence and Incest Reconsidered: Chaucer's Poetic Judgment of his Man of Law', *Papers on Language and Literature: A Journal for Scholars and Critics of Language and Literature* 30.2 (Spring 1994), 132–56 (154–5).

also makes possible the 'discarding [of] anything found disagreeable by a modern reader as the responsibility not of Chaucer but of the fictional teller'.[5] But in the case of the Man of Law's approach to storytelling, what is so 'disagreeable' that it necessitates protecting Chaucer from his narrator's associative voice?

This essay suggests that a significant unexamined part of this critical discomfort results from a cultural discomfort with the intimate ties between money and language and between economics and aesthetics. Money haunts discussions of language: we 'coin a phrase', are in 'debt' or give 'credit' to others for our expressions and inspirations, 'clip' or 'debase' the language and 'counterfeit' the styles and words of others.[6] While the link between money and language is often posited as metaphorical, the relationship is more than symbolic; as Marc Shell has argued, money is an 'internal participant' in the organization of language. Put another way, money and language reside in one another not because they are metaphorically alike, but rather because they are structurally so.[7] Barbara Herrnstein Smith has made a similar argument about the links between aesthetics and economic value. While it is acknowledged that art is produced under specific economic conditions, and that it can itself be a valuable commodity, critics, producers, and consumers of art often desire to distinguish between the supposedly intrinsic value of a piece of art, and its economic worth – to separate its 'use value' from its 'exchange value', to import Marx's terminology. Thus, Smith notes, 'an aesthetician deplores a pun on "appreciation" appearing in an article on art investment and warns of the dangers of confusing "the uniqueness

---

5   A. C. Spearing, 'Narrative Voice: The Case of Chaucer's *Man of Law's Tale*', *New Literary History* 32 (2001), 715–46 (718). Dramatic readings allow for it to seem, as George Lyman Kittredge puts it, that 'Chaucer always knew what he was about': Kittredge, *Chaucer and his Poetry* (Cambridge, MA, 1915), 151. On the role Kittredge plays in the development of dramatic readings, see Kathy Cawsey, *Twentieth-Century Chaucer Criticism: Reading Audiences* (Farnham, 2011), 19–38.

6   Diane Cady, 'Symbolic Economies', in *Oxford Twenty-First Century Approaches to Literature: Middle English*, ed. Paul Strohm (Oxford, 2007), 124–41 (124).

7   Marc Shell, *Money, Language and Thought: Literary and Philosophical Economies from the Medieval to the Modern Era* (Berkeley, 1982). See also Shell, *Art and Money* (Chicago, 1995). For a discussion of how the intersections between money and language reflect a 'style of thinking' prevalent in Western metaphysics, see Jean-Joseph Goux, *Symbolic Economies: After Marx and Freud*, trans. Jennifer Curtiss Gage (Ithaca, NY, 1990), 9–63.

of a painting that gives it scarcity value [...] with its unique value as a work of art'".[8] Yet that such confusion is possible belies the fantasy that these spheres are separate; that the confusion is described as 'dangerous' suggests the ideological stakes in this phantastic separation.[9]

The reason that some imagine this separation between aesthetics and economics, and worry about their conflation, has much to do with the Enlightenment roots of contemporary categorical conceptions of both commerce and aesthetics. During the seventeenth century a number of economic practices, including creative financing, the use of paper money, and currency debasement, produced new questions about the nature of money, its stability (or lack thereof), and the source of its value. Political economy as a discipline emerges in the eighteenth century in part to grapple with these questions. Scholars such as James Thompson note that Enlightenment thinkers were contending with other questions of value at the same time. For example, eighteenth-century theorists pondered the question of what gave a woman value in the marriage market: was a woman's potential value contained in the property that she could bring to her marriage? Or in her virginity? Or did she possess intrinsic value? Just as money and its value became at this time the subject of a separate discourse – political economy – so questions of women's value became the subject of a separate realm, the novel.[10] The separation of these explorations of value helped to obscure the ways in which they were (and continue to be) linked. As Thompson writes:

> across this period, with all of its monetary experiments and innova-
> tions in banking, credit, and paper currency, political economists were
> gradually forced to acknowledge that, in effect, silver was not always

8   Barbara Herrnstein Smith, *Contingencies of Value: Alternative Perspectives for Critical Theory* (Cambridge, MA, 1988), 30–5 (33).

9   Marc Shell makes a similar point in *Art and Money*, observing that 'precisely how such confusion occurs, if it does not already exist, is not so clear' (141 n. 1). Similarly, in 'Pennance profytable', Laurel Hendrix describes the Man of Law's blurring of spiritual and commercial metaphors in the language of 'danger' (144) and 'risk' (147). R. A. Shoaf explores the links between commerce and language in Chaucer's and Dante's work, only to insist that both authors view those links as strictly metaphorical, avoiding the 'baneful confusion' of seeing them as structurally the same: *Dante, Chaucer, and the Currency of the Word: Money, Images, and Reference in Late Medieval Poetry* (Norman, OK, 1983), 13.

10   James Thompson, *Models of Value: Eighteenth-Century Political Economy and the Novel* (Durham, NC, 1996), 15–22.

silver, but novelists came to insist that love was always love, because value as such originated in the home and companionate marriage.[11]

Occupying a time before this gestural split, the Middle Ages provide unique insight into the now occluded (yet always present) relationships between money and language and gender and value. Medieval writers and thinkers also grappled with categories of money, value, gender, and aesthetics, but they did so in crucially different ways. For medieval writers these questions stemmed from practices that highlighted, rather than obscured, money's instability and conventionality.[12] However, unlike their Enlightenment counterparts, medieval writers did not compartmentalize discussions of value. Rather, one finds in medieval texts a promiscuous commingling of realms that will later be separated into distinct discursive categories. This commingling tendency explains, for example, why in a work like the C-text of *Piers Plowman* Holy Church can move so seamlessly in a mere sixteen lines from a discussion of false speech to a discussion of monetary malpractice to a discussion of lechery.[13]

11   Ibid., 22.

12   One such example is the debasement of currency, the process by which the metal content of coinage is reduced, resulting in a reduction of the weight and fineness of a nation's currency. Although this was not a new practice in the fourteenth century, Peter Spufford identifies this period as a time of 'violent debasements' ('The Scourge of Debasement', in *Money and its Use in Medieval Europe* (Cambridge, 1988), 289–318 (289)). Hampered in part by the lack of a direct system of taxation, the king of France found himself turning increasingly to debasement as a way to raise funds as the Hundred Years War raged on for longer than any of its participants could have imagined. Debasement never reached the levels in England that it did on the Continent. However, in response to Parliament's resistance to raising taxes, Edward III embarked on a series of debasements in 1344. By 1351 he had debased the coinage three times, reducing its precious-metal content by 6%. Opponents of debasement, such as Nicholas Oresme, advocated a return to what they called 'strong money', money that remained 'fixed' in its weight and fineness. See *The De Moneta of Nicholas Oresme and English Mint Documents*, trans. Charles Johnson (London, 1956).

13   William Langland, *Piers Plowman: The C-Text*, ed. Derek Pearsall, repr. edn (Exeter, 1994), Passus II, lines 80–96. For a discussion of this moment in the context of isomorphic links between money, language, and sexuality, see Cady, 'Symbolic Economies', 135–6. On the relationship between gender ideology and money, see Diane Cady, 'The Gender of Money', *Genders* 44 (Fall 2006), unpaginated.

In this essay I argue that the conflict between economics and story-telling that critics locate in the *Man of Law's Tale* is a product more of post-Enlightenment critical positionality than Chaucer's satirical pen. In the prologue and opening scenes of the *Man of Law's Tale* Chaucer draws upon a wide range of medieval writers and rhetoricians who present the telling of stories as an activity analogous to the trading of goods. In these texts, much like in the *Man of Law's Tale* itself, stories are commodities and those that are new, or at least can be made to appear new through the transformative power of rhetoric, have the most value in the literary marketplace. Merchants are often deemed particularly gifted storytellers, not only because their travels expose them to new stories, but also because rhetorical prowess is essential to their profession.

Such a reading might help us to better understand two questions about the prologue that have puzzled generations of scholars: the tale's mercantile concerns and its obsession with incest. In the prologue, I see the Man of Law as lamenting not poverty *per se*, but rather his perceived poetic dearth resulting from Chaucer's supposed poetic prowess. His compliment to merchants is not to their financial wealth, but to their literary possessions, which they are able to acquire through their extensive travel. The Man of Law's eschewing of incest is intimately tied to this poetic economy. In a move that oddly anticipates Harold Bloom's theory of the anxiety of influence,[14] Chaucer combines the idea of poetic property with the threat of incest: to be in a state of poetical need is depicted in the *Man of Law's Tale* as both economic and sexual.

Examining the economics of storytelling not only helps us better understand this enigmatic tale and medieval investments in storytelling, but also invites us to think about our own relationship to poetics and economics. If there is a perceived danger in collapsing the economic with the aesthetic, and the monetary with the poetic, there is also a danger in not acknowledging their structural links: in both, we see an effacement of gender ideology. Medieval writers depicted texts not just as commodities but also as feminine corpora, and used stories are likened both to inferior goods and to sexually 'used' women. These damaged goods can be sold by repackaging them in rhetorical techniques that risk exposure to a violence often depicted in sexual terms and described in economic ways. My essay suggests that such renderings are not a

14   Harold Bloom, *The Anxiety of Influence* (Oxford, 1997).

product of a particularly economic outlook of individual storytellers like the Man of Law, but rather are embedded in the very structure of storytelling as understood and described by a wide variety of medieval authors. Labelling the Man of Law as the 'mercantile' poet, and Chaucer as the non-mercantile and thus 'real' poet, obscures the ways in which gender ideology undergirds all storytelling.

Gender and economics are linked to storytelling in this tale in another way as well. To be in the position of telling another's story not only places one in a position of poetic need, but also of effeminacy. Ironically, if, as many scholars now believe, Chaucer obtained the story of Custance from Gower, it is very likely that it is Chaucer, and not his narrator, who finds himself in a state of poetical poverty, since he is not the originator of the story. Chaucer's solution to this dilemma resembles that proposed by Harold Bloom: he creates a rivalry between himself and the Man of Law to obscure his own secondary position. I read the Man of Law not as Chaucer's dupe, but rather as his doppelganger, one from whom he attempts to distance himself by creating a fictional rivalry between himself and the Man of Law. Generations of readers have assisted Chaucer with this project, not only by distancing Chaucer from the Man of Law, but also by creating a second rivalry between Gower and Chaucer. While this rivalry has long been discredited, it still retains a certain haunting currency, a currency that helps to maintain the portrait of Chaucer as an independent and 'masculine' poet.[15]

To engage this reading, I begin with a section that explores the economy of narrative by sketching how a wide variety of medieval writers imagine storytelling and merchandizing as analogous enterprises. In the second section, I examine how that economy intersects with the gender ideology that undergirds medieval storytelling to produce a structure in which texts are imagined as both feminine corpora and feminized commodities. Finally, in the third section, I link the Man of Law's aversion to incest with anxieties about poetic property, anxieties that, I argue, are as likely to be Chaucer's as they are the Man of Law's.

---

15   For a discussion of the persistence of the idea of a rivalry between Gower and Chaucer, and its gendered implications, see Carolyn Dinshaw, 'Rivalry, Rape and Manhood: Gower and Chaucer', in *Chaucer and Gower: Difference, Mutuality, Exchange*, ed. R. F. Yeager (Victoria, B.C., 1991), 130–52.

A Very Lord of Merchants: Poetry and Rhetoric in the Late Middle Ages

In recent years, a growing number of scholars have analysed the presence of merchants in Chaucer's London and their influence on late medieval literature.[16] In this essay, my focus is primarily on travel narratives, the role that they play in the cultural imaginary, and the synergies between the marketing of goods and the telling of stories. Specifically, I am interested in the way that travel narratives stage the gathering of stories as the particular work of merchants. More importantly, travel narratives are a genre that meditates, self-reflexively, on the role that rhetoric plays in the successful selling of stories. These ideas resonate not just with the Man of Law's presentation of storytelling and the literary marketplace, but with that of late medieval culture as well.

We have no way of knowing whether Chaucer had first-hand knowledge of particular travel narratives like John Mandeville's *Travels* or Marco Polo's *Travels*. But we do know that Chaucer came from a family with mercantile connections and concerns, and critics have found echoes of Mandeville's writings in particular in Chaucer's work.[17] Given the wide circulation of travel narratives in the fourteenth century, it seems likely that Chaucer would have had exposure to such works. Travel narratives were extremely popular in the fourteenth century, making them, as Kathryn Lynch has noted, part of the 'cultural geography' of a

16   See, for example, Roger A. Ladd, *Antimercantilism in Late Medieval English Literature* (New York, 2010); Craig E. Bertolet, *Chaucer, Gower, Hoccleve and the Commercial Practices of Late Fourteenth-Century London* (Burlington, VT, 2013); and Jonathan Hsy, *Trading Tongues: Merchants, Multilingualism, and Medieval Literature* (Columbus, OH, 2013).

17   On the possible influence of Mandeville's *Travels* on Chaucer's work, see Hugo Lange, 'Chaucer und Mandeville's *Travels*', *Archiv für das Studium der Neuren Sprachen und Literaturen* 74 (1938), 79–81; Josephine Waters Bennett, 'Chaucer and Mandeville's *Travels*', *MLN* 68 (1953), 531–4; C. W. R. D. Moseley, 'Chaucer, Sir John Mandeville, and the Alliterative Revival: A Hypothesis Concerning Relationships', *Modern Philology* 72.2 (1974), 182–4; David May, '*Mandeville's Travels*, Chaucer and the *House of Fame*', *Notes & Queries* 34.2 (June 1987), 178–82; and Kathryn L. Lynch, 'East Meets West in Chaucer's Squire's and Franklin's Tales', *Speculum* 70.3 (1995), 530–51. In this essay I follow the practice of Ronald Latham and refer to Marco Polo's text as *The Travels*, rather than *The Description of the World*. See Marco Polo, *The Travels of Marco Polo*, ed. and trans. Ronald Latham (Harmondsworth, 1958).

writer like Chaucer.[18] There are 150 extant manuscripts and fragments of Polo's *Travels* and an astonishing 300 copies of Mandeville's *Travels*, and both texts were translated into over a dozen languages. Such facts suggest that travel narratives had the potential to be a very valuable commodity – sometimes quite literally. In London, Paris, and Bruges, for example, Mandeville's *Travels* could be used as a fair medium of exchange.[19]

One reason travel narratives were so popular is that they enabled people to visualize objects and places that they could not see with their own eyes. As Patricia Parker observes, in a travel narrative a writer's words must stand in for direct, ocular experience. Such a situation requires the skilful use of *evidentia*. Etymologically linked to the verb *video*, *evidentia* enables the reader or listener to 'see' by means of

18 Lynch, 'Storytelling, Exchange, and Constancy', 410.

19 On the idea of Mandeville's *Travels* as commodities, see *The Travels of Sir John Mandeville: A Manuscript in the British Library*, ed. Joseph Krása, trans. Peter Kussi (New York, 1983), 13. Marco Polo's *Travels* was originally written in French or Franco-Italian and, twenty years after its first appearance, existed also in Venetian, Latin, German, and Tuscan. For a description of these versions of Marco Polo's text, see John Larner, *Marco Polo and the Discovery of the World* (New Haven, 1999), 105–15. Mandeville's *Travels* was translated from French into over a dozen languages, including Welsh, Old Irish, and Czech. A pictorial edition of the *Travels* even exists. For a discussion of the various versions of the *Travels*, see M. C. Seymour, *Sir John Mandeville*, Authors of the Middle Ages 1 (Aldershot, 1993), 8–49; and Iain Macleod Higgins, *Writing East: The 'Travels' of John Mandeville* (Philadelphia, 1997), xii–xiii. For the general influence of Mandeville on medieval texts and audiences, see Rosemary Tzanaki, *Mandeville's Medieval Audiences: A Study on the Reception of the Book of Sir John Mandeville (1371–1550)* (Aldershot, 2003). C. W. R. D. Moseley notes that the popularity of Mandeville's *Travels* extended beyond the Middle Ages and well into the early modern period. The text was printed more than any other non-religious work, suggesting that printers were well aware they had a valuable commodity on their hands: 'Early printers, for whom speculative commercial production *does* become a reality, would have known that Mandeville was a book for which there would be sure demand. These many manuscripts created, in fact, both market and taste for the multiple copies made by the new technology': Moseley, '"New things to speak of": Money, Memory, and *Mandeville's Travels* in Early Modern England', *The Yearbook of English Studies* 41.1 (2011), 5–20 (9). On the influence of Mandeville's *Travels* on early modern literature, see the essays collected in *A Knight's Legacy: Mandeville and Mandevillian Lore in Early Modern England*, ed. Ladan Niayesh (Manchester, 2010).

language what she cannot see with her own eyes.[20] As Marcus Fabius
Quintilian explains in the *Institutio oratoria*, *evidentia* is 'imago quoda-
mmodo verbis depingitur' ('an image painted with words'), 'ab aliis
[evidentia] dicitur proposita quaedam forma rerum ita expressa verbis,
ut cerni potius videatur quam audiri' ('a representation of facts that
appeals to the eyes rather than to the ears'), and a technique that enables
one to see something 'oculis mentis': literally, in the mind's eye.[21]

Given their extensive travel, merchants were particularly well
positioned to obtain stories about distant places and, once home, to
paint evocative pictures of those places in the minds of their listeners or
readers. In Book 15 of his *Travels*, John Mandeville depicts a scene that
illustrates the importance of storytelling as part of merchants' labour.
During a private audience with the sultan of Damascus, 'Mandeville' is
asked by the sultan about the moral conduct of Christians in England.[22]
While Mandeville insists that English Christians are morally upright,
the sultan demurs and rattles off an extensive list of English vices,
including gluttony, licentiousness, and extravagant dress. Perhaps wisely,
Mandeville does not refute these charges, but he is perplexed: how does
the sultan know so much about the habits of a people so far away?

> And than I asked him how he knew the state of Cristene men. And he
> answerde me that he knew all the state of alle contres of Cristene kynges
> and princes and the state of the comounes also be his messangeres, that
> he sente to all londes, in manere as thei weren marchauntes of precyous

20   Patricia Parker, *Literary Fat Ladies: Rhetoric, Gender, Property* (London
1987), 138–40.
21   Marcus Fabius Quintilian, *Institutio oratoria*, ed. and trans. H. E. Butler
(Cambridge, MA, 1921), 8.3.63, 9.2.40, 8.3.62.
22   Much like the *Man of Law's Tale*, Mandeville's *Travels* has a complicated narrative structure that makes it difficult for the reader to distinguish
'Mandeville' the author (a person yet unidentified by scholars), from 'Mandeville'
the narrator. Although scholars often treat Marco Polo's *Travels* as more accurate
than Mandeville's *Travels*, Marco Polo's possible co-authorship with the romance
writer Rustichello of Pisa, and the text's constantly shifting pronouns, blur the
lines between narrator, author, and character as well; see Larner, *Marco Polo*,
46–58. On how these qualities contribute to the texts' post-modern effects,
see Paul Smethurst, 'The Journey from Modern to Postmodern in the *Travels
of Sir John Mandeville* and Marco Polo's *Divisament dou Monde*', *Studies in
Medievalism XIII: Postmodern Medievalisms*, ed. Richard Utz and Jesse G. Swan
(Cambridge, 2005), 159–79.

stones, of clothes of gold and of othere thinges, for to knowen the manere of euery contree amonges Cristene men.[23]

The sultan's response is revealing. While one might assume that the primary business of merchants is to buy and sell goods, in his kingdom merchandizing is actually a cover for merchants' real business: collecting information about distant lands and people.

Mandeville does not address the role rhetorical prowess plays in successfully rendering one's travel experiences into narrative. However, an early scene in Marco Polo's *Travels* suggests its importance. Polo observes the great interest that the khan takes in foreign lands and cultures, and the khan's dismay that his emissaries do such a poor job conveying in language what they see and experience while travelling on his behalf. Polo sees an opportunity in his colleagues' deficiencies: on his next business trip for the khan, he makes careful note of what he sees and hears and, when he returns, provides a detailed report of his experiences. The khan is pleased and Marco Polo becomes an important emissary, one who not only conducts the khan's business but also successfully 'brings back word of many novelties and curiosities'.[24] The khan's desire for 'novelties' and 'curiosities' suggests both why travel narratives might be popular and the importance of rhetoric in translating supposed first-hand knowledge into narrative. While it was a well-known fact that many travellers' tales were embellishments at best and out-and-out fabrications at worst, the desire to learn something new is what gives them their value.[25]

---

23 John Mandeville, *Mandeville's Travels*, ed. M. C. Seymour (Oxford, 1967), Book 15, lines 19–25.

24 Marco Polo, *The Travels*, 41.

25 Christian Zacher notes that critics of medieval pilgrimages often claimed that curiosity, and not religious fervour, was the primary motivation for travelling on pilgrimages. Curiosity was seen as a sensation that could be satisfied especially through sight. Travel narratives, with their painted rhetoric, would be one way for those back home to satisfy their curiosity, albeit at second hand. Christian Zacher, *Curiosity and Pilgrimage: The Literature of Discovery in Fourteenth-Century England* (Baltimore, 1976), 19–33. Zacher notes that to be 'busy' is one delight of the curious, and Mandeville himself is always 'busy': for example, he stresses that he 'did great busyness' at the kahn's court to learn the trick of making metal birds dance and sing. Zacher, *Curiosity and Pilgrimage*, 157. The links between curiosity and 'busyness' provide another interpretive lens for reading the lines in the portrait of the Man of Law, which state that, 'Nowher

The links among travel, trade, and rhetorical prowess suggested by Mandeville's and Polo's texts converge in Hugh of St Victor's description of commerce in *The Didascalicon*, and underscore the synergy between merchandizing and storytelling:

> Navigatio continet omnem in emendis, vendendis, mutandis, domesticis sive peregrinis mercibus negotiationem. Haec rectissime quasi quaedam sui generis rhetorica est, eo quod huic professioni eloquentia maxime sit necessaria. Unde et hic qui facundiae praeesse dicitur, Mercurius, quasi mercatorum kirrius, id est, Dominus appellatur. Haec secreta mundi penetrat, litora invisa adit, deserta horrida lustrat, et cum barbaris nationibus et linguis incognitis, commercia humanitatis exercet.

> (Commerce [literally, navigation] contains every sort of dealing in the purchase, sale, and exchange of domestic or foreign goods. This art is beyond all doubt a peculiar sort of rhetoric – strictly of its own kind – for eloquence is in the highest degree necessary to it. Thus the man who excels others in fluency of speech is called a Mercurius, or Mercury, as being a mercatorum kirrius (+ kyrios) – a very lord of merchants. Commerce penetrates the secret places of the world, approaches shores unseen, explores fearful wildernesses, and in tongues unknown and with barbaric peoples carries on the trade of mankind.)[26]

Hugh of St Victor's brief definition of trade is striking in a number of ways. While it is clear from the first sentence that Hugh intends

---

so bisy a man as he ther nas, / And yet he semed bisier than he was', *General Prologue*, lines 321–2.

26   Hugh of St Victor, *Didascalicon: De studio legendi*, ed. Brother Charles Henry Buttimer, Studies in Medieval and Renaissance Latin 10 (Washington, DC, 1939), Book 2, ch. 23, lines 10–17. The translation is from Jerome Taylor, *The Didascalicon of Hugh of St Victor: A Medieval Guide to the Arts* (New York, 1961), 76–7. Taylor notes the idea of a 'mercatorum kirrius' in Remigius of Auxerre's comments on Martianus Capella: 'Mercurius dictus est quasi […] mercatorum kyrios, id est dominus, quia sermo maxime inter mercatores viget. […] Mercurius in similitudine facundie et sermonis.' An alternative etymology might be found in the third Vatican mythographer, who, drawing on Fulgentius, states that 'Fulgentius Mercurium megotiis praeesse dicit; ideo Mercurium dictum quasi merces curantem, quod negotiatores, quibus praeest, ercibus semper invigilent […] quod disserere interpretatur, eo quod negotiatori maxime linguarum dissertio sit necessaria.' Taylor, *Didascalicon*, 205–6 n. 72.

to describe trade (the purchase, sale, and exchange of goods), he calls it 'navigatio' (literally, navigation), rather than the more common *commercium* (commerce) or *mercatum* (trade; traffic). Such a choice makes travel synonymous with trade. In addition, he anthropomorphizes trade, making it a kind of traveller itself, one that criss-crosses the globe, penetrating, exploring, and approaching 'the secrets of the world' and its supposedly 'barbaric' people. Much like Mandeville and Polo, Hugh of St Victor calls attention to one of trade's less obvious commercial aspects: the trafficking in stories. Indeed, Hugh aligns commerce with literary endeavours by describing it as an art and 'a peculiar sort of rhetoric', one that greatly depends on fluent speech. Nor is the relationship between merchandizing and rhetoric unilateral: Hugh dubs anyone who skilfully deploys rhetoric as a successful merchandizer – 'a very lord of merchants'.[27]

Hugh of St Victor never elaborates on why 'eloquentia' is essential to commerce, nor does he explain why a rhetorically effective person is like a successful merchant. However, a clue to their relationship is offered by Hugh's contemporary, Alberic of Montecassino. In his *Flores de rhetorici*, Alberic defines metaphor in similarly commercial terms:

> Suum autem est metaphorae modum locutionis a proprietate sui quasi detorquere, detorquendo quodammodo innovare, innovando quasi nuptiali amictu tegere, tegendo quasi praecio dignitatis vendere. Quid enim aliud nisi vendere dixerim, dum historiam in sui simplicitate vilem, quadam altitudine variationis celebras, semper novam semper gratam repraesentas?

> (Metaphor's way of speaking is, as it were, a twist away from the proper meaning: a twist, so to speak, for innovation; innovation as if for dressing in a nuptial gown; and such dressing as if for selling at a dignified price

---

27 As Eugene Vance notes in a discussion of this passage from *The Didascalicon*, it is impossible to trace precisely how and by what means the languages of commerce and rhetoric influenced one another: 'the multiple discourses that constitute any given speech community not only develop together; they also act upon and interfere with each other, even though we cannot always be sure in which discourse new concepts first arise, and even though certain innovating discourses of the past are not audible to us now. There obviously *was* a specifically mercantile discourse in the twelfth century, and the *oratores* obviously *heard* it, if from a distance' (Eugene Vance, *Mervelous Signals: Poetics and Sign Theory in the Middle Ages* (Lincoln, 1986), 118).

[lit: price of dignity]. For what else is it, shall I say, except for selling,
when, a story base in its simplicity, you celebrate by a kind of snootiness
of variety and variation, representing it as always new, always pleasing?)[28]

Much like Hugh of St Victor in his depiction of trade, Alberic imagines
rhetoric as an active agent, twisting away from proper meaning – an
effect that is intensified by his use of anadiplosis in this passage. Alberic
describes less valuable stories as 'vilis', a word that not only means base,
but also 'low-priced' and 'well-known'. Alberic simultaneously deploys
all three of these definitions when he suggests that if a number of people
have access to a story or to information, that story or information
becomes something common and thus less valuable. Metaphor is a way
to cover inferior goods – stories that are cheap because they are too
familiar. To cover a base, low-priced story with rhetoric is, quite literally,
to renew it ('innovare') and to transform it into something desirable that
can be sold for an inflated price. Through Alberic's language we can see
more clearly the link between rhetoric and merchandizing suggested by
Hugh of St Victor: a successful merchant is a skilful rhetorician, just as
a popular storyteller effectively merchandizes his or her poetic wares
through rhetoric.

In the opening scenes of the *Man of Law's Tale*, Chaucer makes a
number of changes to his sources, changes that, collectively, highlight
the role of merchants and rhetoric in the merchandizing of stories. One
of these changes is to alter the reason the merchants are summoned
before the sultan when they return from Rome. In both Gower's and
Trevet's versions, the sultan orders the merchants to appear so they can
explain why they converted to Christianity. In Chaucer's text, no such
conversion takes place. Instead, as David Wallace notes, in the *Man of
Law's Tale* the merchants' audience with the sultan appears routine:[29]

> Now fil it that thise marchantz stode in grace
> Of hym that was the Sowdan of Surrye;
> For whan they cam from any strange place,
> He wolde, of his benigne curteisye,

---

28   Alberic of Montecassino, *The Flores rhetorici*, ed. D. M. Inguanez and E. H.
Willard, Miscellanea Cassinese 14 (Montecassino, 1938), Book VI, line 45. The
translation is from Shoaf, *Dante, Chaucer, and the Currency*, 116.
29   David Wallace, *Chaucerian Polity: Absolutist Lineages and Associational
Forms in England and Italy* (Stanford, CA, 1997), 185.

Make hem good chiere, and bisily espye
Tidynges of sondry regnes, for to leere
The wondres that they myghte seen or heere.

(lines 176–82)

Chaucer's language in this passage underscores the importance of both alterity and novelty in the merchants' storytelling. Much like the sultans described in Mandeville's and Polo's texts, the sultan of Syria expects his merchants to report to him whenever they come from any 'strange place'. The word 'strange' contains multiple senses – 'foreign' as well as 'new' or 'unknown'[30] – and since the merchants travel to 'strange place[s]', they pick up 'strange' stories, stories of 'wondres' unknown to those back home. Chaucer further emphasizes the importance of innovation with the word 'tydinges'. Middle English 'tydinges' underwent a shift in the late fourteenth century: the word no longer meant just new, but also stories – and, in particular, new stories.[31]

As Jonathan Hsy suggests, in the *Man of Law's Tale* the acquisition of new stories is not a casual enterprise. If the merchants wish to stand 'in grace' with the sultan, they will not return to Syria empty-handed or silent-tongued. The stories that they collect on their travels are as much a part of the 'chaffare [...] so thrifty and so newe' (line 138) as the silks and spices they peddle around the world.[32] 'Thrifty' is a telling word in this regard: it means both 'suitable' and 'profitable',[33] and it is precisely because the merchants' stories are 'newe' (or, perhaps more importantly, appear new) that they are suitable for the sultan's consumption and therefore profitable for the merchants to tell. Thus, while part of the merchants' business in Rome is to sell merchandise, it is essential that they make another kind of purchase while they are there: that they collect new stories that they can dilate before the sultan's eager ears much as Marco Polo does before the khan's.

30 See *Middle English Dictionary*, ed. Hans Kurath and Sherman McAllister Kuhn (Ann Arbor, 1952), s.v. *strange* (definitions 2a and 2b), 872.
31 R. C. Goffin, 'Quiting by Tidings in the *Hous of Fame*', *Medium Aevum* 12 (1943), 40–1. In *Curiosity and Pilgrimage*, Christian Zacher quotes Mandeville, whose language suggests this link between novelty and tydynges: 'men han gret liking to have speke of strange thinges' and that 'newe things and newe tydynges ben plesant to here' (*Curiosity and Pilgrimage*, 228).
32 Hsy, *Trading Tongues*, 68.
33 See entry for 'thrifty' in *A Chaucer Glossary*, ed. Norman Davis et al. (Oxford 1979), 154.

Custance is just the kind of 'thrifty' tale sought by the merchants. In another alteration to his sources, Chaucer has his heroine enter the tale not as a character, but rather as a narrative. This change underscores Custance's role as both narrative and commodity in the text.[34] The merchants first learn of Custance through the praise of others: it is the 'commune voys' of Rome that she is the most beautiful and virtuous woman in all the world (lines 155–9). As Nancy Vickers observes, to praise something is to put a price on it,[35] a relationship neatly conveyed in the Middle English word *pris*. The cause and effect between praising and selling is connected to the relationship between verbal display and merchandizing. Rhetorical embellishment helps sell something (whether a material object or a literary product) by inciting desire. As Alberic of Montecassino observes, praising something profusely, even if it is a story, base in its simplicity, transforms it into something with a high price. By reporting Custance's *pris* in the streets (her 'excellent renoun', line 150), the 'commune voys' of Rome establishes her value. The economic consequences of the townspeople's praise are revealed in the word 'rekene': by recounting Custance's virtues, they calculate a high price for her (line 158).[36] The merchants, in turn, recount the tale of Custance before the sultan:

---

34   In Gower's text, Custance is considerably more active, and converts the merchants to Christianity. On Custance as narrative, see Carolyn Dinshaw, *Chaucer's Sexual Poetics* (Madison, 1989), 95. On the commodification of Custance, see also Sheila Delany, 'Womanliness in *The Man of Law's Tale*', *The Chaucer Review* 9.1 (1974), 63–72; and Laurel Hendrix, 'Pennance profytable'. Not every reader views Custance as a passive object, however. David Raybin, for example, argues that Custance uses her speeches in order to get back at her tormenters, including her parents (Raybin, 'Custance and History: Woman as Outsider in Chaucer's *Man of Law's Tale*', *Studies in the Age of Chaucer* 12 (1990), 65–84). Robert B. Dawson also sees Custance's rhetoric as more complex and aggressive than it might seem at first, and argues that, in turn, the Man of Law might be a more complex narrator than he at first appears (Dawson, 'Custance in Context: Rethinking the Protagonist of the *Man of Law's Tale*', *The Chaucer Review* 26.3 (1992), 293–308).
35   Nancy Vickers, '"The blazon of sweet beauty's best": Shakespeare's *Lucrece*', in *Shakespeare and the Question of Theory*, ed. Patricia Parker and Geoffrey Hartman (London, 1985), 95–115. I will return to Vickers's argument and the gendered implications of such selling later in this essay.
36   Wallace, *Chaucerian Polity*, 185, notes that 'this term *rekenynge* is a curious one: in the C[anterbury] T[ales] it denotes the kind of detailed calculations associated (mostly commonly) with mercantile trade, astrology, or the state of

Amonges othere thynges, specially,
Thise marchantz han hym toold of dame Custance
So greet noblesse in ernest, ceriously,
That this Sowdan hath caught so greet pleasance
To han hir figure in his remembrance,
That al his lust and al his bisy cure
Was for to love hire while his lyf may dure.

(lines 183–9)

As these lines suggest, Custance is among the 'thynges' with which the
merchants return to Syria. Like 'the commune voys', their enthusiastic
praise advertises Custance as a valuable commodity. Here, Chaucer
highlights the role of rhetoric in this process. Much like his counterpart
in Mandeville's *Travels*, the sultan in the *Man of Law's Tale* is able to
'bisily espye' (line 180) the 'wondres' (line 182) of the world, thanks to the
merchants' verbal reports. 'Espye', which derives from French *espionner*,
means to discover not only in a general sense, but also in a specifically
visual sense, as Modern English *spy* would suggest.

The term 'figure' further underscores the role of rhetoric in marketing
Custance's story. As Carolyn Dinshaw observes, it denotes both a
person's form and a rhetorical trope.[37] Given that the sultan proclaims
his love for Custance after having only visualized her by means of the
merchants' painted rhetoric, it is clear with which 'figure' he really falls
in love. We might extrapolate that the merchants follow Quintilian's
advice, skilfully using *evidentia* so that the sultan sees 'hir [Custance's]
figure in his remembrance' – that is, sees her 'figure' in his *oculis mentis*
(mind's eye). The merchants, on the other hand, see Custance's actual
'figure', but it seems to have little impact on them.[38] For the merchants,
life returns to normal and they 'doon hir nedes', part of which is to return
to Syria and tell the sultan the most breath-taking stories they can. There
they prove through their rhetorical prowess to be the kind of 'lord[s] of
merchants' that Hugh describes.

the soul. It appears three times in the G[eneral] P[rologue]: the Shipman is said
to "rekene wel his tydes" (line 401); the Reeve makes his own "rekenynge" of his
young master's stock value (line 600); and the pilgrims pay their "rekenynges"
before leaving the Tabard (line 760)'.

37   Dinshaw, *Chaucer's Sexual Poetics*, 95.

38   Winthrop Wetherbee, 'Constance and the World in Chaucer and Gower', in
John Gower: Recent Readings, ed. R. F. Yeager (Kalamazoo, MI, 1989), 65–93 (84).

If we accept the premise that the prologue and opening of the tale are at least in part an exploration of the economics of storytelling, the Man of Law's lament about poverty and his panegyric to merchants and their wealth begin to make sense. At the end of the prologue the Man of Law says of merchants:

> Ye seken lond and see for yowre wynnynges;
> As wise folk ye knowen al th'estaat
> Of regnes; ye been fadres of tidynges
> And tales, bothe of pees and of debaat.
>
> (lines 127–30)

In these lines Chaucer emphasizes the importance of travel to commerce as much as does Hugh of St Victor: merchants must journey over land and sea in pursuit of their profits. As a consequence merchants are 'wise folk', because they have a particular kind of wealth – they know stories, and thus are 'fadres of tidynges and tales'. The presence of the word 'tidynges' hints that, in the prologue, the Man of Law is praising precisely what is demonstrated by the tale he tells: merchants have access to new stories because of their travels; they are wise and 'ful of wele' (line 122) because they possess such a valuable commodity.

While travel keeps the merchants in the *Man of Law's Tale* well stocked in stories, Chaucer's narrator regrets to inform his fellow pilgrims that he does not possess such good fortune. Due to Chaucer's industriousness, little literary material remains from which to choose:

> I kan right now no thrifty tale seyn
> That Chaucer, thogh he kan but lewedly
> On metres and on rymyng craftily,
> Hath seyd hem in swich Englissh as he kan
> Of olde tyme, as knoweth many a man;
> And if he have noght seyd hem, leve brother,
> In o book, he hath seyd hem in another.
> For he hath toold of loveris up and doun
> Mo than Ovide made of mencioun
> In his Episteles, that been ful olde.
> What sholde I tellen hem, syn they been tolde?
>
> (lines 46–56)

Chaucer-as-the-Man-of-Law presents Chaucer-as-poet as a writer who, albeit 'lewed', is more prolific than Ovid, a striking piece of self-promotion that I will return to later in this essay. For now, note that 'olde' is repeated twice in these lines: what the Man of Law seems to regret is the fact that there are no new stories left to tell. It is revealing that the Man of Law describes his problem as want of a 'thrifty tale'. It is precisely the newness of stories (or the appearance of newness) that makes them 'thrifty'. As the Man of Law asks, why should he retell a story that everyone already knows?

With this reading in mind, the plaint against poverty also begins to make sense. Just as it is not material wealth that the Man of Law praises, but merchants' access to a wealth of stories, so it is not literal poverty that he deplores, but his lack of a new story. The complaint immediately follows the Man of Law's musings, for a second time, on what story he is going to tell. He describes poverty as a condition that requires one to 'stele, or begge, or borwe thy despence!' (line 105). Borrowing (or perhaps stealing?) is precisely what the Man of Law does when he repeats a story told to him by a merchant:

> I were right now of tales desolaat,
> Nere that a marchant, goon is many a yeere,
> Me taughte a tale, which that ye shal heere.

(lines 131–3)

It is fitting that the story he tells comes from a merchant, a person whose business, at least in part, is storytelling.

'Desolaat' is a word that appears only one other time in the tale, in a description of David's dilemma as he stands before Goliath:

> O Golias, unmesurable of lengthe,
> Hou myghte David make thee so maat,
> So yong and of armure so desolaat?

(lines 934–6)

Rodney Delansata notes that this is a misreading of the David and Goliath story, because David chooses to remove the armour given to him by Saul.[39] One could therefore read these lines as an example of the

---

39   Rodney Delasanta, 'And of Great Reverence: Chaucer's Man of Law', *The Chaucer Review* 5.4 (1971), 288–310 (296).

kind of misreading and misstatement made by the Man of Law and often attributed to Chaucer's satire.[40] But like the other changes that I have traced thus far, this alteration makes sense if one sees the economics of storytelling as a central concern of the tale. David may have chosen to remove his armour, but the Man of Law does not imagine he has a choice: he sees himself as a helpless child before Chaucer, who seems a literary giant. If he had not been equipped with the story from the merchant, he would be, like Custance, bobbing helplessly in a rudderless boat. Anxiety is always a possibility in the project of storytelling; one wishes to tell a story that is deemed valuable to readers and the literary marketplace more generally. While often the anxiety expressed here is read as that of the Man of Law, I will argue in the final section of this essay that there is good reason to read this anxiety as Chaucer's as well.

'What nedeth gretter dilatacioun?' Rhetoric, Gender, and Bringing Stories to Market

So far in this essay, I have focused primarily on the relationship between rhetoric and merchandizing. That is not, however, the only structure undergirding medieval storytelling. As many scholars have noted, story-telling in the Middle Ages has a decidedly gendered structure as well. Texts are often imagined as feminine corpora to be read and interpreted by male readers, and such reading and interpreting is rendered in decidedly heterosexual and heterosexist terms.[41] What interests me here

40   These misreadings and misstatements include the Man of Law's promise to 'speke in prose' (line 96), only to deliver a tale in rhyme royale; and his ample citation of Pope Innocent III's *De miseria condicionis humane*, in a prologue that copiously praises merchants and their riches. In addition, the Man of Law questions the function of rhetorical amplification, asking at one point, 'What nedeth gretter dilatacioun?' (line 232). Despite this protest, he engages in ampli-fication to such an extent that, with the exception of the Wife of Bath, he is one of Chaucer's most prolix narrators. Finally, the Man of Law promises to avoid discussing incest, only to bring the subject up so frequently that it cannot help but be in the forefront of the reader's mind. These last two issues – dilation and incest – are intimately tied to the poetic economy I have been outlining, and will each be the subject of a section of this essay.
41   On texts as feminine corpora, and the gendered structure of medieval poetics more generally, see, for example, Dinshaw, *Chaucer's Sexual Poetics*, 3–27; Paul Allen Miller, 'Laurel as Sign of Sin: Laura's Textual Body in Petrarch's *Secretum*', in *Sex and Gender in Medieval and Renaissance Texts: The Latin*

are the ways in which this gendered structure works with the poetic economy I have been outlining. Texts in the Middle Ages are presented simultaneously as both feminine bodies and literary commodities. By examining the synergy between these gendered and economic renderings, we develop a fuller picture of ideas about literary value and readerly desire.

We can see these gendered and economic structures at work in Alberic of Montecassino's use of the term 'vilis' in the *Flores*. As noted earlier, Alberic advocates using rhetoric as a way to restore used goods, stories that are 'low-priced' or 'common' due to their overexposure on the marketplace. However, 'vilis' not only means 'low-priced' and 'common' in the sense of well known, but also 'common' in the sense of sexually known by a number of people. Alberic plays on this third meaning of 'vilis' when he describes metaphor as a kind of nuptial gown through which tired goods are disguised ('innovando quasi nuptiali amictu tegere'). What gives stories their value is the same characteristic that makes women a valuable commodity on the marriage market in the Middle Ages – their virginity. In the case of narratives, a virginal story is one that has not circulated to the point where it has become 'common', or at least one that appears to be virginal because it has been transformed by rhetoric's regenerative powers.

The regenerative possibilities of rhetoric are explored in Boccaccio's story of Alatiel in *The Decameron*, a possible analogue for the story of Custance.[42] Like Chaucer's heroine, Alatiel drifts from port to port.

Tradition, ed. Barbara K. Gold, Paul Allen Miller, and Charles Platter (Albany, NY, 1997), 139–63; Jill Ross, *Figuring the Feminine: The Rhetoric of Female Embodiment in Medieval Hispanic Literature* (Toronto, 2008), 13–14, 44–9; Robin R. Hass, '"A picture of such beauty in their minds": The Medieval Rhetoricians, Chaucer, and Evocative Effictio', *Exemplaria* 14.2 (2002), 383–422; and Mary Frances Brown, 'Critique and Complicity: Metapoetical Reflections on the Gendered Figures of Body and Text in the "Roman de la Rose"', *Exemplaria* 21.2 (2009), 129–60.

42 Giovanni Boccaccio, 'The Seventh Story on the Second Day', in *The Decameron*, ed. Aldo Rossi (Bologna, 1977). All citations in Italian are from this edition. Chaucer's and Boccaccio's heroines share a number of similarities: both women are given to husbands to solidify political bonds, both are desired by men who have only heard of their beauty (rather than seeing it first-hand), both women circulate in a boat, both leave violence in their wake, and both hesitate to reveal their identities at various moments in the tale. On the links between the two stories, see T. H. McNeal, 'Chaucer and the *Decameron*', *MLN* 53 (1938), 257–8; and Robert W. Hanning, 'Custance and Ciappelletto in the Middle of

Unlike Chaucer's heroine, Alatiel does not remain 'unwemmed': she is raped by nearly every man she encounters.[43] Her situation alters when she reunites with her native countryman, Antigono. He is not only the first person she can communicate with (none of her captors speaks her language), but he is also the first man she encounters who sees her value in different terms: not in terms of how her beauty can give him personal pleasure, but rather in terms of how he can curry favour with her father by returning her to him. In this way, Antigono is much like the merchants in the *Man of Law's Tale*, who see Custance's value in commercial rather than sexual terms. Alatiel wants to return home, but is terrified her father will reject her if she is not returned 'pristino stato'. Antigono reassures her that he will return her without anyone knowing about her ordeal and, in the process, will make her even more dear to her father than she was before: 'Madonna, poi che occulto è stato nei vostri infortunio chi voi siate, senza fallo piú cara mai vi renderò al vostro padre.' ('Madame, [...] since in your misfortunes it has been hidden who you are, I will, without fail, restore you, dearer than ever, to your father.')[44] Alatiel's restoration involves Antigono creating an alternative story that narrates what has transpired since she left home, one that has her spending the entire time living chastely in a convent. The sultan of Babylon accepts the story, rewards Antigono, and marries Alatiel to her betrothed, the king of El Gharb. The text ends with these telling words, 'Bocca baciata non perde ventura, anzi rinnuova come fa la luna' ('Lips for kissing forfeit no favour, no, they renew as the moon does ever').[45]

it All: Problems of Mediation in *The Man of Law's Tale* and *Decameron 1:1*', in *The Decameron and the Canterbury Tales: New Essays on an Old Question*, ed. Leonard Michael Koff and Brenda Deen Schildgen (London, 2000), 177–211.

43 A significant difference between the women is that Alatiel is Muslim and Egyptian, and Custance is Christian and Italian. The implications for the different ways in which these stories are presented by their authors are disturbing: if Alatiel were European and Christian, like Custance, would she have escaped 'unwemmed' as well? Indeed, when Custance is faced with rape at the hands of a 'theef', both Mary and Christ come to her aid, and her attacker is thrown overboard (lines 915–24). Alatiel receives no such protection. The ways in which these two European writers market their stories not only point to the role that gender ideology plays in that marketing, but also to how the national and religious identity of a character – and an audience – impact the way in which that story is marketed.

44 Boccaccio, 'The Seventh Story on the Second Day', 254–5. The translation is from John Payne's edition of *The Decameron* (Berkeley, 1982), 149.

45 Boccaccio, 'The Seventh Story', 258; Payne, 153.

Thanks to Antigono's skilful storytelling, Alatiel is renewed and restored as a valuable commodity.

While the story of Alatiel suggests the restorative power of rhetoric, it also illustrates its dangers. Covering a 'used' text/woman with rhetoric may restore it/her to a seemingly new and valuable state, but in order to adequately sell a text, one needs to create desire by opening at least a portion of it to the curious gaze of the reader. *Dilatio* is one rhetorical technique writers can use to create such desire. To dilate a text is to open it up and extend its length through digressions, metaphor, and other rhetorical devices. As Patricia Parker has noted, the word derives from the same Latin root as Derrida's 'différance', and it contains the same combination of difference and deferral, expansion and dispersal, both in terms of time and space.[46] Just as with 'vilis', *dilatio* has a decidedly gendered meaning, as well. The term not only describes a technique that opens a text to the mind of the reader, but also one that opens a woman's body to the gaze of a spectator, as the word's use in gynaecological treatises would suggest.[47]

Rhetoric's power to take a used story/used woman and renew it/her provides an alternative lens for reading Harry Bailey's meditation on time in the opening of the *Man of Law's Tale*. Time, the Host claims, is more valuable than 'gold in cofre' (line 26) because, like virginity, it supposedly cannot be replaced:

46   Parker, *Literary Fat Ladies*, 9. Early modern writers will make explicit the economic potential inherent in this kind of rhetorical opening. The early modern period referred to *dilatio* as '*copia*', a word that etymologically makes clear its link to wealth and power. See Terrence Cave, *The Cornucopia Text: Problems of Writing in the French Renaissance* (Oxford, 1979), 3. In his treatise on *copia*, Desiederius Erasmus explains precisely how rhetorical abundance can elicit desire and, consequently, sell a text:

> The first method of enriching what one has to say on any subject is to take something that can be expressed in brief and general terms, and expand it and separate it into its constituent parts. This is just like displaying some object for sale first of all through a grill or inside a wrapping, and then unwrapping it and opening it out and displaying it fully to the gaze.

See Desiederius Erasmus, '*Copia*: Foundations of the Abundant Style', in *Collected Works of Erasmus*, ed. Craig R. Thompson, trans. Betty I. Knott, vol. 24 (Toronto, 1978), 280–659 (574).

47   Parker, *Literary Fat Ladies*, 15.

For 'Los of catel may recovered be,
But los of tyme shendeth us', quod he.
It wol nat come agayn, withouten drede,
Namoore than wole Malkyne's maydenhede,
Whan she hath lost it in hir wantownesse.

(lines 27–31)

However, as we have seen, the Host's observations are not exactly true. Spending time by expanding a text through the use of rhetoric will increase its value by taking a story, base in its simplicity, and turning it into a rejuvenated, virginal narrative. Rhetoric is the 'gold in cofre' that can increase a text's value, taking damaged goods and converting them into valuable property.

The link between opening a text to sell it and opening a woman's body to view it invites us once again to consider how gender and economics merge in medieval rhetoric, and the ramifications of that merger. Outlining the economy of early modern sonnets, Nancy Vickers observes that when sonneteers praise their lovers in front of others, they are turning those lovers into commodities for purchase: 'the relationship so constructed involves an active buyer, an active seller, and a passive object for sale'. The problem arises when a person or object is praised before another without the intention to sell it. Doing so 'dangerously flirts with theft'.[48] It is the reason that, as Vickers notes, the narrator of Shakespeare's *Rape of Lucrece* will ask plaintively:

Why is Collatine the publisher
Of that rich jewel he should keep unknown
From thievish ears, because it is his own?[49]

If the intention is not to sell, one should keep one's possessions to oneself, for rhetoric excites desire and invites violence. In many medieval and early modern texts, this incitement is depicted in sexually violent terms. We see this situation occur repeatedly in Boccaccio's story of Alatiel. Alatiel's beauty is a narrative that becomes a subject of public knowledge, either by the praise of the person who possesses her at a

---

48   Vickers, 'The blazon of sweet beauty's best', 97.
49   William Shakespeare, *The Rape of Lucrece*, in *The Norton Anthology of Shakespeare*, ed. Stephen Greenblatt et al. (New York, 1997), lines 33–5.

given moment or by the general praise of others. Each time that she is praised in front of someone else, she is stolen.[50]

The languages of rhetoric, selling, and violence are not solely in the purview of medieval discussions of storytelling; they inform post-medieval political economy as well. A telling moment appears in Book 1 of *Capital* where, in a short chapter on exchange, Karl Marx describes the process by which commodities are brought to market. In language similar to Nancy Vickers's description of the economy of early modern sonnets, Marx outlines the buyer–seller–commodity triangle:

> Commodities cannot themselves go to market and perform exchanges in their own right. We must, therefore, have recourse to their guardians, who are the possessors of commodities. Commodities are things, and therefore lack the power to resist man. If they are unwilling, he can use force; in other words, he can take possession of them.[51]

Here commodities are passive things that must be taken to market by 'their guardians' because they cannot take themselves. Commodities are unable to resist the advances of their buyers. If unwilling they must be forced.[52] But why does Marx have recourse to such language, and what might this language tell us about the economics of storytelling? I believe that the reason he depicts commodities as feminine and lacking

50 On rhetoric and literary rape, see R. Howard Bloch, *Medieval Misogyny and the Invention of Western Romantic Love* (Chicago, 1991), 111; and Hass, 'A picture of such beauty', 396. I am mindful of the danger of collapsing metaphors of sexual violence with actual physical violence perpetrated against women and men. However, as Carolyn Dinshaw notes, they cannot be entirely separated either: 'To equate reading with rape would be to underestimate drastically the transgressive reality of rape, on the one hand, and to slight the potentially positive value of literary interpretation, on the other. But this fact also invites us to consider causal relationships between gendered representation and actual social relations between men and women; it invites us to consider the relations that form the bases for figurative discourse and that, in turn, are affected by literary representation' (Dinshaw, *Chaucer's Sexual Poetics*, 11).

51 Karl Marx, 'Exchange', in *Capital*, vol. 1: *A Critique of Political Economy*, ed. Frederick Engels, trans. Samuel Moore and Edward Aveling (New York, 1967), 88–96 (88).

52 On the sexual violence embedded in this description of exchange, see Karen Newman, 'City Talk: Women and Commodification: *Epicoene* (1609)', in *Staging the Renaissance: Reinterpretations of Elizabethan and Jacobean Drama*, ed. David Scott Kastan and Peter Stallybrass (New York, 1991), 181–95 (183).

resistance is the same reason that medieval poetics renders stories as feminine corpora: women and stories are viewed as passive goods to be displayed and consumed by men. Although it may be tempting to think that only bad storytellers – like Shakespeare's Collatine, Boccaccio's Panfilo, or Chaucer's Man of Law – turn women into stories and stories into commodities, all storytelling is undergirded by this same economy and haunted by this same kind of violence. Imagining some stories and some storytellers as economic and others as disinterested occludes that structure.

Early on in the *Man of Law's Tale*, Chaucer's narrator seems to reject the role of rhetoric in advertising stories when he announces somewhat peevishly, 'What nedeth gretter dilatacioun?' (line 232). As made clear by the travel narratives and rhetorical treatises discussed above, every writer needs 'dilatacioun' to elicit desire and to add value to a text. Indeed, while Chaucer has his narrator reject dilation, the Man of Law engages in it extensively, making him one of Chaucer's most prolix narrators.[53] Chaucer is aware of the delicate balance to be achieved. While a text must be dilated in order to return a used text to a whole, virginal state, ironically, too much display can make a text 'too familiar', and therefore like a cheap commodity or sexually 'used' woman. Rather than hoarding the story of Custance because the Man of Law has mercantile concerns that make him a bad storyteller, Chaucer, as a good storyteller, is acutely aware that he needs to merchandize effectively – and therefore carefully – this familiar story of a Christian heroine.

Narrative Dearth, Anxiety, and 'Unkynde Abomynaciouns'

Perhaps the only element of the *Man of Law's Tale* that has puzzled scholars as much as its mercantile concerns is its odd treatment of incest. Incest does not appear in either Trivet's or Gower's versions of the story of Custance, versions that we know were probably Chaucer's

53   It is perhaps not surprising that another of the narrators who indulges in rhetorical embellishment is also one of the *Canterbury Tales*' most prolix: the Wife of Bath. She is the pilgrim who insists that her body is still of value, though she concedes that it is perhaps now worth less than when she was 'new'. On the role of dilation in the tale, see Lee Patterson, '"For the wyves love of Bathe": Feminine Rhetoric and Poetic Resolution in the *Roman de la Rose* and *The Canterbury Tales*', *Speculum: A Journal of Medieval Studies* 58.3 (July 1983), 656–95.

direct sources for the tale. Consequently, Chaucer might have been unaware of the pivotal role that incest played in the story's analogues. However, given the popularity in the fourteenth century of the so-called 'accused queen' genre, of which the story of Custance is a type, that scenario seems unlikely.[54] The Man of Law's prudishness is one explanation often offered for his rejection of incest narratives. However, as Carolyn Dinshaw asks, if this is the case, why is incest the particular focus of the Man of Law's opprobrium, as opposed to some other form of sexual transgression, such as adultery or sodomy? Dinshaw sees in the Man of Law's insistence that he will avoid incest 'if that I may' (line 89) a nervous adumbration: a recognition that incest narratives may not easily be avoided.[55]

In the pages that follow, I argue that the discomfort with incest expressed in the prologue is intimately tied to the gendered economy of storytelling that I sketched above. Specifically, the state of poetical poverty that the Man of Law laments requires him to retell the stories of others, a situation that he describes in terms of incest. While it seems that this is the Man of Law's exclusive concern, I argue that Chaucer's presentation of himself in the prologue as the Man of Law's rival betrays the poet's own anxiety about possibly slipping into incestuous poetics.

We might understand the link between incest and storytelling in the context of the long history of the connection of poetics with sex. Sodomy is perhaps one of the most frequently analysed topics in this regard. Thanks in large part to Michel Foucault, as critics we readily recognize

54   In the 'accused queen' stories, the heroine often flees her homeland to avoid her father's sexual advances. For a discussion of the popularity of this genre in the Middle Ages, see Margaret Schlauch, *Chaucer's Constance and Accused Queens* (New York, 1927); Elizabeth Archibald, 'The Flight from Incest: Two Late Classical Precursors of the Constance Theme', *Chaucer Review* 20 (1986), 259–72; and Nancy Black, *Medieval Narratives of Accused Queens* (Gainesville, FL, 2003). Carolyn Dinshaw suggests that vestiges of these older incest narratives might linger in the *Man of Law's Tale*, accounting for Custance's reluctance to identify herself to those around her both in Northumbria and upon her return to Rome (Dinshaw, *Chaucer's Sexual Poetics*, 101–2). For other discussions of incest's role in the *Man of Law's Tale*, see Marc M. Pelen, 'Providence and Incest Reconsidered'; R. A. Shoaf, 'Unwemmed Custance'; and Elizabeth Scala, 'Canacee and the Chaucer Canon: Incest and Other Unnarratables', *The Chaucer Review* 30.1 (1995), 15–39.

55   Dinshaw, *Chaucer's Sexual Poetics*, 94–5. Dinshaw reads the gaps and disruptions inherent in patriarchal ideology in the Man of Law's admission that incest may not be avoidable (*Chaucer's Sexual Poetics*, 90).

sodomy as a mobile signifier, one that can represent a panoply of behaviours well beyond the sexual. Alain de Lille's conflation of sodomy with bad grammar, which brings together sexual and poetic practice, is perhaps one of the most frequently analysed by medievalists.[56]

Although less frequently discussed, incest, much like sodomy, is a slippery signifier, one that has a much broader meaning in medieval culture than it does today. Formed from the Latin *castus* with the negative prefix *in-* and the vocalic alternation of /a/ and /e/, incest originally signified sexual transgression more generally, particularly debauchery or defilement that would make one unable to perform a religious ritual. Like sodomy, incest is conflated with a variety of transgressions. For example, the fourteenth-century writer Robert of Flamborough depicts sleeping with an infidel as incestuous.[57] Thus incest, like sodomy, encompasses a range of behaviours that extend well beyond the sexual, making it equally mobile and flexible as a signifier.

56   For example, in the opening of *The Complaint of Nature*, Alain de Lille's narrator complains that:

> The active sex shudders in disgrace as it sees itself degenerate into the passive sex. A man turned woman blackens the fair name of his sex. The witchcraft of Venus turns him into a hermaphrodite. He is subject and predicate: one and the same term is given a double application. Man here extends too far the laws of grammar. Becoming a barbarian in grammar, he disclaims the manhood given him by nature. Grammar does not find favour with him but rather a trope. This transposition however, cannot be called a trope. The figure here more correctly falls into the category of defects.

See Alan of Lille, *Plaint of Nature*, trans. James J. Sheridan (Toronto, 1980), 67–8. For other moments when Alain's text conflates certain grammatical excesses with sodomy, see pp. 133–4, 156–9, and 164. For an excellent discussion of the links between sex and writing generally, and in Alain's text in particular, see Jan Ziolkowski, *Alan of Lille's Grammar of Sex: The Meaning of Grammar to a Twelfth-Century Intellectual* (Cambridge, MA, 1985).

57   Anna Walecka, 'The Concept of Incest: Medieval French and Normative Writings in Latin', *Romance Languages Annual* 5 (1993), 117–23. The example of sex with an infidel as a type of incest seems counterintuitive, given that such an act might be read as ultra-exogamous, rather than endogamous. It therefore serves as a useful example of how the label is less about specific acts and practices, and more about the representation of those acts and practices. On incest and intercultural relations, see Leslie Dunton-Downer, 'The Horror of Culture: East West Incest in Chrétien de Troyes's *Cligés*', *New Literary History* 28.2 (1997), 367–81.

Like Alain de Lille (with whose works we know Chaucer to have been intimately familiar), I speculate that Chaucer draws on sexual practice – in this case, incest – as a way to explore concerns about writing – in this case, poetic poverty. This reading is supported by the prologue's very structure. The subject of incest, which appears in the prologue in lines 77–89, is framed by the two speeches of the Man of Law in which he expresses his need for a story, lines 45–76 and lines 90–8, respectively. This positioning invites the reader to contemplate incest in conjunction with his lack of a 'thrifty' tale, and the 'cursed stories' (line 80), which he assures the reader Chaucer would avoid at all costs, with not only narratives that depict literal incest, but also those that represent a figural incest: stories that are incestuous in the sense that they have already been told. What worries Chaucer's narrator is that he will be forced to repeat someone else's story because Chaucer has already told all the 'thrifty' tales: 'Of swiche unkynde abhomynacions, / Ne I wol noon reherce, if that I may' (lines 88–9). His choice of the word 'reherce' is revealing in this respect: while 'reherce' can mean 'tell', it also more specifically means to repeat. The 'if that I may' tagged on the end of line 89 may serve as an admission that his lack of a 'thrifty' tale might make incestuous poetics impossible to avoid.

Further evidence linking incest and the retelling of stories can be found in the Man of Law's second complaint about his lack of a 'thrifty' tale:

But of my tale how shal I doon this day?
Me were looth be likned, douteless,
To Muses that men clepe Pierides –
Metamorphosios woot what I mene;
But nathelees, I recche noght a bene
Though I come after hym with hawebake.
I speke in prose, and lat him rymes make.

(lines 90–6)

These lines are, initially, puzzling. Given the Man of Law's stated insecurity about his poetical skills, wouldn't the Muses be precisely the entities he would wish to be 'likned' to? As the *Riverside Chaucer* notes, Chaucer's narrator is probably confusing the nine Muses (called Pieria, from their birthplace) with the daughters of King Pierus, who, swollen with pride, challenge the Muses to a poetry contest at the end of Book

V of the *Metamorphoses*.[58] The daughters narrate the battle between the gods and the giants, describing the beastly shapes the gods adopt in order to hide from Typhoeus. The Muses, on the other hand, tell a tale that, technically, is a tale of incest: the abduction of Proserpina by her uncle, Pluto.[59] The Muses win, and the nine sisters are changed into magpies, creatures that can only imitate what they hear.[60] The contest between the Muses and the nine women echoes the 'contest', at least as the narrator presents it, between himself and Chaucer. The Man of Law tries to approach the situation with bravado: 'I recche noght a bene / Though I come after hym with hawebake' (lines 94–5). Yet he is acutely aware that he is too late – that he 'come[s] after' the supposedly more prolific poet who has already rendered into English all possible tales. His concern is not that if he tries to compete with Chaucer he will be compelled to tell literal stories of incest, as the victorious Muses do, but rather that he will tell figurally incestuous ones – twice-told tales. He is 'looth be likned' to the magpies that lose their contest with the Muses and consequently can only 'reherce' (line 89) the words of others.

While dated, Bloom's 'anxiety of influence' provides a fascinating lens through which to consider this conflation of sexual impropriety and poetic property in the *Man of Law's Tale*. Bloom famously relies on the trope of incest to describe the anxiety a writer feels when he encounters his artistic vision in the work of his literary 'forefathers' (never foremothers). Less discussed is how Bloom frames this anxiety in economic terms, as well as sexual. As in the *Man of Law's Tale*, new stories are the most valuable merchandise in *The Anxiety of Influence*.

58   Benson, *Riverside Chaucer*, 856 n. to lines 91–2.
59   Book V of *Metamorphoses* begins with a story of thwarted uncle–niece incest as well (the battle between Phineus and Perseus), making incest the frame of the entire book. Whether the relationship would be considered incestuous in Chaucer's time is unclear; sexual relationships between uncle and niece were not necessarily considered illegal (Benson, *The Riverside Chaucer*, 1074 n. to line 2602). H. A. Kelly observes that authorities may have thought such relations were illegal due to a misinterpretation of 'neptis' for niece rather than granddaughter. See H. A. Kelly, 'Canonical Implications of Richard III's Plan to Marry his Niece', *Traditio* 23 (1967), 269–311. See also Kelly's 'Shades of Incest and Cuckoldry: Pandarus and John of Gaunt', *Studies in the Age of Chaucer* 13 (1991), 121–40. Kelly argues that Pandarus and Criseyde's relationship would be read as incestuous by Chaucer's audience.
60   See Ovid, *Metamorphoses*, ed. and trans. Frank Justus Miller (Cambridge, MA, 1984), Book V, line 299.

Being first with an idea places a poet in a position of power because 'the commodity in which poets deal, their authority, their property, turns upon *priority* [Bloom's emphasis]'.[61] Being a latecomer, on the other hand, leaves a poet in a state of 'poverty' (35), 'bankrupt' (70), and experiencing an 'anxiety of indebtedness' (5).

As in Alberic of Montecassino's text, in Bloom's *Anxiety of Influence* the characteristic that makes stories valuable property is their apparent 'purity', as well as priority. Bloom likens the discovery of one's ideas in another's work to sexual betrayal: 'he is compelled to accept a lack of priority in creation [...] his word is not his word only, and his Muse has whored with many before him' (61). If one is a latecomer, one not only lacks the priority and thus the property, but one is also a cuckold.

Bloom's poetic economy is gendered in another way as well. 'Weak' poets succumb more readily to the temptation of incest. They are more likely to acknowledge their literary forefathers 'through a generosity of the spirit' (43). 'Strong' poets, on the other hand, do not: 'the stronger the man, the larger his resentments'. To be a strong poet is to be a masculine poet: 'he who will not work does not get the bread but remains deluded, as the gods deluded Orpheus [...] deluded him because he is effeminate, not courageous, because he was a cithara-player, not a man' (72–3). As Bloom makes clear throughout his text, rivalry is the only way to resist incest's 'enchantment'.

This depiction of incestuous poetics as something feminine or feminizing might give us another lens for reading the incestuous desires of the mothers-in-law in the tale. Although there is nothing directly in the mothers-in-laws' behaviour that points to incest, the Man of Law encourages the reader to view their actions in this way, particularly in the case of the sultaness. The Man of Law associates her with Semiramis, a woman not merely 'famed for her wickedness', as *The Riverside Chaucer* notes, but for a very particular wickedness: marrying her son.[62] The Man of Law's complaints about the mothers-in-law echo his earlier descriptions of incest in the prologue. He lambasts Donegild with 'Fy, mannish, fy!' (line 782) and 'Fy, feendlych spirit' (line 783), lines that recall the Man of Law's dismissal of incest narratives: 'Of swiche cursed stories I sey fy!' (line 80). 'Cursed' is also a word used to describe both women. The sultaness is described as a 'cursed krone' and her plot to kill the

---

61   Bloom, *Anxiety of Influence*, 64. All subsequent citations are from this edition and are referenced parenthetically.
62   Benson, *The Riverside Chaucer*, 860 n. to line 359.

sultan and his followers as a 'cursed dede' (lines 432–3). The Man of Law also states that Donegild 'thoughte hir cursed herte brast atwo' when she learns of Alla's plan to marry Custance (line 697).

At first, the behaviour of the mothers-in-law is depicted as decidedly unfeminine. The sultaness, for example, is described as a 'virago' (line 359), a serpent in the guise of a woman (line 360), and a 'feyned womman' (line 363); Donegild, in turn, is criticized for being 'mannysh' (line 782) and possessing a 'feendlych spirit' (line 783). Yet, one can trace a counter-narrative in the Man of Law's condemnations. He describes the sultaness as a 'welle of vices' (line 323), the 'roote of iniquitee' (line 358), and one in whom 'al that may confounde / Vertu and innocence [...] Is bred [...] as nest of every vice' (lines 362–4). Rather than behaving unnaturally, the Man of Law suggests that their evil stems from their very essence: it is bred in them, and the very 'roote' of their wickedness.

We might read this incestuous framing of these foreign women as a form of projection, one used by the narrator to further distance himself from the threat of incestuous poetics. By mapping incest onto Donegild and the sultaness and by connecting it to their very bodies, both Chaucer and his narrator, as men and Europeans, can distance themselves from its feminine and foreign taint.

It is tempting to locate this anxiety about incestuous poetics and these acts of projection in the Man of Law. It is, after all, the Man of Law who complains in the prologue about 'coming after' Chaucer. However, it is generally accepted by scholars that it is Chaucer who is the 'latecomer' to the story of Custance, likely borrowing the tale from Gower. Chaucer's solution to the incestuous potential of such a borrowing is to deploy the same method Bloom argues adopted by 'strong poets': he creates a rivalry between himself and another 'poet', in this case, the Man of Law. By presenting himself in the *Man of Law's Tale* as the industrious rival of its narrator, Chaucer distances himself from the possibility of not being his own man, poetically speaking. The Man of Law's complaint about Chaucer's productivity becomes a deft form of advertising, making Chaucer a more prolific writer than Ovid. The Man of Law's guarantee that Chaucer would never recount stories of incest reassures the reader (and perhaps Chaucer himself) that incestuous poetics will not happen on Chaucer's watch.

Generations of scholars have assisted Chaucer in this project of avoiding incestuous poetics. An early article by Alfred David, significantly titled 'The Man of Law vs. Chaucer: A Case in Poetics', begins with the observation that Chaucer may very well be feeling anxious as he begins the *Man of Law's Tale*:

> The Man of Law's doubts about his ability to tell a 'thrifty' story may, therefore, reflect Chaucer's own uncertainty on the same score [...] It looks as though, after a brilliant beginning with his first fragment, Chaucer [was] no longer entirely sure. The Lawyer's discussion of poetry can be construed as a humorous projection – with serious implications – of Chaucer's own search for fit materials to carry out his great plan.[63]

This insightful observation occurs on the first page of David's study. But the remainder of the article is dedicated to distancing Chaucer from it, and from the Man of Law, as far as possible. In David's reading (one that helped launch some forty years of reading Chaucer's portrait of the Man of Law satirically), Chaucer's narrator becomes Chaucer's worst critic, someone sententious and strait-laced, too morally uptight to enjoy the humour found in the bawdier *Canterbury Tales*. David adds another rivalry as well: the supposedly real-life figure behind the critic becomes 'moral Gower'. Chaucer's comments about incest in the prologue become a 'good-natured' joke: 'The implication that the author of the *Confessio Amantis* was, like the Man of Law, humourless and pedantic, hits close to home.'[64]

A quarrel between Gower and Chaucer has long been discredited. But the idea has had a surprisingly long shelf-life. Dinshaw observes that the terms of that imagined rivalry are far from gender-neutral. Traits associated with Gower – dullness, fickleness, insincerity, passivity, timidity, and unctuousness – are traditionally seen as 'feminine' attributes in Western society. This 'femininity' was thought to permeate Gower's writing as well, writing often criticized for being obsequious, imitative and didactic. Chaucer, on the other hand – who, in this narrative, refused to ingratiate himself with the new court – demonstrates the 'masculine' traits of sincerity, integrity, and strength. Such 'manly' behaviour leads to superior verse: unencumbered by self-interest, Chaucer's work expresses pure poetry, language, and aesthetics. What goes unacknowledged in this critically constructed rivalry, Dinshaw argues, is how masculine identity necessitates that expulsion of the feminine, and the violence that such

---

63   Alfred David, 'The Man of Law vs. Chaucer: A Case in Poetics', *PMLA* 82.2 (1967), 217–25 (217).
64   Ibid., 220.

an expulsion reveals and reflects.[65] While in our own critical moment we have dispensed with the quarrel between Gower and Chaucer, we have replaced it with an equally productive quarrel, the quarrel between Chaucer and the Man of Law. As a result, Chaucer can continue both to hold onto his poetic property and, at the same time, to be his own man.

Admittedly, we have no way of knowing if Chaucer was anxious about his status as an author in the ways that I have imagined in this essay. Would a late medieval writer like Chaucer have a sense of poetic property? After all, writers like Chaucer retell the stories of others all the time. Certainly, ideas of originality in the Middle Ages do not exist in the same imaginative way that we might conceive of them today. However, as Stephanie Trigg has argued, late medieval authorship may be more complicated than previously recognized. Trigg identifies three independent models of authorship coexisting in late medieval culture, one of which is the writer as a professional author striving to establish the terms of his posterity. She argues that Chaucer engages in a more complicated way with models like Petrarch and Boccaccio, desiring to 'place himself and his own writerly authority at center stage'.[66] My point is that if we can read the Man of Law as someone anxious about his poetic deficiencies (or even Gower, for that matter) it follows that we can imagine that the authorial voice of Chaucer is anxious as well. It is this failure of imagining that interests me. I see in it a nostalgic longing for a poetics that is free from the taint of the economic, for an aesthetic that does not collude with gendered systems of value.

In *Forms of Capital*, Pierre Bourdieu observes that:

Economic theory has allowed to be foisted upon it a definition of the economy of practices which is the historical invention of capitalism; and by reducing the universe of exchanges to mercantile exchange, which is objectively and subjectively oriented toward the maximization of profit, i.e., (economically) self-interested, it has implicitly defined the other forms of exchange as noneconomic, and therefore disinterested.[67]

65   Dinshaw, 'Rivalry, Rape and Manhood', 34.
66   Stephanie Trigg, *Congenial Souls: Reading Chaucer from Medieval to Postmodern* (Minneapolis, 2002), 50–5. David Wallace also observes that in the *Man of Law's Tale*, a 'sense of commercial aspects of fiction writing – storytelling as commodity production – places him [Chaucer] much closer to Boccaccio than to Petrarch' (*Chaucerian Polity*, 205).
67   Pierre Bourdieu, 'The Forms of Capital', in *Handbook of Theory and Research for the Sociology of Education*, ed. John E. Richardson, trans. Richard Nice (New

As I have argued in this essay, the *Man of Law's Tale* is, indeed, mercantile in its outlook. However, that outlook is not due to the Man of Law's flaws or Chaucer's satirical pen. Rather, Chaucer's tale, and medieval poetics more broadly, are invested in a very particular economy of storytelling, one in which commodification and desire are entwined with ideologies of gender and value. The problem arises when we attempt to quarantine storytelling from economics. This attempt is rooted in the same nostalgic desire that led Enlightenment writers to imagine, as James Thompson describes it, a place where 'silver was not always silver, but [...] love was always love'.[68] The result is that economics (perhaps much like Chaucer's narrator) bears the brunt of self-interest, which allows other realms, like storytelling and romance, to masquerade as non-economic and therefore disinterested in the ways that Pierre Bourdieu describes. Ironically, although the Man of Law has been lambasted for his poor storytelling, this story, perhaps more so than any other in the *Canterbury Tales*, exposes those interests.

York 1986), 241–58 (242). In a recent, excellent analysis of gift exchange in the *Shipman's Tale*, Robert Epstein sketches some of the limitations of Pierre Bourdieu's idea of 'disinterest' when applied to the tale. Chief among them is that for Bourdieu, all social relations and exchanges are marked by competition and materialism, leaving very little room for other kinds of motivation, such as love and friendship (Robert Epstein, 'The Lack of Interest in *The Shipman's Tale*: Chaucer and the Social Theory of the Gift', *Modern Philology* 113 (2015), 27–48). As a reader of the *Man of Law's Tale*, I continue to find Pierre Bourdieu's observations about disinterest particularly useful, not because storytelling and romance *cannot*, theoretically, be read as disinterested, but rather because it is almost always assumed that they *are* disinterested. Perhaps the larger question is why do we read interest or disinterest in some of the tales (and in certain social and cultural institutions and relations) and not in others? What ideological work is being done in these readings?

68 Thompson, *Models of Value*, 22.

6

Gower's Bedside Manner

JOE STADOLNIK

A priest stands at the deathbed of Richard Whittington, the London mercer and the City's great benefactor, in an illustration of his death in 1423. Poised behind the clergyman (probably the rector of St Michael's Paternoster, Whittingon's parish priest and confessor) stands a physician holding aloft a flask of urine for inspection in the iconic fashion of a medical professional.[1] Whittington's death scene juxtaposes two kinds of expert care that often came into contact in the course of medieval English life. At the bedside, confessors attending to the souls of the dying regularly rubbed shoulders with attending physicians whose expertise might still have managed a cure. The *De instructione medici*, a guide to medical house visits, recommends that the physician be sure the patient confesses at the start of treatment.[2] (To suggest confession later can only diminish a patient's confidence in the physician and his prognosis.) The surgeon Henri de Mondeville advised battlefield surgeons against removing arrows from wounds before patients had confessed.[3] These medical best practices accorded with ecclesiastical mandate. A decree of the Fourth Lateran Council (1215) instructed physicians to encourage patients' confession before undertaking medical treatment.[4] In medieval hospitals, where lay care-

---

1   See Amy Appleford, 'The Good Death of Richard Whittington', in *The Ends of the Body*, ed. Jill Ross and Suzanne Conklin Akbari (Toronto, 2013), 86–112 (86–8).
2   For the Anglo-Norman translation, see *Anglo-Norman Medicine*, vol. 2: *Shorter Treatises*, ed. Tony Hunt (Aldershot, 1997), 21.
3   Carole Rawcliffe, *Medicine and Society in Late Medieval England* (Stroud, 1995), 78.
4   See Canon 22 of Lateran IV in *Decrees of the Ecumenical Councils*, ed. Norman P. Tanner (Washington, D.C., 1990), 245–6.

givers nursed inmates alongside clergy tasked with the cure of their souls, confession was commonplace.[5]

This practical proximity corresponded to a persistent metaphorical comparison between confessional and medical expertise. The Fourth Lateran Council formalized a requirement for all Christians to confess annually, and this decree articulated the spiritually curative task of the confessor by analogy with the expertise of the physician: 'The priest shall be discerning and prudent, so that like a skilled doctor he may pour wine and oil over the wounds of the injured one.'[6] The characteristic qualities of the good *sacerdos* – be *discretus, cautus, peritus* – are illustrated most saliently by the good *medicus*.[7] The decree draws this vivid analogy between confessional and medical expertise particularly in comparing their conversation. Careful inquiry (*diligenter inquirens*) facilitates a discriminating consideration of a sin's circumstances (*prudenter intelligat*) and then the provision of proper advice (*consilium*). Discretion and caution, for both confessor and doctor, were aspects of talk. Clerical and lay discourses of confession articulated a form of dialogic examination that proceeded as measured and discerning talk of spiritual disease, and was thus akin to the inquisitive method of a skilled doctor. Medieval confessional discourse depended upon this analogy not only to express an ideal relation between confessor and penitent, but also to delineate the ideal practices of language to mediate it.

John Gower adopts these inquisitive discursive methods to inaugurate the frame of his long Middle English poem *Confessio Amantis*. 'Tell thi maladie', says Venus to Amans, the recently revived speaker and Gower's newly adopted poetic persona.[8] A diagnostic conversation ensues, in which Amans professes to suffer from lovesickness. Venus soon refers him to Genius, her 'own clerk', to confess. She tells Amans, 'In aunter if thou live, / Mi will is ferst that thou be schrive.'[9] This couplet, rhyming

---

5   See Faye Marie Getz, *Medicine in the English Middle Ages* (Princeton, 1998), 90–1; Rawcliffe, *Medicine and Society*, 19. Confession to the warden of St Mary's in Leicester, for instance, was a prerequisite for admission into the royal hospital.
6   Canon 21 of *Decrees of the Ecumenical Councils*, ed. Tanner, 245–6.
7   See Alexander Murray, 'Counselling in Medieval Confession', in *Handling Sin: Confession in the Middle Ages*, ed. Peter Biller and Alastair Minnis (York, 1998), 63–77.
8   I refer throughout to the text of Gower's *Confessio Amantis* as printed in *The English Works of John Gower*, ed. G. C. Macaulay, EETS e.s. 81, 2 vols (Oxford, 1969; first published 1900), Book I, line 164.
9   *Confessio Amantis*, Book I, lines 189–90.

'live' and 'shrive', recalls in miniature that deathbed conjunction of medically critical talk and administration of last rites as the poem turns from a 'telling of malady' to an account of sin through shrift. Genius's careful and conscientious administration of confession then frames and organizes the exemplary tales of the *Confessio*, which he narrates to facilitate Amans's education and correction as a lover. Gower invokes the medieval conventions for skilful conversation with both the confessing and the sick, conventions which formalized the process and manner of that conversation's conduct, as he institutes the process and manner of his book.

When the poem turns from Venus's diagnostic interview of Amans to a confession before her clerk, Genius, Gower interpolates a Latin quatrain that raises the prospect of a restorative experience to be had by Amans, and possibly, in the poem's reading:

Confessus Genio si sit medicina salutis
    Experiar morbis quos tulit ipsa Venus
Lesa quidem ferro medicantur membra saluti
    Raro tamen medicum vulnus amoris habet.

(Book I, versus iii, lines 1–4)

(Having made confession to Genius, let me test this as if it were a cure for the sickness that this very Venus has brought me. At least limbs mangled by steel are healed to health, yet there's seldom a physician for love's wound.)[10]

The experimental quality inherent to medical practice expresses the experimental quality of the poem's attempt at rehabilitating the lovesick Amans; the subjunctive mood of '*experiar*' ('Let me test this as if it were a cure [...]') inflects Gower's undertaking with a note of uncertainty and purpose. In presenting his poem as a curative exercise, Gower recalls some literary precursors: Boethian consolatory dialogue, with its therapeutic intervention by a goddess; and Ovidian instruction in the cures for love in the *Remedia amoris*. But readers expecting this to be followed by a philosophical *prosimetrum* or a direct and cynical argument against love will be disappointed. These implicit affiliations are never drawn out; Gower fashions a confessional conversation into

10   I use my own translation here, aided by that of Andrew Galloway in *Confessio Amantis*, vol. 1, ed. Russell Peck (Kalamazoo, MI, 2006).

the poetically curative regimen for the lovesick Amans. This quatrain is surely a statement of the poem's therapeutic ambitions: readers can find solace in their reading.[11] Yet Gower's opening invites readers to understand this poem not only as therapy, but also as an experiment in making poetry with therapy's familiar discursive procedures. This poem might be medicine to the sick, but it also sounds like and works like professionally mannered therapeutic talk.

The medieval analogy between expertly curative conversational practice – not just the analogy of cure itself – might prompt us to rethink what is experimental about the Middle English poem's confessional frame. By expert conversation, I mean a practised style and pattern of speech instrumental to the advisement and the treatment of an inexpert clientele; these manners are governed by professional codes of comportment and honed with long experience. While confessional manuals illustrated a conversational ideal with reference to the questioning of a good physician in some detail, medieval medical texts, too, coached their readers to talk expertly with the sick. These medical texts made careful and discreet practices of language a part of their therapeutic repertoires. Crucially, this advice in therapeutic speech also made varieties of literary language and performance – the telling of different tales, the recital of poetry – the useful instruments of medical practice. Some medical texts recommended practices of narrative selection and formal artifice in good 'bedside manner', those practices of talk being calibrated for pragmatic curative effect. I argue here that Gower, in the opening moments of Book I, appeals to these trained styles and patterns of expert conversation as informing logics behind the ensuing style and arrangement of his compendious English work. This scene dramatizes for readers the poem's adoption of these medieval forms of expert colloquy. Gower makes the particular kinds of conversations good confessors and good physicians were meant to have (connected here by his persona's serial encounters with Venus and Genius, as well as by metaphorical proxy) the organizing premises for the composition of the poem and the literary experiences it might produce. In the process, Gower performs a versatile vernacular authority, as he variously inhabits

---

11   Gower's therapeutic aims, of course, have not gone unnoticed by earlier critics. See for instance James M. Palmer, 'Bodily and Spiritual Healing through Conversation and Storytelling: Teaching Genius as Physician and Confessor', in *Approaches to Teaching the Works of John Gower*, ed. R. F. Yeager and Brian Gastle (New York, 2009), 53–8.

the familiar learned roles of confessor, doctor, and counsellor to kings
to guide his readers through profitable and pleasurable encounters with
the poem. I look to medieval training in bedside manner to show how
the poem's act of impersonation grounds its admittedly 'plain' style and
invites readers to range across and around the text to avail themselves
of the its instruction and pleasure – its 'lust and lore' – as desired or
required.

When Genius promises to shrive the lovesick Amans 'after the
forme' of his priesthood (Book I, line 275), this confessor alludes to a
set of forensic practices of speech that were defined 'after the form' of
doctors' bedside manner. Confessional literature produced in the wake
of the 1215 Lateran decree conventionalized confessional conversation,
in its language and methods, with special reference to medical interview.[12] Guides for confession written for confessors and laypeople alike
provided instruction for those eager to master their assigned colloquial
role, and appealed to notions of professional medical manner in conversation for a metaphorical expression of confessor's expertise. Echoing
the Lateran decree the *Summula* of Walter Cantilupe, a Latin confessor's
manual (c.1240), advocates the scrupulous gathering of the details of
'who, what, when', etc., with specific analogy to the medical professional:

> Just as it is proper for a person to undress completely to show his bodily
> wounds to a doctor or surgeon, since confession is the healing of injuries
> done to the soul it is proper for someone to reveal all his inner wounds to
> his spiritual doctor – in other words, all those circumstances and every-
> thing which could aggravate the sin in any way.[13]

The *Summula* figures sins as wounds and the confessor as a 'doctor or
surgeon', the observer and reader of these manifested signs charged with
their redress, and equipped with the expertise to do so. If the penitent
seems reluctant, 'the discerning priest should supply what the penitent

---

12   Recapitulating the history of medieval confessional literature is beyond the
scope of this article, but for an overview with specific reference to England, see
Masha Raskolnikov, 'Confessional Literature, Vernacular Psychology, and the
History of the Self in Middle English', *Literature Compass* 2 (2005), 1–20.
13   *Pastors and the Care of Souls in Medieval England*, ed. John Shinners and
William J. Dohar (South Bend, IN, 1998), 170–85 (178). On its ascription to
Walter, see Joseph Goering and Daniel S. Taylor, 'The *Summulae* of Bishops
Walter de Cantilupe (1240) and Peter Quinel (1287)', *Speculum* 67.3 (1992),
576–94.

has ignored by asking questions with discretion' (182), with the *circum-stantiae* of the rhetorical tradition styled anew into the confessor's interrogative arsenal.[14] These norms for confessional practice required confessors to speak with all kinds of care: a rhetorician's care for composition, a doctor's care for injury, a curate's care for sinfulness.

Confessional texts intended for lay readership describe the responsibilities of the confessor towards those under his care by medical analogy as well. When Laurent de Orléans, in his *Somme le roi* (c.1279), advises his lay reader to search out signs of a curate's competence, he turns to medical metaphor: '[S]echen þe beeste phisicions and þe wisest þat he may haue.'[15] Laurent counsels readers to confess openly, turning to the same metaphor:

> for but a sek man telle and schewe openliche his siknesse to þe phisicion, elles þe phisicion ne may not worche ne do hym no good, ne þe leche ne may not hele a wounde but he see openliche al þe wounde.
>
> (176)

The penitent should take care to 'do after the ordenaunce and counseil of þe schrift-fadre', just as 'þe sek schal bi resoun obeien to þe phisicion for to haue soon heele' (184). The reader should respond to confessional counsel with trusting obedience to expert prescriptions, as one heeds medical advice. Throughout the *Somme le roi*, this analogy between the work of the confessor and that of the physician is reasserted in refrain. Even further, the *Somme's* lay readers are told to cultivate mastery in telling openly of their sins, 'for vse makeþ maistre, as it scheweþ in oþere craftes' (182). In the *Summula* and the *Somme le roi*, the defining model for confession's discursive forensics is the physician's expert manner of inquiry, by which the *medicus* asks the right questions and through which the *phisicion* assures the patient of the care-giver's wisdom.

14 See Rita Copeland, *Rhetoric, Hermeneutics, and Translation in the Middle Ages* (Cambridge, 1991), 66–73.

15 I quote from the edition of the Middle English translation, *The Book of Vices and Virtues*, ed. W. Nelson Francis, EETS o.s. 217 (London, 1942), 173. Laurent was the royal confessor to Philip III, and surely the prestige of *Somme le roi* traded not only on the status of its dedicatee and first reader but also on the expertise of its author at the pinnacle of his profession. The *Somme le roi* and its many translations into European vernaculars instructed lay readers in the substance of requisite Christian knowledge; for its pastoral readers, it modelled an instructional regimen with remarkable specificity.

While confessional literature drew on medical conversation to imagine an ideal form of expert colloquy, medieval medical texts instruct readers directly in bedside manner, articulating principles of best practice in talking to patients about their conditions, prognoses, and courses of treatment. Circumspect – and sometimes tactical – talk with patients could be an essential tool. To supplement what can be gleaned from the patient's pulse, urine, and complexion, inquiry must discover those facts of the condition that must be divulged by the patient: the duration of the suffering and affected senses or appetite.[16] The *Repetitio super Canone Vita Brevis* of Arnald of Villanova, for example, outlines what should and should not be said, and even how it should be said.[17] Medically expert speech should be guarded and well composed when answering the patient (*ordinatus in respondendo circumspectus*). At the bedside the physician should be discreet and discerning (*discretus*), careful in his speech (*diligens in sermone*), and modest in his disposition (*modestus in affectione*). Specific instructions are given for taking medical histories; in order that his interrogation into symptoms might produce a diagnosis, the physician designs the inquiry carefully to discover specific facts of the condition. For Villanova, a measured and meticulous clinical conversation naturally reassures the patient, whereas the other tools of diagnosis may worry them. As a result he gives conversation priority among these tools.

For the medical practitioner of late medieval England, manner mattered away from the bedside as well. In his prologue to the *Practica*, the fourteenth-century English surgeon John of Arderne occupies himself with defining and modelling the proper 'manere of þe leche'[18] from the moment of his acquaintance with the prospective patient's case:

---

16   See Michael McVaugh's wide-ranging treatment of the subject, 'Bedside Manner in the Middle Ages', *Bulletin of the History of Medicine* 71.2 (1997), 201–23 (212).

17   Text in Henry Sigerest, 'Bedside Manner in the Middle Ages: The Treatise *De Cautelis Medicorum* Attributed to Arnald of Villanova', *Quarterly Bulletin of Northwestern University Medical School* 20 (1946), 136–43.

18   I quote from the Middle English translation in *Treatises of Fistula in Ano*, ed. D'Arcy Power, EETS o.s. 139 (Oxford, 1910), 1. The quoted material here is found in the rubric of London, British Library, MS Sloane 6, fol. 141v. On John Arderne, see Peter Murray Jones, 'Arderne, John (b.1307/8, d. in or after 1377)', *Oxford Dictionary of National Biography*, ed. H. C. G. Matthew and Brian Harrison (Oxford, 2004).

When seke men, forsoth, or any of tham bysyde comeþ to the leche to
ask help or counsel of hym, be he noȝt to tham ouer felle ne over homely
but mene in beryng after the askyngis of the personeȝ; to som reuerently,
to som comonly.[19]

John's ideal doctor speaks with a restrained demeanour and discretion
when responding to the petitions of the sick. One's tone of speech
should be neither too familiar nor too severe, sometimes courteous
and sometimes casual. Elsewhere John includes further advice for
manner as it pertains to specific, sensitive discomforts: 'a leche ow to
be circumspecte in his askyngis' (14), he writes, when asking about
urethral abscesses. He further recommends being a mild-mannered
dinner guest:

And be he curtaise at lordeȝ bordeȝ, and displese he noȝt in wordes or
dedes to the gestes sytting by; here he many þingis but speke he but fewe
[...] And whan he speke, be the wordeȝ short, and, als mich as he may,
faire and resonable and withoute sweryng.

(6-7)

At the table, the good doctor speaks pleasantly, wisely, and respectably.
In the *Practica*, the medical man's clinical manner is but one element of
general professional deportment and social grace.

This was not only a matter of appearances; practically, bedside
manner worked. Whereas the other tools of diagnosis may worry
patients, a well-composed and circumspect manner counters their
anxieties with reassurance about the quality of their care. Bedside
conversation was a theatre for the practitioners' expertise, a site in
which the physician could perform competence and build trust. A
physician's practised and confident language indexed his qualifications
as physician. This assurance paid practical dividends. 'He to whom
patients entrust themselves cures most illnesses', said no less authority
than Galen; accurate diagnosis and prognosis from the outset helps the
patient confide in the doctor.[20] John Mesue, in one of his axioms, held
that answering patients' questions too quickly fosters doubt ('Si

---

19 *Treatises of Fistula in Ano*, ed. Power, 5.
20 Commentary on Hippocrates's *Prognostics*; qtd. and trans. in McVaugh,
'Bedside Manner', 208, 210.

interrogatus semper velociter respondeas, dubitandus es').[21] In the *Repetitio* Arnald describes how the prudent physician always communicates his planned regimen of treatment so as to distract the patient, and his or her attendants, with minor points of progress.[22]

As for the substance of speech at the bedside, John of Arderne's *Practica* equips the reader with a conversational repertoire composed of useful and versatile fragments of pragmatic talk. He recommends learning proverbs to use in conversation with patients in order to comfort them in treatment, or convince them to swallow the bitter pill. He gathers for the reader a number of anonymously attributed proverbs ('gode prouerbeȝ pertenyng to his craft').[23] John scripts exemplary proverbial citation for his readers' sake, imagining conversations in which the leech points to the proverb's original authority almost as a template: 'ȝif pacientes pleyne that ther medicynes bene bitter or sharp or sich other, than shal the leche say thus: "It is redde in the last lesson of matyns of the natiuitè of oure lord that [...]"'.[24] He introduces this snatch of imagined talk with a construction – 'than shal the leche say þus' – that both trains the leech in a manner of speaking and implies that this manner makes the leech. This prescriptive cue appears elsewhere, and John makes this implication more explicit:

> Also say to the pacient þus: 'I wote þat þe kynde of the fistule is soche þat [...]', ffor suche pronosticacions sheweþ and tokneth to þe pacient þat þe leche is experte in þe knowing of þe fistule, and so þe pacient wil better trist vnto hym.
>
> (14)

John not only describes a correct course of treatment, but scripts the words by which to communicate that medical regimen to the patient and cultivate a salutary confidence in the care-giver's ability. Showing oneself to be 'expert in the knowing' of medical matters requires expertise in their expression to the patient.

Gower adopts a confessional structure for his poem's frame, but with that structure comes an associated conversational mode that inflects

21   See Yūhannā ibn Māsawayh, *Le Livre des axioms médicaux*, ed. Danielle Jacquart and Gérard Troupeau (Geneva, 1980), 149.
22   Quoted in McVaugh, 'Bedside Manner', 216.
23   Arderne, *Practica*, 7.
24   Ibid.

his style with its modestly confident tones. These medieval manners of expert conversation allow Gower to craft a poetic voice in English that is at once natural and formally composed, as adept as it is familiar. At the opening of Book I, the poet forewarns of this stylistic shift from the abstract to the familiar and close at hand: 'I may noght strecche up to the hevene / Min hand, ne setten al in evene / This world [...]' (Book I, lines 1–3). Scholars of the *Confessio* have read these lines as an important transitional moment from the Prologue's political concerns to the exemplary treatment of the ethics of love.[25] Gower reorients his poetic 'compass' towards what, we learn, is within reach: love, a natural thing subject to natural laws. But as he embarks upon this poetic project, love figures as an unnatural physical condition – 'a diseased health, a sweet wound, a soothing ill' – which garners the forensic attentions of Venus and Genius. Gower assumes the persona of Amans to address a woeful complaint to the reader, which in turn makes way for the speech traded between a goddess and her thrall, then a patient and paramedic, then a priest and penitent. Conversation precedes and then arranges the poem's exemplary narratives, as well as its digressions into expository and didactic genres.

The *Confessio*'s opening occupies itself with the self-exposure of Amans so compelled by the forms of expert conversation taught by Walter of Cantilupe and Arnald of Villanova alike. Venus sets out conditions for Amans's response to her entreaty to him:

What is thi Sor of which thou pleignest?
Ne hyd it noght, for if thou feignest
I can do the no medicine.

(Book I, lines 165–7)

Here Venus asks Amans to 'tell his malady', but she also sets the terms of this telling. He must not hide his sickness, and must feign nothing. Only then might she 'do him medicine'. Venus warns Amans against counterfeiting lovesickness, like the many 'faitours' who by 'feintise' reproduce its symptoms for the goddess for show (Book I, lines 173–6). The conversation between Venus and Amans is not only concerned with the matter at hand, but also with clarifying the terms of its language – what is spoken truly and what is feigned, not only what but *how* things

25 Simpson describes this as an abrupt transition from the personal, political concerns of the Prologue in *Sciences of the Self* (Cambridge, 1995), 140–1.

should be said. Venus's practical experience has taught her to approach
new cases of claimed lovesickness with a practical prudence. Her speech
here is as much a reassuring performance of expertise as it is an instance
of its exercise. She speaks with a multivalent authority: as muse and as
figment of allegorical vision, but also as something less abstract. In this
pragmatic context, Venus's speech is textbook bedside manner, coaxing
out an account of Amans's 'sor' while articulating the logic of doing so
and her qualifications to do it.

Amans's response to Venus's attentions reveals his own sense of her
familiarity with the conventions of medical conversation, a familiarity
Venus acquired working with both the authentically lovesick and its
'faitours'. He too pads his own speech with reflexive references to the
progress of conversation. Amans's report of their exchange attends to
how her speech is both a mode of discovering the truths of a case, and
also a way of demonstrating her deliberate tact:

> And natheles sche wiste wel,
> Mi world stod on an other whiel
> Withouten eny faiterie:
> Bot algate of my maladie
> Sche bad me telle and seie her trowthe.
> 'Ma dame, if ye wolde have rowthe',
> Quod I, 'than wolde I telle yow'.
> 'Sey forth', quod sche, 'and tell me how;
> Schew me thi seknesse everydiel.'

> (Book I, lines 177–5)

Venus tailors her conversational manner to facilitate rehabilitation and
foreground her therapeutic qualifications. He detects in her response a
strategic insistence on his own telling of his own affliction; she feigns
ignorance of what she knows well. She goes through the motions, and
requires that Amans 'say the truth' himself: 'Schew me thi seknesse
everydiel.' The lovesick patient tells of the malady; the expert auditor
urges his speech's production, directs it, and hears it, even if this is a
matter of course rather than discovery.

Venus directs Amans to show his sickness as a part of her 'doing
medicine'. With this scene, Gower invokes one aspect of the congruence
of confessional and medical conversation: the deliberate invitation
to expose one's affliction, for the sake of the showing. Venus insists
on a forthright account of the malady, like the metaphorically useful

physicians of the *Somme le roi* who aid patients who 'telle and schewe openliche' of sickness. Venus's mannered performance as attending physician lasts for only a few dozen lines before she refers her lovesick patient to confess his sins to Genius. However brief the encounter, this scene of diagnosis of lovesickness introduces a vernacular register of expertise – that of conventional bedside manner – that is but one of several vernacular registers inhabited by Gower throughout the poem. Venus's paramedical performance parleys itself into Genius's confessional regimen, which is itself interrupted by the register of princely advice in Book VII.

After her brief medical attentions, Venus refers her lovesick patient to Genius, to 'say forth' his sins rather than his sickness. Amans petitions his confessor to be discerning and searching in his talk, too. Amans asks Genius for expert guidance in telling of his desperate condition:

> I prai the let me noght mistime
> Mi schrifte, for I am destourbed
> In al myn herte, and so contourbed,
> That I ne may my wittes gete,
> So schal I moche thyng foryete.
>
> (Book I, lines 220–4)

The disciplinary methods of the confessor shape the content and form of the lover's confession, a narrative otherwise vulnerable to the distortions of the lovesick patient's addled wit. For a brief moment, Gower's poem threatens to become the record of a faulty and incomplete confession by a 'destourbed' and 'contourbed' penitent, the inner turmoil of the penitent likely to produce a disturbed and mistimed narrative. With this anxiety not to 'mistime' his confession, Amans begs for formal correction from his confessor; this formal correction will take the form of conversation. He entreats Genius to leave no stone unturned in the conversational practice of his office:

> Bot if thou wolt my schrift oppose
> Fro point to point, thanne I suppose,
> There schal nothing be left behinde.
> Bot now my wittes ben so blinde,
> That I ne can miselven teche.
>
> (Book I, lines 225–9)

Moving from 'point to point', this 'opposing' (or questioning)[26] will be the scrupulous exercise demanded of Genius's discipline and expected by penitents. The confessor's examination promises to rescue the *Confessio* from the threat of Amans's morbid misprisions. Amans fears that his bungled shrift will deepen his lovesick condition, either in its faulty arrangement or in its omissions. The urgency of medical crisis looms over the procedures of this shrift, and affirms the metaphorical equivalence that tied confessional and medical manners to one another as genres of expert conversation.

While Amans's lovesickness provides the occasion and material for confession, it is the work of the disciplined confessor to impose upon it a right form. Genius promises to minister to his lovesick charge through auricular confession in a manner prescribed by his discipline:

> Of my Presthode after the forme
> I wol thi schrifte so enforme,
> That ate leste thou schalt hiere
> The vices, and to thi matiere
> Of love I schal hem so remene
> That thou schalt knowe what thei mene.
> For what a man schal axe or sein
> Touchende of schrifte, it mot be plein,
> It nedeth noght to make it queinte,
> For trowthe hise words wol noght peinte.

> (Book I, lines 275–84)

In informing Amans (and the reader) of these designs, Genius cites his vocation as an explanatory pretext for the poem's modest style, its directness, and the way it will proceed through its many and various subjects. The aims and procedures of his priestly office are to 'enforme' – in this Middle English sense, 'to give shape to' – the poem as shrift, one composed of plain questions met with plain answers. Painted words are foregone, as is an over-elaborate, 'queinte' style. The confession must also be 'plein', or full and complete (the Middle English word's sense here resembling French *plein*).[27] Genius will arrange the matter of the poem and its style of expression – 'enforme' it – according to his discipline's

---

26   See *Middle English Dictionary*, s.v. 'opposicion, n. (c)'.
27   *Middle English Dictionary*, s.v. 'plain(e), adv.' The *Oxford English Dictionary* records a number of uses of the Middle English 'plein' in the modern sense of

manner of asking and saying, a manner as discerning and well ordered as it is unadorned and accessible.

The meticulous 'opposing' of Amans proceeds from 'point to point' throughout the poem, and this conversational procedure is often linked to the poem's plain and unadorned style. Gower's term to describe the style of this confessional speech and of his Middle English elocution, 'plein', contains that link within itself, with its dual senses of 'complete' and 'unadorned'. Yet the poem's 'plein' style is everywhere tied to the functional conventions of discursive practices of careful examination by 'opposition'. Early on Amans promises to 'pleinly telle [...] oute' an account of his calamitous love, 'fro point to point I wol declare' (Book I, lines 71 and 73); Genius asserts that all asked or said in shrift must be 'plein' and unpainted (Book I, lines 282–4); he further indexes the plainness of his speech when reminding Amans of its didactic aims:

> That I wole axe of the forthi,
> My Sone, it schal be so pleinly,
> That thou schalt knowe and understonde
> The pointz of schrifte how that thei stonde.
>
> (Book I, lines 285–8)

Again, a point-by-point conversation organizes the 'plein', compendious material of the poem. Again, this will be effected by a functional, plain style that facilitates understanding. This style, of course, is a vernacular one. The plainness of English recommends it for the expert interrogative mode of the *Confessio* that Gower proposes as the fundamental structure of his poetic composition.

While Genius anticipates proceeding plainly, point by point, through the catalogue of Amans's sins of love, the *Confessio Amantis* elsewhere imagines alternative interactions between the audience and the poem, alternatives that are hardly so exhaustive. In his prologue, Gower sets out to write a versatile work that can furnish selective entertainment and education:

> I wolde go the middel weie
> And wryte a bok betwene the tweie,
> Somwhat of lust, somwhat of lore,

clear and unornamented, in Chaucer, Gower, and Trevisa (including to mean a plain style of writing).

That of the lasse or of the more
Som man mai lyke of that I wryte.

(Prologue, lines 17–21)

Elsewhere Gower resolves to:

[W]rite in such a maner wise,
Which may be wisdom to the wise
And pley to hem that lust to pleye.

(Prologue, lines 83–5*)

The material collected in the *Confessio* suits such personally selective readings. Gower announces the *Confessio* as an assemblage of narrative forms in his Prologue. A Latin prose commentary in the First Recension describes it as a 'little book', 'zealously compiled […] from various chronicles, histories, and sayings of poets and philosophers, like a honeycomb gathered from various flowers'.[28] Gower collects the poem's component parts from diverse genres and from diverse sources, and arranges them into a work which promises to provide pleasure and education. Pleasure *or* education, too – his readers will come to the text seeking lust or lore in different measures. Some look for wisdom, others for play. But these experiences are facilitated by the certain 'maner wise' through which this wisdom and play are presented.

Gower's various 'flowers' of narrative are not gathered unsystematically into a bundle, but compiled according to the dialogic, confessional structure inaugurated in Book I. Medieval bedside manner prescribed its own 'maner wise' for administering narrative, to be practised by those attending to the sick. John of Arderne recommended that his readers complement the practices of good professional speech outlined above with a repertoire of talk of a different kind:

Also it spedeth þat a leche kunne talke of gode taleȝ and of honest that may make þe pacientes to laugh, as wele of the biblee as of other

---

28   I quote Andrew Galloway's translation of the marginal prose commentary of the Prologue as preserved in the margins of Second Recension manuscripts of the *Confessio*, annotating line 34 of the Prologue. The Latin, in Macaulay's edition, reads: 'set tanquam fauum ex variis floribus recollectum, presentem labellum ex variis cronicis, historiis, poetarum philosophorumque dictis, quatenus sibi infirmitas permisit, studiosissime compilauit'.

tragedie3; & any othir of which it is no3t to charge while3 þat þey make
or induce a li3t hert to þe pacient or þe sike man.

(8)

The leech, then, needs to be a circumspect tale-teller. His store of
good and honest tales should be diverse. Some of these tales should
make patients laugh. Both biblical tales and tragedies can potentially
alleviate a heavy heart, though John's reader should be discerning in
selecting them. Fictions of different kinds belong in the leech's repertoire of speech, to be called upon in moments of medical crisis during
which a little levity would do the patient good. John trains readers in
the pragmatic literary practices of medical speech, with little respect
for distinctions that oppose comedies to tragedies ('gode tale3 [...]
that may make þe pacientes to laugh' and 'tragedie3'). Tales to provoke
laughter, tales of the Bible, and tragedies share equal status as rudiments
of useful medical narration. The 'good and honest tale' becomes one
more component of medically expert speech among the many John
recommends: the introduction, the table comment, the proverb, the
prognostication, the occasional tale.

Specific medical crises could call for storytelling. In the *Confessio
Amantis*, Amans's lovesickness attracts Venus's concerned – and explicitly
medical – attentions. Lovesickness is one such crisis of health that calls
for narrative treatment. Stories, songs, and poems prevent the patient
from sinking into the 'excessive thoughts' symptomatic of the lovesick
one's fixation upon a beautiful form.[29] Avicenna recommends drinking
wine, conversation, and admiring beautiful gardens or people in his
Canon medicinae. The *Viaticum* includes among these prescriptions the
recitation of poetry to the patient.[30] The lovesick condition of Amans,
then, is not merely an ornamental trope, decorating the poem's narratives around their edges; lovesickness inflects the immediate relation
between its component narratives and its readers with a pragmatic
quality. A medical crisis conditions and necessitates a narrative regimen,
and so Amans's predicament points directly to the salutary quality of the
enjoyment of these tales.

29   See Mary Wack, *Lovesickness in the Middle Ages* (Philadelphia, 1996), 39–40.
See also Ellen Shaw Bakalian, *Aspects of Love in the 'Confessio Amantis'* (New
York, 2004).
30   Wack edits and translates Constantine the African's translation of Ibn al
Jazzar's *Viaticum* in *Lovesickness*, 45–6.

The enjoyment of fictions – judiciously selected and well told – was not only a means of critical intervention but a wholesome pastime.[31] First, it was thought healthy to be happy. 'Take away your heavy cares, and refrain from anger', instructs the very first stanza of the *Regimen sanitatis*, a popular regimen of health; consult that good doctor, the 'joyful mind'.[32] In Pseudo-Aristotle's mirror for princes, the *Secreta secretorum*, the recommended means to gladness are familiar ones from the cures of lovesickness: 'behold beauteuous parsonis, and delectabil bookis, and here pleasaunt songis, and be in cumpany of such as a man louith'.[33] These recommendations of good company (for both admiration and conversation) and of pleasant entertainment in the *Secreta* again emphasize the enjoyment of pleasures as an efficacious and crucial aspect of hygienic rectitude, and, by extension, of good princely conduct. The Latin *Secreta* recommends reading books, watching games or plays (*ludis*), admiring beautiful things, donning recreational raiment, and listening to music, all as means to salutary royal *gaudium*.[34] Pseudo-Aristotle adds, at another point, conference with 'wise people, seeking after matters of past and future' and 'strengthening the powers of reason'.[35] Roger Bacon glosses the verb *conferre*: 'id est, confabulare', denoting a more explicitly engaged form of conference.[36] Bacon's clarification insists that the king take pleasure in active participation in conversation, beyond paying gracious attention. The king is to enjoy conversations on topics of policy and virtue, with suitably wise interlocutors, just as he is to enjoy poetry, games, and good company.

Confabulation as talk with the wise brought salutary pleasures. Fictions, too, were incorporated in this health-giving species of literary enjoyment. The *Tacuinum sanitatis* (*Tables of Health*) prescribes 'confabulatio', administered as narrative, as a remedy for insomnia: 'doctors advise people with cold hearts to have stories told to them that provoke

---

31   See chapter 1 of Glending Olson, *Literature as Recreation in the Middle Ages* (Ithaca, NY, 1982).
32   Quoted and translated in Olson, *Literature as Recreation*, 52.
33   *'Secretum secretorum': Nine English Versions*, vol. 1, ed. M. A. Manzalaoui, EETS o.s. 276 (Oxford, 1977), 8.
34   *Secretum secretorum*, ed. Robert Steele, *Opera hactenus inedita Rogeri Baconi*, fasc. V (Oxford, 1920), 82, 95. Translations are mine.
35   *Secretum secretorum*, ed. Steele, 95.
36   See Charlton T. Lewis and Charles Short, *A Latin Dictionary* (Oxford, 1879), s.v. 'confabulor'.

anger, and those with hot hearts stories that entail pity.'[37] The mind then tires in responding with delight or anger. This bedside conversation should be 'delightful, with fitting verbal adornment' ('delectabiles debent esse ornatu verborum').[38] Crafting such a discerning and well-composed conversation requires special expertise, and the *Tacuinum* recommends the employment of a professional practitioner of narrative therapy, or a *confabulator*, whom it describes at length:

> *Confabulator*: A teller of stories should have good discernment in knowing the kind of fictions in which the soul takes delight, should be able to shorten or extend his presentation of stories as he may choose, and to decorate, amplify, and arrange them as is fitting. He should not alter his appearance in conversation, nor should the purpose of the confabulator be interfered with by too much talking. A *confabulator* should be proper in manner and in courtesy, be able to stay awake, be a good judge of discourses (not only histories of great princes but also delightful stories that provoke laughter) and be conscious of verses and rhymes, so that through these things a prince may gain an abundance of pleasures. For his digestion will improve because of them, and his *spiritus* and blood will be purified, and he will be freed from all sorts of troubling thoughts, and his memory sharpened for the common talk and occurrences that well up around him.[39]

The *confabulator* of the *Tacuinum* must inform his practice with a familiar kind of expert discernment, answerable to both literary sensibility and pragmatic, medical *savoir-faire*. The confabulator must be a deft versifier who can tailor verse forms to the occasion, and employ the rhetorical strategies of decoration and amplification to good effect. The stuff of *fabula* becomes the raw material for the confabulator's artful remaking into a colloquial regimen. The desired effect is the salutary

---

37   The Arabic *Tacuinum sanitatis* (*Tables of Health*) of Ibn Buṭlān was translated into Latin in the thirteenth century. It circulated in aristocratic circles as a personal guide for hygiene; many sumptuously illustrated copies are extant, mostly in Italy. A thirteenth-century copy of the work, Paris, Bibliothèque nationale de France, MS Lat. 6977, is known to have been in the French royal library in the early fifteenth century, but found its way into the hands of poet Charles d'Orléans some time after the dissolution of the library in 1429. Quoted in Olson, *Literature as Recreation*, 81.

38   Olson, *Literature as Recreation*, 82.

39   Translated in Olson, *Literature as Recreation*, 82–3.

delight of the soul. The *Tacuinum* teaches readers to expect a confabulator who can converse with purpose and with careful professionalism. The confabulator's manner is marked by staid restraint in gesture and appearance, an aversion to small talk, and courtesy. Along with effecting an improvement in the patient's physical condition, the confabulator's art assures the listener a freedom from troubling thoughts and a sharper acuity with which to respond to everyday talk (*rumoribus*) and occurrences (*eventibus*). The confabulator's literary craft promises to hone the mind for cutting through the disorderly speech of social life.

The confabulator's practice manipulates both genre and form as crucial dimensions of a particular medical expertise, and puts the formal and generic character of literary speech in the pragmatic service of bedside manner. While John of Arderne intends for the surgeon's diverse tales to lighten the heart similarly, the *Tacuinum* imagines the various pleasures of various narratives as discrete – and even opposed – accidents of the soul. The pleasures of an enraging tale and those of a pitiful one manifest bodily as accidents of opposite effect. The confabulator uses discretion to select poems and tales with generic precision, recognizing the 'kinds of fiction' proper to the circumstances. The 'histories of great princes' have their place at the bedside; so too do 'delightful stories that provoke laughter'. The conversational expertise of the confabulator in the *Tacuinum* motivates and structures this seeming riot of genres – the collection of princely histories together with the lighter fare of comic tales.

Medieval instructions in bedside manner articulated a set of conventions for the expert and discerning composition of a narrative course of treatment. Bedside manner prescribed uses for literary genres like histories and good tales of the Bible. But in the end, all these generic narratives are constituent elements of a genre of a higher order, an expert form of forensic conversation designed for pastoral and medical practice. These medieval colloquial genres have their own conventions, which shape how readers would approach an encounter with a lengthy collection of narrative and didactic material. How might Gower's introductory impersonation of these genres of expert conversation in Book I orient his readers to the reading experience before them?

In this sense, these genres of expert conversation themselves operate generically in the poem. Genres entail an implicit understanding between a text and its reader, by invoking some familiar conventional standard. A text may present itself as a history of a great prince; the reader proceeds with expectations for this narrative learned through some prior experiences with other histories of great princes. Genres, then, propose 'provisional schema[ta]' that promise to structure the experience to come, as genres do in E. D. Hirsch's classic formulation.[40] Fredric Jameson, too, imagines genres to signal to readers a certain understanding: they are 'social contracts between a writer and a specific public, whose function is to specify the proper use of a particular cultural artifact'.[41] But Gower enters into one new generic contract after another as Genius narrates one tale after another. The *Confessio* is a mélange of narrative forms we would call genres – like the popular romance, the philosophical anecdote, and *exemplum* – interspersed with digressions into mythography and *fürstenspiegel*.[42] Criticism has responded to this puzzling conglomeration by proposing an authorial logic at work behind the seemingly haphazard, even antagonistic, arrangement of diverse narrative genres. George Shuffleton describes (and challenges) a variously articulated critical consensus that the *Confessio Amantis* stages a conflict between the escapism of romance and the poem's thoroughgoing moral vision, with its imposition of readerly self-reflection.[43] Shuffleton rightly argues that Gower, rather than exploit generic conflict, integrates narrative genres; there is a 'remarkable *lack* of conflict at the "surface" of the text, where different genres and styles interact without a hint of tension or even explicit acknowledgment that such differences exist' (81). Through all this debate about genre in the *Confessio*, though, 'genre' has remained a term of taxonomy that sorts the poem's narratives into different kinds, and gives them the name of, say, romance. But Gower's conversational frame for all these narratives might be understood to entail a genre concept of its own, which specifies to readers how to use the text.

What is the 'proper use' of the *Confessio*, then, proposed by the poem's opening affiliation with the genres of pastoral and medical *conversatio* in Book I? With this more expansive sense of what genres

40   E. D. Hirsch, *Validity in Interpretation* (New Haven, 1967). Quoted in Paul Strohm, 'Middle English Narrative Genres', *Genre* 13 (1980), 379–88 (385).

41   Fredric Jameson, *The Political Unconscious* (Ithaca, NY, 1981), 106.

42   These final three can be found respectively in the *Confessio Amantis* at Book IV, lines 2396–56 and 2606–71; Book V, lines 47–1496; and the whole of Book VII. On the first, see Ernst Robert Curtius, *European Literature and the Latin Middle Ages*, trans. Willard R. Trask (New York, 1953), 548.

43   George Shuffleton, 'Romance, Popular Style and the *Confessio Amantis*: Conflict or Evasion?', in *John Gower: Trilingual Poet*, ed. Elisabeth Dutton (Cambridge, 2010), 74–84.

do in mind, we can begin to see that the pragmatic kinds of conventionalized expert conversation which introduce and frame Gower's dream
vision themselves function as literary genres. His poetic rendition of
conversation suggests its own provisional schema for the reading of
the *Confessio*, in proposing to imitate these conventional scripts of
dialogic encounter to structure the literary experience to come. When
a medieval literary work frames its own narrative regimen with a dual
appeal to these two conversational genres, it implies the conversational
expertise of the *medicus* and *sacerdos* in the logic of its composition and
asks the reader to understand its structure on those terms. The *Confessio
Amantis*, then, might be reconsidered as a textual confabulation; it
invites its readers to see in its frame a practical logic underpinning its
idiosyncratic assembly of diverse genres. The poem encourages readers
to profit from a 'confabulated' experience with the text's lust and lore.

The confessional frame facilitates diverse ways of navigating across
the poem's vast territory according to readers' momentary concerns and
caprices. The practical realities of medieval literary culture habituated in
readers a historically specific literacy fit to cope with such conglomerate
productions. As Julie Orlemanski reminds us, medieval readers' generic
sensibilities were cultivated by reading *florilegia*, collections of *exempla*,
and miscellaneous manuscript compilations which invite 'eclectic
performances of reading' of precisely the kind I argue for here.[44] These
conglomerate textual forms trouble the phenomenological notion of
genre, which assumes literary reading to be a linear experience wherein
generic expectations are initiated, and then fulfilled or flouted over its
course.[45] A readerly feel for genre must cooperate with medieval texts'
other organizing patterns and paratexts, which medieval literacy attuned
readers to expect, utilize and respond to. These conglomerate kinds
of text index how literary practitioners (authors, compilers, scribes)
encouraged and enabled the reader to move freely, discriminately, and
uniquely across the text's terrain. By these lights, the *habitus* of medieval
literacy draws its own itinerary through an experience with the text.[46]

---

44   Julie Orlemanski, 'Genre', in *A Handbook of Middle English Studies*, ed.
Marion Turner (Chichester, 2013), 216.
45   See Hans Robert Jauss's classic account of genre and the horizon of expectations in 'Literary History as a Challenge to Literary Theory', *New Literary History*
2.1 (1970), 7–37.
46   On Pierre Bourdieu's concept of *habitus*, see *A Handbook of Middle English
Studies*, ed. Turner, 212–3.

This has consequences, then, for how we understand the frame's effect on the experience of reading the poem. Gerald Kinneavy argued some time ago that confessional technique is the 'organizing' and 'working principle' of the *Confessio*, a poem that we 'read through [...] and arrive at the end' of.[47] Reading like this assumes that the poem's confessional regimen dictates a linear reading process. Much criticism of the *Confessio Amantis* takes for granted such a practice of linear reading, and Gower's accommodation of it, in offering readings that trace the moral education and rehabilitation of Amans over the long course of its eight books.[48] The poem's confessional frame, however, equally abets readings that fork and wind through the poem, permuting its narratives into a bespoke literary experience of pleasure and moral profit. In response critics have argued for more eclectic ways to read the poem. Siân Echard describes a tendency of early readers to 'ransack' the *Confessio* for their favourite tales.[49] Indeed, Gower seems to have left his poem conspicuously well stocked, unlocked, and unattended. The genres of expert conversation that open the *Confessio* actively invite these eclectic readings that ransack the poem according to whim, circumstance, and an impulse to readerly experiment. Readers are invited not to read it from the beginning to arrive at an end but to ransack it for the literary experience they want, or need, or both.

This argument elaborates upon scholarship on the *Confessio* that encourages us to imagine less exhaustive practices of reading the poem. The poem's confessional frame facilitates this mode of reading in cooperation with the interpolated Latin verses and prose commentaries by the author, as well as the non-authorial indexes that eventually accreted to the poem, and have been described by Echard.[50] Throughout the poem, Genius and Amans pause between

47   Gerald Kinneavy, 'Gower's *Confessio Amantis* and the Penitentials', *Chaucer Review* 19.2 (1984), 144–61.

48   Readings in this vein include C. S. Lewis, *Allegory of Love* (Oxford, 1936); Simpson, *Sciences and the Self*, in which the *Confessio* is seen as a *bildungsroman* that subordinates its narratives to a 'psychological allegory of the individual soul' (13); and Peter Nicholson, *Love and Ethics* (Ann Arbor, 2005), in which the confessional frame 'imposes comprehensiveness' (96).

49   Siân Echard, 'Dialogues and Monologues: Manuscript Representations of the Conversation of the *Confessio Amantis*', in *Middle English Poetry: Texts and Traditions*, ed. A. J. Minnis (York, 2001), 57–76 (59).

50   See Siân Echard, 'Pre-texts: Tables of Contents and the Reading of John Gower's *Confessio Amantis*', *Medium Ævum* 66.2 (1997), 270–87.

tales to reflect upon the deliberate, instructive ends of its narratives. These pauses for conversation recollect the narrated material to arrive at some newly articulated conclusion; in this way, Gower serially dramatizes moments of generic and thematic inflection and reorientation where readers move from one narrative to the next. In its moralizing, the *Confessio* proposes certain remedial effects imagined for each tale while mimicking expert dialogic practice. But these moments of reflective exchange also mark out the poem's divisions into exemplary tales. Genius and Amans point to this function of their 'opposition' when the conversation pivots toward new topical and thematic material and certain moral realities are expounded.[51] The Latin speaker markers that signal shifts in the conversational voice of the frame conveniently flag these points on the manuscript page for readers. 'Amans', 'Confessor', and sometimes 'Opponit Confessor', 'Respondet Amans', collect in the manuscript margins of copies of the *Confessio*, often in red ink, to flag for readers where one tale ends and another will soon begin.[52] The framing conversation, then, turns the impersonated speech of these expert genres into a tissue of cues and comment that, visually and discursively, dismantles the poem into its exemplary narrative units for readers' selective enjoyment and education. The manuscripts of the *Confessio* aided readers in experiencing the poem as textual confabulation, and in fashioning a bespoke literary encounter, by presenting the text's lust and lore on the page in such a way as to facilitate such selection.

Gower himself built the poem for dynamic performance contexts that would have invited confabulation, as curated by professional literary expertise. Joyce Coleman has argued that the poem's 'hard Latin' would have required a learned translator – an 'interpres' whom Gower names in its opening Latin verse heading – to present the poem in its bilingual fullness to a courtly audience.[53] This *interpres*, Coleman imagines, was an aural performer who might 'enliven [...] the event with periodic bouts of code-switching, turning from a relatively restrained reading of the English to a showier style of prelection appropriate to the

51   See, for instance, Book IV, lines 884–6: 'Bot yit of Slowthe hou it hath ferd / In other wise I thenke oppose, / If thou have gult, as I suppose.' Other such moments occur at Book I, lines 569–74, 1227–34, 2384–93, and 2678–80.

52   See Echard, 'Dialogues and Monologues'.

53   'Ossibus ergo carens que conterit ossa loquelis / Absit, et *interpres* stet procul oro malus.' Book I, versus I, lines 5–6, emphasis mine.

self-display of the Latin verses'.[54] Coleman argues that Gower designed the *Confessio* with this kind of court reading in mind, crafting its hard Latin for an *interpres* to then reshape for the 'social reality' of its reception through adept public performance (233). The job of the *interpres* was no easy one, requiring a 'combination of academic, literary, and pastoral skills and interests'.[55] Candidates for such a position in the Lancastrian affinity included Richard Maidstone (d.1396), translator of the Penitential Psalms, deft versifier of the Anglo-Latin *Concordia*, and confessor to John of Gaunt. Men like Maidstone, occupied by both literary and pastoral activity, have been cast in the role of 'literary confessor' by Coleman and others, performing a role in John of Gaunt's court to mirror the fictive one of Genius within the poem.[56] So the *interpres* curates one performance of a poem for a particular readership with particular effects in mind. In imagining and enabling this form of presentation, Gower provided the flexible material for the salutary, courtly *confabulatio* recommended by Pseudo-Aristotle in his *Secreta secretorum*. The poet would have, after all, seen in that wise adviser something of a model: it was thought that Aristotle wrote the *Secreta* as a textual surrogate for his presence at the prince's side. Pseudo-Aristotle, like Gower, suffered from debilitating sickness, and instead sent a book for Alexander's sake.[57]

When Gower impersonates confessional conversation to write a poem after that form, he transposes its discursive conventions and forms of address into his poetic manner as a style of literary address. When he frames his poem's confessional conversation with a medical conversation, he invites readers to not only remember their analogical relationship as expert practices of forensic speech, but also to approach the text mindful of the pragmatic ends of the expert's circumspect style and language. Gower invokes the manner of medical talk to recast his

---

54   Coleman, 'Lay Readers and Hard Latin: How Gower may have Intended the *Confessio Amantis* to be Read', *Studies in the Age of Chaucer* 24 (2002), 209–34 (229).

55   Ibid., 230.

56   Ibid., 232; Carlson, 93–109; Irvin, 93.

57   In a Middle English translation of the *Secreta*, the prologue describes Aristotle's reasons for compiling a text of princely advice: 'This book made this forseyd Aristotille in his gret age, whan he myght not travayle ne done the nedis that he had in charge of Alexandre.' See Robert Steele, *Three Prose Versions of the Secreta Secretorum*, EETS e.s. 74 (London, 1898), 3. Middle English translation from the French in London, British Library, MS Royal 18 A vii, fol. 2.

own literary practice as an expert practice of making language into something that is both useful and pleasant. His poetry becomes useful because it is pleasing. In this way he recommends himself as confabulator to princes with this achievement in plain style and judicious choice of entertainments. (So we see some logic in Gower's interruption from his penitential scheme with a digression into *fürstenspiegel* in Book VII.) Gower imbues his vernacular poetry with an expert potency to claim the attentions of its imputed sovereign reader and dedicatee, Richard II. And for those of his readers who are mere subjects, he encourages a vicarious readerly practice that can simulate that expertly eclectic practice of confabulation, and curates an experience with its own abundance of pleasures, whether that pleasure is found in the poem's tracts of wisdom or stretches of play.

7

Vitreous Visions

Stained Glass and Affective Engagement in John Lydgate's *The Temple of Glass**

BOYDA JOHNSTONE

Stained glass features prominently in both Geoffrey Chaucer's celebrated dream vision *The House of Fame* and John Lydgate's fifteenth-century adaptation of it, *The Temple of Glass*. How are we to understand its function in these poems? While the walls of Venus's temple in *Fame* contain a single narrative of Troy, Lydgate's walls in *Temple* are packed with detail:

> I sawe depeynted upon every wal,
> From eest to west, many a feyre ymage
> Of sondry lovers, lyche as they were of age
> Sett by ordre right as they were truwe,
> With lyfly colours wonder fresshe of huwe.
>
> $(44–8)^1$

---

* I am deeply thankful for the input of various readers throughout the process of writing and revising this article, especially Jocelyn Wogan-Browne, but also Nina Rowe, Megan Cook, David Coley, Alexandra Verini, David Klassen, and the very thorough and generous comments of the anonymous readers of *NML*. This project grew out of a conference panel organized by Tom Goodmann at the 2014 New Chaucer Society congress in Reykjavík, Iceland.

1 In this article, I quote from Julia Boffey's edition of *The Temple of Glass* in *Fifteenth-Century English Dream Visions*, which treats London, British Library, Additional MS 16165 as its base text (Oxford, 2007). I have also relied upon her edition for modern translations of difficult passages. Mitchell's edition is based on the alternative version found in Oxford, Bodleian Library, MS Tanner 346 (*Temple of Glas*, TEAMS Middle English Texts Series (Kalamazoo, MI, 2007)). The main difference between the two versions is the ending, though Boffey's version from Add. MS 16165 also situates the lady within a broader community

By my count, *Temple* makes explicit note of twenty-two stories captured in the walls, and even these are only a selection; the space is crowded with 'many an hundred thousand here and there' (144) who bring their complaints and supplications to Venus. This article, then, attempts to make sense of Lydgate's refashioning of Chaucer's temple as an almost excessively detailed and teeming environment.

A brief detour through the extant stained glass of Lydgate's era will help illustrate my reading of the aesthetic programmes of these texts. Great Malvern Priory in Worcestershire, England holds the largest complete collection of fifteenth-century stained glass on display in a parish church. But visitors eager to experience this remarkable reserve may soon be disappointed when they discover that, in fact, much of the glass has been subject to slipshod reconstructive techniques. Although the glass survived the dissolution of the monasteries under Henry VIII, by the nineteenth century the windows were in need of major repairs due to environmental damage, graffiti, and the general effects of time. Consequently, gaps in larger panels were filled with medieval glass from smaller windows, and a generally haphazard reconfiguration carried out by inexperienced glaziers has produced, in the present, something resembling a poorly executed jigsaw puzzle.[2]

Yet the windows are still magnificent in their arrangement. It is not just the contents of the windows that convey meaning, but also the effect of light streaming through them, and the collective power of the ensemble. Like medieval drama, which does not depend on realism for its appeal but rather on the moral and ludic effects it has on its audience, medieval glass too found means of acting upon its beholders beyond conveying information or symbolic iconography.

---

of victimized women and establishes jealousy as a universal problem among men (see lines 496–516, not found in Mitchell). An article by Norton-Smith remains influential in accounting for the three separate versions of the poem, though Mitchell notes that Norton-Smith's theory that Lydgate's three versions represent a process of revision has been discredited (John Norton-Smith, 'Lydgate's Changes in the *Temple of Glas*', *Medium Ævum* 27 (1958), 166–72; cf. Mitchell's Introduction to his edition of *Temple of Glas*, unpaginated). Rather it seems that the poem was occasionally altered and revised by readers, and fragments extant in manuscripts – including the major sixteenth-century Scottish anthology, the Bannatyne Manuscript – further indicate that 'the poem was something to be plundered and used piecemeal' (Mitchell, Introduction to *Temple of Glas*).
2 Katherine Wells, *A Tour of the Stained Glass at Great Malvern Priory* ([Malvern], 2013), 7.

It was designed additionally to influence visitors' emotions and usher them into a more personal, sacred experience of the interior space; both distinct from and opening a channel to the outside world, it combines iconographic mythology with light in colour to enclose visitors in a dazzling, heightened architectural experience. And Great Malvern Priory's vitreous programme, the victim of centuries of environmental damage, careless reconstructions, and removal and storage during the Second World War, still emanates these effects, being breath-taking and sobering in its scale and intricacy.

Gothic architecture, with its large-scale designs and multiple windows, had goals beyond conveying the edifying details of biblical stories. According to Grodecki and Brisac, it aimed to construct 'walls of light, like the Heavenly Jerusalem of the Apocalypse, built of translucent precious stones'.[3] Viewers confronted with these glittering walls may have been 'overcome by the expressive force of the ensemble rather than by an analysis of details'.[4] Anne Harris similarly focuses on stained glass's performative qualities as a medium for the play of light and colour. She asserts that 'unlike other visual media, which remain within the discrete boundary of their material frames, stained glass exceeds its materiality. Its colours steal beyond its architecture, marking sunlight; its tracery is heavy or light, plotting characters and stories, or dissolving narrative into a kaleidoscopic array'.[5] Geoffrey Chaucer himself demonstrates his familiarity with these effects when, in the *Book of the Duchess*, the narrator describes how within the dream:

My wyndowes were shette echon
And throgh the glas the sone shon

3   Louis Grodecki and Catherine Brisac, *Gothic Stained Glass, 1200–1330* (Ithaca, NY, 1984), 18. Grodecki and Brisac argue that many stories depicted in the Sainte-Chapelle in Paris, for instance, are repetitive and 'incomprehensible […] it is rare to find intact a unified iconographic program inspired by a single directing thought' (ibid., 22).
4   Ibid., 24. See also Beth Williamson's discussion in 'Sensory Experience in Medieval Devotion: Sound and Vision, Invisibility and Silence', *Speculum* 88.1 (2013), 1–43 (32–3).
5   Anne Harris, 'Glazing and Glossing: Stained Glass as Literary Interpretation', *Journal of Glass Studies* 56 (2014), 303–16 (303). See also Nancy Thompson's 'Close Encounters with Luminous Objects: Reflections on Studying Stained Glass', in *Transparent Things: A Cabinet*, ed. Maggie M. Williams and Karen Eileen Overbey (New York, 2013), 57–67.

Upon my bed with bryght bemys,
With many glade gilde stremys.[6]

Light shining through glass works to draw the disparate objects of
interior spaces together in synchronic moments. As time passes, light
changes and alters its environment, even though the physical space
remains the same. Stained glass is thus distinct in its ability to reach
beyond its materiality and dazzle the eye with walls of light, intentionally
incorporating affective response within its aesthetic agenda. It is a
medium at once fixed and rigid in its architectural casing – its glass and
its lead struts – and yet highly fluid and dynamic in its performance as a
wielder of light, working in tandem with the surrounding architectural
assemblage to shape the viewer's response.

Medieval poetry, too, has effects beyond the symbolic nature of its
contents and narrative action, and it shares with stained glass certain
formal features, such as narrative fragmentation and an emphasis on
emotion and affect as constitutive elements of the reception experience.
Stained glass typifies both the paratactic but unglossed logic of
dream events joined together without explanation, and their ability
nonetheless to engage and transform response. This article suggests
that a deeper understanding of stained glass can supply revealing
insights into the performance of medieval dream visions, particularly
those that themselves position glazed programmes as a central feature
of their dreamer's encounter with oneiric material. I will examine two
representative visions, Chaucer's *The House of Fame* and Lydgate's
underappreciated remobilization of it, *The Temple of Glass*, in order to
demonstrate the power that stained-glass aesthetics could enact within
late medieval texts. In both poems, stained glass plays a prominent role
in engaging the dreamers in a journey of understanding and affective
disorientation; in essence, these texts translate a visual aesthetic into
a literary aesthetic. After analysing the hermeneutic significance of
Geffrey's sensorial absorption within the walls in Book I of *Fame*, I
trace in *Temple* the play of light through the walls and characters in
order to position Lydgate's use of stained glass within fifteenth-century
debates about the power and dangers of art and its performances, both
for devotional practices and in courtly love. Light streaming through

6   Geoffrey Chaucer, *The Book of the Duchess*, ed. Helen Phillips, in *Chaucer's
Dream Poetry*, ed. Helen Phillips and Nick Havely, Longman Annotated Texts
(London, 1997), lines 335–8.

the walls and suturing together the bodies and ontologies of characters contributes to a sense that *Temple* in all its dreamlike wonder is more impressionistic than realist, enacting the expressive power of stained glass.

This study, then, is more interested in effect and experience than detail and literary allusion, which is perhaps more in tune with how poems would in the fourteenth and fifteenth centuries have been read or listened to by ordinary people. While Lydgate's poetry is character-istically thick with allusions, stock phrases, and epithets, fixating on those details fails to recognize that the sum of the whole can amount to more than that which these cultural symbols signify. John M. Bowers ruminates on this question of reception and the necessary level of education needed for full textual comprehension: 'for those of us who labor diligently in the classroom to instruct our students in the basics of our own culture, we cannot help wondering whether medieval audiences, too, needed teachers to educate them in this sophisticated and often obscure pictorial language'.[7] Medieval audiences, especially those who *listened to* rather than individually read poems, would not all have possessed the training necessary to comprehend the rich cultural layering that characterizes late medieval literary texts, but this does not mean they would not have enjoyed them. In fact, a lack of understanding of the symbolism may offer certain advantages to approaching medieval poetry, clearing space for the atmospheric disorientation that can only come from a new artistic experience.

Medieval Stained Glass and *The House of Fame*

Chaucer in *The House of Fame* demonstrates his familiarity with the effects of glass by characterizing the walls in Venus's temple as materially permeable and emotionally captivating. It is inevitable that he as well as other medieval authors would have been influenced by the splendid

---

7   John M. Bowers, 'Speaking Images? Iconographic Criticism and Chaucerian Ekphrasis', in *The Art of Vision: Ekphrasis in Medieval Literature and Culture*, ed. Andrew James Johnston, Ethan Knapp, and Margitta Rouse (Columbus, OH, 2015), 55–76 (59). V. A. Kolve makes similar comments about the relative privilege and rarity of medieval 'close reading' practices whereby all allusions could be traced (*Chaucer and the Imagery of Narrative: The First Five Canterbury Tales* (Stanford, CA, 1984), 17–18).

imagery they encountered in major architectural structures. Twelfth-and thirteenth-century designs encouraged affective engagements with the contents and effects of the panes, surpassing the contemplative, detached, and hierarchical systems of previous layouts. Abbot Suger's twelfth-century alterations made the stained glass of the cathedral at Saint-Denis more immediately accessible to viewers by placing it within a 'closer, taller, wider medium with radically less masonry' separating the glass surfaces, thereby creating an 'overwhelming effect of sensory saturation, as opposed to the independently working, isolated windows cut off by deep chapels of the older design'.[8] Similarly the thirteenth-century construction of the façade of Wells Cathedral depended on polychromatic design for its windows and sculptures, in an evocation of the dreamlike structures of heaven.[9] The Becket Miracle windows (1205–20) in Canterbury Cathedral detail various miracles posthumously performed by the saint and position these images close to the viewer's eye, in contrast to older allegorical versions of saints and biblical figures, such as the twelfth-century Genealogy of Christ series. The windows participate in the transformation of the cathedral from 'elite (contemplative) to popular (performative) culture' as they coaxed pilgrims closer to the saint and his stories – even as other areas, such as the clerestory, remained difficult to perceive.[10]

The fourteenth and fifteenth centuries saw stained glass appearing in both religious and secular spaces, featuring in churches, chapels, manor houses, palaces, and university colleges; by the fifteenth century, stained glass was more omnipresent and multifaceted than ever before. Windows in churches such as Merton College at Oxford, the great York Minster, Exeter Cathedral, Eaton Bishop church, St Stephen's chapel and St Edmund's chapel at Westminster, and a priory church at Chetwode

8   Conrad Rudolph, *Artistic Change at St-Denis: Abbot Suger's Program and The Early Twelfth-Century Controversy Over Art* (Princeton, 1990), 67. See also Robert Rosewell, *Medieval Wall Paintings in English and Welsh Churches* (Woodbridge, 2008); and Christopher Woodforde, *The Norwich School of Glass-Painting in the Fifteenth Century* (London, 1950).

9   See Carolyn Marino Malone, *Façade as Spectacle: Ritual and Ideology at Wells Cathedral* (Leiden, 2004), esp. ch. 3, 'The Production of Signs'.

10   Anne Harris, 'Pilgrimage, Performance, and Stained Glass at Canterbury Cathedral', in *Art and Architecture of Late Medieval Pilgrimage in Northern Europe and the British Isles*, ed. S. Blick and R. Tekippe (Leiden, 2004), 243–81 (255, 254). See also Wolfgang Kemp, *The Narratives of Gothic Stained Glass*, trans. Caroline Dobson Saltzwedel (Cambridge, 1997).

in Buckinghamshire, were developed in the fourteenth century, and the fifteenth century saw vitreous programmes constructed at Eton College, King's College Cambridge, Eltham Palace, the Beauchamp Chapel, and Great Malvern Priory, among others.[11] Silver (sometimes called yellow) stain, a combination of silver sulphide and white glass which turns yellow when fired, reached England from Normandy in the early fourteenth century, allowing for multiple colours to be achieved in one piece of glass, and attaining greater sculptural, luminescent effects.[12] By the end of his reign, the rooms of Henry III's palace were filled with glazing, though decorated glass remained a luxury item.[13] Additionally, payment in 1431–2 by the Earl of Oxford makes references to repairs made to a room evocatively called the 'Glaschambre'.[14] Henry IV's study at Eltham Palace, rebuilt in the early fifteenth century, contained seven impressive stained-glass windows, decorated with birds, beasts, various saints, and devotional scenes, created by the same glazier who supplied glass for Westminster Hall, their area totalling 78 feet 4 inches square.[15] Medieval people had regular access to the wonders of decorated glass, and sometimes commissioned works that bridged the divide between material and literary arts: in a window at All Saints' church in York, portions of *The Prick of Conscience* dealing with the fifteen signs of doomsday were rendered, in both textual and visual form, around 1410–20.[16]

Even though Chaucer's and Lydgate's temples are not exclusively made of vitreous materials, glass is a predominant material within both poems and a key to understanding their uncertain properties. Consider the well-known description in *The House of Fame*:

> But, as I slepte, me mette I was
> Withyn a *temple ymade of glas*,

---

11   See Richard Marks, *Stained Glass in England during the Middle Ages* (Toronto, 1993).

12   Ibid., 38.

13   C. M. Woolgar, *The Great Household in Late Medieval England* (New Haven, 1999), 72–3.

14   Ibid., 73.

15   Jenny Stratford, 'The Early Royal Collections and the Royal Library to 1461', in *The Cambridge History of the Book in Britain*, vol. 3: *1400–1557*, ed. Lotte Hellinga and J. B. Trapp (Cambridge, 1999), 255–66 (260).

16   For more on this window, see Robert Rosewell, 'The Pricke of Conscience or the Fifteen Signs of Doom Window in the Church of All Saints, North Street, York', *Vidimus* 45 (2010), unpaginated.

> In which ther were moo ymages
> Of golde, stondynge in sondry stages,
> And moo ryche tabernacles
> And, with perré, moo pynacles [gemstones]
> And moo curiouse portreytures
> And queynte maner of figures
> Of olde werk then I sawgh ever.
> For certeynly, I nyste never
> Wher that I was, but wel wyste I
> Hyt was of Venus, redely.[17]

Since the walls of the temple are glass, some or all of the 'portreytures and queynt figures' (125–6) seen by the narrator can reasonably be inferred to appear in the medium of stained glass, and are thus appropriately referred to in terms of painting; other 'ymages […] stondynge in sondry stages' (121–2) seem to be three-dimensional. The *Middle English Dictionary* glosses 'portraiture' as exclusively referring to painting, according with Chaucer's use of it in *The Knight's Tale*, but this term may retain vitreous qualities or even denote glass itself because stained glass in the Middle Ages was technically at once both glazing and painting.[18] Richard Marks points out that the term 'stained glass' 'is in itself misleading, for almost until the Reformation the English glass-painter did not stain glass'; rather, he painted pigments on coloured sheets which were then fired and fixed into the glass.[19] So the painted murals, the *portreytures*, may in fact be superimposed onto the temple's predominantly vitreous surface; they may be paintings on glass. But there is a reason Chaucer is not clearer: material indeterminacy and plurality are features both of stained glass and of Chaucer's mode of inquiry in the poem.

Geffrey becomes transfixed in the presence of the glass walls. His response, though conventional in its inexpressibility topos, combines

---

17   Geoffrey Chaucer, *The House of Fame*, ed. Nick Havely, in *Chaucer's Dream Poetry*, ed. Helen Phillips and Nick Havely, Longman Annotated Texts (London, 1997), lines 119–30. All quotations from *Fame* are taken from this volume.

18   Even in *The Book of the Duchess*, then, when the materials seem to be clearly differentiated, the walls 'Ful wel depeynted' might actually involve a melding together of painting and glass: 'my chambre was / Ful wel depeynted; and with glas / Were al the wyndowes wel yglasyd' (321–4). These materials need not be 'either/or'; there is nothing to suggest that these painted walls 'with colouris fyne' are not also the transparent material of glass.

19   Marks, *Stained Glass in England*, 38.

awe with productive confusion, treating the architectural materials as a composite of parts that cannot be fully comprehended or accessed. Scholars have noted that the Temple of Venus has significant analogies with contemporary medieval cathedrals: Chaucer's description, noting spires, pinnacles, images, and tabernacles, recalls reliquary churches such as the Sainte-Chapelle in Paris.[20] These correspondences are suggestive but not reductive; that is, we are meant to envision a cathedral-like space with all its aggregated elements, but not a cathedral itself. The description of the space thwarts our attempts to recreate it in our minds: the superlative and echoed phrase 'moo [...] than I sawgh ever' captures the reader's attention to evoke a dazzling but only partially read and perhaps unreadable environment. Superlatives, according to Allen, serve to 'distort [the] object of description'; the superlative is used to 'transform its object by virtue of its poetic mediation'.[21] Chaucer's ekphrastic technique translates the walls beyond their material form into the enigmatic dreamscape Chaucer is conjuring here. The passage seems to demand that we consider the impact of seeming contradictions as it juxtaposes the phrase 'nyste never / Wher that I was' with the following phrase, 'but wel wyste I / Hyt was of Venus' (even if we can understand the literal meaning as confusion regarding the precise location of Venus's temple). 'Nyste' and 'wyste' are parallel terms that both undermine and confirm the dreamer's comprehension of his dream, acting as an epistemological cue to understanding the dreamer's journey: he is both unsettled and captivated, committed to attaining further understanding even though that attainment only produces increased bewilderment.

I thus read Book I of *Fame* as an intentional aggregation of disparate materials and sources, inspired by the fragmented nature of glass that treats knowledge as indeterminate and shifting. This reading is somewhat in contrast with that of those who would read Book I as embodying medieval theories of *memoria* in which knowledge (*rerum*) is organized into architectural *loci*.[22] Knowledge *might* be installed systematically into

20   Mary Braswell, 'Architectural Portraiture in Chaucer's *House of Fame*', *Journal of Medieval and Renaissance Studies* 11 (1981), 101–12 (103). Chaucer was associated with Henry Yevele, the leading English master mason of the fourteenth century, and was constantly surrounded by masons, carpenters, craftsmen, labourers, and gardeners (ibid., 103).

21   Valerie Allen, 'Ekphrasis and the Object', in *The Art of Vision: Ekphrasis in Medieval Literature and Culture*, ed. Andrew James Johnston, Ethan Knapp, and Margitta Rouse (Columbus, OH, 2015), 17–35 (27).

22   See Mary Carruthers, 'Italy, *Ars Memorativa*, and Fame's House', *Studies*

the wall of Venus's temple, but readers are conspicuously prevented from accessing the forms in which it appears, and, as many have noted, the selection of sources is inconsistent.[23] The walls bearing the story of the *Aeneid* in *The House of Fame* Book I present seemingly contradictory accounts of Dido's victimhood as taken from Virgil's *Aeneid*, Ovid's *Metamorphoses*, and the narrator's own exposition. Coley shows how seeming contradictions in the narrative, such as the joining together of the accounts of Virgil and Ovid, do not confuse or subvert meaning, but open up additional layers of material for engagement. I suggest additionally that in *Fame* meaning is meant to be partially confused, and that *amplificatio* (found in the glass of Sainte-Chapelle by Alyce Jordan) is an effect that can function in tandem with disorienting material.[24] This

in the Age of Chaucer, Proceedings no. 2 (1986), 179–88; and Beryl Rowland, 'Bishop Bradwardine, the Artificial Memory, and *The House of Fame*', in *Chaucer at Albany*, ed. Rossell Hope Robbins (New York, 1975), 41–62 (48–9). For more on medieval mnemonic theory, see Mary Carruthers, *The Book of Memory: A Study of Memory in Medieval Culture*, 2nd edn (Cambridge, 2009). Rebecca Davis also applies memory theory: 'Fugitive Poetics in Chaucer's *House of Fame*', *Studies in the Age of Chaucer* 37 (2015), 101–32 (106).

23   With this claim I do not mean to suggest that the poem is incoherent; I subscribe to Sheila Delany's analysis of the poem as 'establish[ing] for the artist a rhetorical and intellectual stance that can accommodate both traditional material and a skeptical approach to that material'; his stylistic features are 'part of a coherent effort to portray a subject whose salient trait is ambiguity' (Sheila Delany, *Chaucer's 'House of Fame': The Poetics of Skeptical Fideism* (Chicago, 1972), 5). For the admixture of contradictory accounts, see Jacqueline Miller, 'The Writing on the Wall: Authority and Authorship in Chaucer's *House of Fame*', *Chaucer Review* 17 (1982), 95–115 (105); Robert Clifford, '"A man of gret auctorite": The Search for Truth in Textual Authority in Geoffrey Chaucer's *The House of Fame*', *Bulletin of the John Rylands University Library of Manchester* 81 (1999), 155–65 (162–3); Thomas C. Kennedy, 'Rhetoric and Meaning in *The House of Fame*', *Studia Neophilologica* 68 (1996), 9–23 (14); and Katherine H. Terrell, 'Reallocation of Hermeneutic Authority in Chaucer's *House of Fame*', *Chaucer Review* 31 (1997), 279–90 (283).

24   David K. Coley, '"Withyn a temple ymad of glas": Glazing, Glossing, and Patronage in Chaucer's *House of Fame*', *Chaucer Review* 45.1 (2010), 59–84 (81). Coley here draws upon art-historical analysis by Alyce Jordan, who asserts that the windows of the Sainte-Chapelle in Paris employ '*amplificatio*, which involves the amplification or expansion of narrative *materia*', along with other rhetorical techniques drawn from Geoffrey of Vinsauf (*Visualizing Kingship in the Windows of the Sainte-Chapelle*, Publications of the International Center of Medieval Art 5 (Turnhout, 2002), 11). See also Jordan, 'Seeing Stories

is shown through the unspecific material forms in which the story of Dido presents itself. The temple walls, which we know incorporate glass as their basic form, seem additionally to contain some combination of brass carving, paintings, and stained glass, and it is rarely clear at any single moment which part of the story appears in which material. The verb *graven*, which the narrator frequently uses to describe the walls ('Ther sawgh I grave', line 193, also 253, 256, 433, 451, 473), could refer to carvings, decorations, incisions, inscriptions, or even, as suggested by his claim that his dream supplies Dido's lament ('Non other auctour alegge I', line 314), mental impressions (*MED* 'graven'). It is possible that at times the story remains as text while the narrator 'turn[s] the text into visual imagery, thus imitating the psychological response of the reader'.[25] Beside all this material confusion, though, is the basic detail that the temple is 'ymade of glas' (120), and it is this very aesthetic framework that allows for such a blurred integration of aggregate materials.

In *Fame*, Geffrey pauses to allow the shimmering effects of glass to reverberate through his body.[26] Once Geffrey begins reading the walls of glass, the narrative transfers from a focus on his own mediating senses to a more direct encounter with the tale that mirrors the expectation of heightened responses from readers as they delve further into the story. This intimate delving represents the enacting of stained-glass aesthetics. Some variation of the phrase 'I saw' appears nine times in the narrative's first hundred lines,[27] repeatedly calling attention to Geffrey's body; the

in the Windows of the Sainte-Chapelle: The *Ars Poetriae* and the Poetic of Visual Narrative', *Mediaevalia* 23 (2002), 39–60. For another perspective on the decoration of Chaucer's walls, see Michael Hagiioannu, 'Giotto's Bardi Chapel Frescoes and Chaucer's *House of Fame*: Influence, Evidence, and Interpretations', *Chaucer Review* 36.1 (2001), 28–47.

25   Kennedy, 'Rhetoric and Meaning', 12.

26   Cf. Harris's comments that stained glass implements an 'aesthetics of suspension': Harris, 'Glazing and Glossing', 306. Harris does not discuss *Fame*.

27   These are lines 151, 162, 174, 193, 198, 209, 212, 221, 253. For example, '*Ther saugh I* such tempeste aryse / That euery herte myght agryse [shudder] / To see hyt peynted on the walle. / *Ther saugh I* graven eke withalle, / Venus' (209–13). Kathryn McKinley outlines the ambulatory nature of Geffrey's traversal of the space, which mimics the movements of pilgrims through religious struc-tures as well as their affective responses (McKinley, 'Ekphrasis as Aesthetic Pilgrimage in Chaucer's *House of Fame* Book I', in *Meaning in Motion: The Semantics of Movement in Medieval Art*, ed. Nino Zchomelidse and Giovanni Freni (Princeton, 2011), 215–32). My reading of the poem aligns quite closely with McKinley's, sharing her awareness of the vanishing narratorial markers

reassertions of Geffrey's presence in the scene keep readers at a cognitive distance, focusing our imagined gaze on Geffrey's own perceptions and locking the narrative in the past. But from the hortatory 'let us speke of Eneas' at line 293 to Aeneas's departure at line 432 – that is, the narrative of Aeneas's betrayal of Dido and her subsequent suicide – narrative interventions disappear entirely. This phrase ushers in the present tense and inaugurates a new level of immediacy and emotion as readers are given unmediated access to Dido's lament, the emotional climax of Book I, in which she 'rofe hir selfe to the herte / And dyed thorgh the wounde smerte' (373–4). Geffrey paradoxically sees in the walls both spoken dialogue and internal emotion, but rather than just seeing the vivifying effects of this moment as the work of ekphrasis, as other scholars have done,[28] I read these effects as enacting the impact of the glass walls, with implied light streaming through them and giving breath and motion to static images. The walls of Venus's temple become vitalized through the work of light through glass.

Medieval marginalia suggest that readers were more fascinated with the temple's story of Dido than with any of the rest of the poem. *The House of Fame* is the most heavily glossed of all the texts in two of its three manuscripts (Oxford, Bodleian Library, MS Fairfax 16, and Oxford, Bodleian Library, MS Bodley 638), and some of the most interesting marginal notes congregate around the temple and the narrator's experiences there.[29] In contradistinction to Bowers's proposal that '[t]

---

which mark Geffrey's affective engagement within the storified walls. However, her emphasis is on Chaucer's evocation of devotional contemplation and the relationship of the walls to painted religious murals, while I am concerned with the encompassing role of glass and the epistemological confusion it invokes.

28   C.f. Bowers, 'Speaking Images?', 70.

29   See *Manuscript Bodley 638: A Facsimile*, ed. Pamela Robinson, The Facsimile Series of the Works of Geoffrey Chaucer 2 (Norman, OK, 1982); and *Bodleian Library, MS Fairfax 16*, ed. John Norton-Smith (London, 1979). *Fame* is also extant in Cambridge, Magdalene College, Pepys 2006. In both Fairfax 16 and Bodley 638, the section of *House of Fame* that we now call Book I contains eighteen shared glosses. Most marginalia supplement the text with source material from Virgil or Ovid, but in the Dido suicide section there are three notable additions, shared across two manuscripts: first, a piece of cautionary advice in response to the tale ('Cavete vos innocent [*sic*] mulieres', or 'Beware you innocent women' (Bodley 638, fol. 148v; Fairfax 16, fol. 158v)) appears alongside Dido's description of men as desiring 'fame / In magnyfyinge of hys name' (lines 305–6); second, underlining and partial reproduction in the margins of the list of cruel male lovers from Ovid's *Heroides* that follows the story of Dido (Bodley

he dreamer has little affective engagement with what he witnesses, his emotional life as arid as the desert that he finds outside the temple', I suggest that the absence of response is in itself a responsive mode: readers are meant to propel themselves into the drama of the glass walls and thus replicate the narrator's own experience of being lost within them.[30] We are then dealing both with the narrator's interior means of experiencing Dido's lament, and with the capacity for stained glass in performance to overflow and envelop him.

Upon leaving the temple, the hyperbolic terms of Geffrey's entry are simply echoed:

> Yet sawgh [...] never such noblesse
> Of ymages, ne suche richesse
> As [he] saugh grave in this chirche!

(471–3)

The vision unfolding around him remains unprocessed in the moment, and his awestruck response reinforces the entire poem's concerns with epistemological uncertainty – an effect inspired by the radiant impact of stained glass.

Permeable Identities in John Lydgate's *The Temple of Glass*

John Lydgate, in the early fifteenth-century *The Temple of Glass*, takes up not only Chaucer's discourses and figures of love, but also Geffrey's general experience of responding to the absorptive qualities of glass.[31]

638, fol. 151r; Fairfax 16, fol.160r); third, before the list of lovers, the words 'Now of many vntrewe loueres', the only marginal instance of vernacular rather than Latin (Bodley 638, fol. 150v; Fairfax 16, fol. 159v).

30   Bowers, 'Speaking Images?', 72.

31   The precise date is disputed: Boffey places it pre-1420 since John Shirley's anthology, of which *Temple* is a part, dates to the 1420s (Julia Boffey, Introduction to *The Temple of Glass*, in *Fifteenth-Century English Dream Visions*, 15–24 (16)); Mitchell's edition claims the first quarter of the fifteenth century, but he later shifts this range to between 1427 and 1432 in an article proposing that the poem deals obliquely with the amorous affairs of the queen (Mitchell, 'Queen Katherine and the Secret of Lydgate's *Temple of Glas*', *Medium Ævum* 77.1 (2008), 54–76 (63)). It is likely the poem was written for a historical patron – a note by Shirley claims it as 'a delightful dream made at the request of a lover, by Lydgate,

But beyond Geffrey's pure wonder and blind acceptance of the impact
of the glass walls' tale, Lydgate figures his own 'temple of glas' (14) as
slightly more sinister, casting identities as susceptible to the imper-
manent transformations of art. *The House of Fame* is not Lydgate's
sole Chaucerian source for his poem,[32] but there are many similarities
between the two: both dreamers fall asleep in December (rather than
the more conventional spring setting) and explore the interior of
Venus's glass temple, engaging with and responding to the shimmering
and animated depictions on the vitreous walls. Both observe Venus in
similar guise – she is 'fleting in the see' in Lydgate's *Temple* (53), and
'naked, fletyng in a see' in Chaucer's *House of Fame* (133). However,
although Lydgate – like Chaucer – gives a prominent place to Dido
among the lovers represented in his temple, his chief female figure is an
unnamed lady whose love affair is successfully navigated to the point
of mutual acknowledgement during the poem. The lady's resplendent
beauty captures the attention of the dreamer and her melancholic lover,
and she seems to demonstrate a remarkable degree of agency within the
poem, taking the place, it has been argued, of the conventionally male
courtly lover. Scholarship on *Temple* has tended to focus on this figure,

---

monk of Bury' ('une soynge moult plesaunt fait a la request d'un amoreux par
Lidegate Le Moygne de Bury'; Boffey, Introduction, 15–16); however, this study
is not concerned with the circumstances that gave rise to the poem, but rather
with its post-production effects on contemporary readers and debates. It is
unknown whether Lydgate himself gave the poem its title, but the fact that it
appears under this name in most early manuscripts (its appearance as 'Temple
of bras' in Oxford, Bodleian Library, MS Bodley 638 is anomalous) suggests that
even if the title is not authorial, scribes and compilers, and early printers – that
is, early readers with reasons for close engagement of various kinds with the
poem – embraced the name and its literary connections with the temple of glass
in Chaucer's *House of Fame*. Seven manuscripts and five early modern editions
of *Temple* survive, as well as a number of fragments, which indicate it was
excerpted freely and adapted to new contexts. For a shortened list of manuscripts
and early editions, see Mitchell's Introduction to his edition of *Temple of Glas*;
for a fuller list, with some description of the manuscripts and palaeographic
idiosyncrasies, see Josef Schick's Introduction to *Lydgate's Temple of Glas*, EETS
e.s. 60 (London, 1891), xvi–xxx.
32   Larry Scanlon additionally lists *The Book of the Duchess*, *The Knight's Tale*,
The Franklin's Tale, *The Clerk's Tale*, and *The Parliament of Fowls*. See Larry
Scanlon, 'Lydgate's Poetics: Laureation and Domesticity in the *Temple of Glass*',
in *John Lydgate: Poetry, Culture, and Lancastrian England*, ed. Larry Scanlon and
James Simpson (Notre Dame, IN, 2006), 61–87 (63).

but, as I will show, she is far from being Lydgate's only innovation or development in his reading of Chaucer's poem.[33]

Educated at Oxford and widely travelled, Lydgate would have been familiar with glazing both in Suffolk and elsewhere, and the Norman tower at Bury with twelve polychromatic glass windows may have supplied direct inspiration for his poem.[34] Glaziers were based throughout East Anglia, where Lydgate lived and worked, including at least one at Bury St Edmunds itself. Two of his texts appeared in visual form at the Lady Chapel at Holy Trinity in Long Melford, and Lydgate himself inscribed the textual portion of the 'Danse Macabre' wall painting at the Church of the Holy Innocents, Paris, into verse.[35] However, Lydgate must have felt some discomfort over the exorbitant costs of stained glass and its exclusive associations with affluent circles, as well as its support of affective modes of devotion which did not

33   Mitchell proposes that the heroine alludes to Queen Katherine of Valois, who was personally acquainted with Lydgate and whose clandestine marriage to the Welsh squire Owen Tudor supplies compelling parallels with the predicaments of the lovers in this poem (Mitchell, 'Queen Katherine'). Scanlon locates the uniqueness of Lydgate's poem in his conferral of agency onto the lady rather than the man, 'giv[ing] her the capacity of suffering to the full the agonies of the courtly lover, that mark of sublime privilege almost entirely reserved to male figures' (Scanlon, 'Lydgate's Poetics', 86). Tara Williams examines the function of womanhood as a guiding and sometimes restraining principle in the lady's behaviour, as part of her larger project that traces the development of notions of womanhood throughout the Middle Ages (Tara Williams, *Inventing Womanhood: Gender and Language in Later Middle English Writing* (Columbus, OH, 2011), ch. 3).

34   The Norman tower contains sculptures, bronze doors, and stained-glass windows donated by Edward III; there were no fewer than 'twelve brightly-coloured stained-glass windows of the south aisle and the adjoining south transcept': Walter F. Schirmer, *John Lydgate: A Study in the Culture of the XVth Century*, trans. Ann E. Keep (London, 1961), 12. William Rossiter references this detail in '"The light so in my face / bigan to smyte": Illuminating Lydgate's *Temple of Glas*', in *On Light*, ed. K. P. Clarke and Sarah Baccianti (Oxford, 2014), 71 n. 18. By the middle of the fourteenth century, local glaziers were widely distributed around English counties, suggesting that the glass-painting industry remained relatively separate from London until the sixteenth century (Marks, *Stained Glass in England*, 41).

35   Shannon Gayk, *Image, Text, and Religious Reform in Fifteenth-century England* (New York, 2010), 88. For more on this topic, see Jennifer Eileen Floyd, 'Writing on the Wall: John Lydgate's Architectural Verse', PhD diss. (Stanford University, 2008).

accord with his personal ascetic approach. Scholars have identified in the fifteenth century a 'greater sensory concreteness with which the central mystery of Incarnation was experienced', as devotional pieties became more emotional, personal, and embodied, and affective images and icons spread across streets, civic buildings, and sacred spaces.[36] But the proliferation of images was cause for no small consternation among religious officials who were suspicious of the power of imagery to sway and captivate. As Shannon Gayk observes, Lydgate disdained the 'affective, unmediated visual experience' promoted by contemporary models of lay piety and hoped through his religious works 'to promote an altogether different devotional model for the laity – an application of the practice of monastic *lectio* and *memoria*'. Gayk identifies, accordingly, a 'regulatory aesthetics' running through his devotional lyrics in opposition to the predominant 'incarnational aesthetic' of the fifteenth century.[37]

While recent scholarship has focused on the lively performative effects of devotional texts and images,[38] I propose that Lydgate's secular poetry expresses a similar regulatory aesthetic impulse in the absence of explicitly Christian material. The power of art to impact upon and alter viewers should not be viewed as restricted to devotional circles, but was operational in secular or pagan artistic contexts too; as Simon Gaunt remarks, '[o]ur own grounding in secular social structures and ethics perhaps makes it difficult for us to grasp that the opposition we take for granted between secular and ecclesiastic, between sacred and profane, may simply not be operative within medieval society'.[39]

---

36   Gail McMurray Gibson, *The Theater of Devotion: East Anglian Drama and Society in the Late Middle Ages* (Chicago, 1989), 16.

37   Shannon Gayk, 'Images of Pity: The Regulatory Aesthetics of John Lydgate's Religious Poetry', *Studies in the Age of Chaucer* 28 (2006), 175–203 (177, 178).

38   See, for example, Jessica Brantley, *Reading in the Wilderness: Private Devotion and Public Performance in Late Medieval England* (Chicago, 2007); Pamela Sheingorn, 'Performing the Illustrated Manuscript: Great Reckonings in Little Books', in *Visualizing Medieval Performance: Perspectives, Histories, Contexts*, ed. Elina Gertsman (Burlington, VT, 2008), 57–82; Jill Stevenson, 'The Material Bodies of Medieval Religious Performance in England', *Material Religion* 2.2 (2006), 204–33; and Boyda Johnstone, 'Reading Images, Drawing Texts: Performing *The Abbey of the Holy Ghost* in British Library Stowe 39', in *Editing, Performance, Texts: New Practices in Medieval and Early Modern English Drama*, ed. Jacqueline Jenkins and Julie Sanders (New York, 2014), 27–48.

39   Simon Gaunt, 'A Martyr to Love: Sacrificial Desire in the Poetry of Bernart de Ventadorn', *Journal of Medieval and Early Modern Studies* 31.3 (2001), 477–506 (478).

Lydgate thus revises Chaucer's dream world to suit his own ends; more than just carrying out an exercise in epistemological unknowing, in this secular vision Lydgate voices his discomfort with the visual aesthetic of glass and its captivating functions. His vision involves a dream world caught up in a number of affective bodily transformations which are then also reined in. What emerges in Lydgate's poem is a subtle critique of the power of stained glass to transfigure response and unsettle the boundaries of the human.

Since *Temple* is not widely known, I will provide a brief synopsis here. A distraught narrator falls asleep and experiences a vision of a glittering temple of glass positioned on a rock of ice, imagery combined from *House of Fame*'s temple in Book I and ice mountain in Book III. While Chaucer's *House of Fame* and other texts, such as *Book of the Duchess* and *Parliament of Fowls*, use introductory material to foreground questions of the relationship between books and life, and about the nature and significance of dreams as drawn from classical antiquity, Lydgate's *Temple* propels readers directly into the temple, emphasizing the affective drama that occurs within and between the temple walls. Within the temple, a radiant lady, her melancholic lover, and the beneficent Venus as the goddess of love together act out a courtly love pageant which ends with the two lovers bound together, yet denied an official marital union until they have endured a proper degree of suffering. The dreamer awakens at the end, still distraught, and in some versions describes his plan to present his dream in book form to a lady.

Dream visions characteristically aim to engage epistemological and existential questions within a concentrated yet permeable space. *Temple* seems especially intent on isolating questions of love, aesthetics, and authorial agency, as it focuses on Chaucer's temple but expands it into an individual encounter with classical histories of love. As in *Fame*, Lydgate's images '[o]f sondry lovers, lyche as they were of age' cast across 'every wal, / From eest to west' are 'depeynted' on what remains a predominantly glass temple – they are not opaque, but mix their vivified 'lyfly colours' with the captivations of light (46, 44–5, 48). The narrative from the very beginning focuses on the dreamer's perceptions, and his roving gaze becomes the lens through which we understand the relationship between the physical space and the many bodies contained within it:

And whan that I had goon longe and sought
I fonde a wyket and entyrd inne als fast

Into the temple, and myn eyen cast
On every syde, nowe lowe and efft alofft.

(38–41)

The motion of the dreamer's gaze – 'cast / On every syde' – highlights
the aggregate mobility of the glass temple walls. The lamenting Dido
leads the narrator's description of the glass walls' contents, but Dido is
supplemented by examples drawn from a wider range of contexts and
storyworlds than Chaucer's temple walls in *The House of Fame*: Medea's
complaint over Jason, and Penelope, and Alceste, and Griselda in 'al
hir meknesse and hir pacyence' (76) are joined by Isolde lamenting the
torment she suffers for Tristan, and by many others (55–142). Lydgate's
survey of the surfaces in combination with the light shining through
the glass gives a kind of mobility to figures frozen in acts of beseeching,
pursuing, being struck by love, thus enacting a temporal collapse of past
with present. The narrator sees story in the image in a blending picked up
from Book I of Chaucer's *House of Fame* but here generalized to all love-
longing rather than presented as a moment of individual absorption. In
addition to their iconography of lament and supplication, these figures,
at once static and endlessly renewable, supply images of transformation.
Mythological bodies morph from one state into another: Philomene
is turned into a nightingale; Palamon mutates after glancing at Emily;
Daphne changes into a laurel tree; and Jove transfigures himself. They
are *transsfourmed* (73) or *iturned* (99, 116) they *transmewe* (120), and
take shape *by transmutacioun* (121). Human transformation, humanity
subject to the effects of glass, will prove to be a lasting theme throughout
the poem.

The vitreous wall's fixed images, which can nonetheless overflow their
material representation in being perceived and retold, merge with the
ever renewed tide of supplicants within the temple, who in turn echo the
host of amorous pursuits reverberating through the temple walls:

And firthermore in the temple were
Ful many an hundred thousand here and there
In sondri wyse redy to compleyne
Unto the goddesse of hir wo and peyne.

(143–6)

Like those in the glass, these denizens of love exist in every variety of love-
longing, frustration, denial, sorrow and betrayal (146–246), suppliants

whose stories in their very telling represent them as incarnate versions of the walls' repertoire. The narratorial comment that there was in the temple 'mani a story mo than I rekken can' (91) recalls the comparative 'moo curiouse portreytures' of *Fame*, and emphasizes the all-encompassing nature of its contained love-stories. The poem thus blends the glass with the space and events the glass encompasses through beaming light.

That the walls of glass are not separate from the space between them, but rather serve as an active force within the internal drama, is made explicit through the character of Venus, who both inhabits the walls and springs to life independently of them: while Boffey posits that '[t]he painted representation described here is distinct from the goddess whom the dreamer will later see and hear from', I contend that the deity is both preserved within the walls of glass and a living manifestation of her active participation in the space, a reading that accords with Mitchell's comments that Venus's 'variable ontology matches the metamorphoses and miscellaneousness of the lovers on the temple mural and indicates the freedom with which the poet felt he could combine disparate materials'.[40] After dispatching her advice to the unnamed lady, Venus simply 'shooke hir hede / And was in pees, and spake as thoo namore' (544–5), as though becoming immobile again within the glassy surfaces of the walls.[41] Her physical position above the supplicants is suggested through requests that she 'enclyne' to her 'audyence' (822–3), and 'doun streght from thi sete / Us to fortune caste youre streemys sheene' (1119–20). But no throne is explicitly mentioned, suggesting that her 'sete' might simply be a part of the elevated walls of glass.

While it may seem that the aesthetic function of glass ceases after the first 140 lines, then, a closer look indicates that it emerges as an enveloping force through the rest of the poem, enacting an aesthetics of performance that merges the bodies of the characters into each other as well as into the uncertain and shifting qualities of the oneiric landscape. Lydgate's dreamer is visibly pierced and penetrated by what he sees in a way that transcends Geffrey's affectively charged absence from the narrative, and contributes to Lydgate's commentary on the power of art to transform and perhaps even manipulate response. Sensorial piercing is a dominant experience within the poem that is introduced by the blinding sun immediately upon the dreamer's arrival:

40   Boffey, Introduction, 27 n. 53; Mitchell, Introduction.
41   She may also recall painted sculptures carved into cathedral walls, such as inhabited the façade at Wells Cathedral.

As I gan neghe this grisly dredful place
I wex astonyed – the light so in my face
Began to smyte, so *persyng* ever in on
On yche a part wher that I koude gon,
That I ne might nothing as I wolde
Abowten me considerne and byholde
The wondreful hestrys [buildings], for brightnesse of the sonne.

(23–9, my emphasis)

William T. Rossiter has analysed the significance of neo-Aristotelian optical theories for Lydgate's figuration of light as piercing – according to him, these lines evoke 'Ptolemy's "unius puncti" and Bacon's explanation of the emanation of species [rays] from "the whole object" both to "every point of the eye" and "to one point of the eye"'.[42] Lydgate demonstrates his familiarity with theories of visual intromission in which the object of vision pierces the subject, casting erotic desire into scientific terms. But the piercing effects of the sun here demonstrate that the terrain of this dream is not altogether benevolent or inviting, and frame the dreamer's experience of the temple with sensory overload. Indeed the dreamer's sudden removal from waking life carries both violent and spiritual overtones: the verb 'ravyshed' means 'to steal', 'to capture', and 'to entrance' or 'enrapure' as well as the more straightforward meaning in this context of 'to transport' (*MED* 'ravishen' (v.)); its use here prefigures an experience that will offer a secular correlative to a religious vision through its love piercings, as well as an unsettling, even violent, internal journey of enrapturement. That the sun is earlier likened to 'cristal' gives it material form and allows its impact to be likened to that of the temple itself (22).

Unsurprisingly, hiding from the sun within a temple of glass does not prove effective. The sun beams through the coloured windows and radiates through the bodies of the denizens within, particularly the female characters who are shown to be contiguous with the glass walls, as well as with each other. They in fact manifest the heavenly effects of the walls with which I began this study. Both Venus and the lady are described as issuing captivating 'stremys' from their glances, echoing the 'stremys of Tytan' outside the temple (32): the narrator describes the 'stremys of hyre [the lady's] lok [look] so bryght' that 'Surmountyth alle thourgh beaute in myn syght' (263–4), and a few lines later the lady

42   Rossiter, 'The light so in my face', 70.

declares to Venus, 'And with thy stremys canst every thing discerne / Thoroughe hevenly fyre of love that is eterne' (326–7). They are joint extensions of the walls' radiant power, and, as Rossiter claims, the lady 'appears to embody both the light and the medium of light as described in the poem's opening', emitting visual species.[43] Venus absorbs and projects the sunlight from outside (735, 737–8) and is addressed by the lady as 'O blisfull sterre, *persant* and cler of light' (328), even as the lady is described in similar terms by the man ('For with the *perssing* of hir eyen clere / I am wounded I weene so to the hert / That frome the deethe I may not astert' (602–4)). It is not too much of an exaggeration to say that all the characters are interpenetrated by one another in some way. Together, the women exude the blinding energy of the sun and become manifestations of stained glass's effects within the temple, as the lady's 'hye presence' causes the temple to be 'enlumyned envyroun [all around]' (282–3). Similarly, her gown '[e]mbrowded [embroidered] al with stonys and perry [jewels] / So rychely that joye it was to see' (301–2) enacts the kaleidoscopic effects of glazed programmes. Medieval glass, notably, was often decorated with jewels.[44]

Lydgate, in this way, relying upon the penetrative force as treated in medieval optical theory, comments on the ability of stained glass to have such a phenomenological impact on our bodies that it may profoundly change who we are, melding our identities into the environment around us and vanquishing distinctions between ourselves and the multimodal registers of the space.[45] The unifying and absorptive light flowing through the walls made of glass thus sponsors an interconnected, permeable means for the communication and transmission of eroticized desire between the vitreous partitions and the lovers. In this secular context, Lydgate's discomfort may be directed at sensorial devotional practices, as in his religious lyrics, or he may additionally be calling into

43   Ibid., 70. For 'species' as 'rays' see p. 69.
44   Marks, *Stained Glass in England*, 39.
45   This awareness of the collapsing boundaries between bodies in the Middle Ages has found recent purchase in the critical theory of posthumanism; see, as a foundational piece from a medievalist's perspective, Jeffrey J. Cohen, *Medieval Identity Machines*, Medieval Culture 35 (Minneapolis, 2003); or, more recently, J. Allan Mitchell, *Becoming Human: The Matter of the Medieval Child* (Minneapolis, 2014). Appositely, Rebecca Davis's 'Fugitive Poetics' analyses *The House of Fame* as 'a world of becoming' through its collocation of motion and chaos (111). Situating dream visions within this broader critical discourse is one of the objectives of my ongoing work.

question the fickle and bewitching nature of love, capable of subverting rational choice and rendering subjects helpless to its whims. Lydgate uses the temple of glass with its propensity at once to fix and refract colours, 'huwes', and energy to contain the literary traditions of love-longing, and as the appropriate environment for love's combinations of transformation and fixity. The lovers as a group evoke the depicted figures in the glass walls, *turned* and *transmuted* by the life-altering effects of love and eternally beholden to Venus's whims. Lydgate does not just make the dreamer disappear within the vitreous walls, as in *Fame*, but renders characters susceptible to one another's influence as well as to the influence of the walls that contain them.

Within this turbulent atmosphere, the principal characters and the represented figures seek stillness and permanence, and attempt to re-establish lasting autonomy within their newly transformed roles. That is to say, the frenzied atmosphere inside the temple results in emotional paralysis and a desire for stability rather than interminable change – the characters seek, in a sense, to escape the glass even while retaining its piercing effects, to find in love a place of security. In the second part of the poem the crowd becomes so oppressive that the dreamer must seek respite outside:

> Withinne the temple me thought that I say [saw]
> Gret part of folk with murmour wonderful
> So heve and shove (the temple was so ful),
> Everyche ful bysy in his owen cause,
> That I ne may shortly in a clause
> Descryben al the ryte [activity] and the gyse [manner].
>
> (552–7)

The dreamer and the lover exhibit overlapping identities, and the latter also experiences discomfort in response to the temple's impact. He describes himself as wounded to the point of death by his desire for the lady, 'dismayed in a traunce, […] For Drede I trowe I dare not oon worde speke' (679, 81). Later, after Venus instructs the lover to approach and beseech the lady who has captured his attention, the dreamer experiences a corresponding paralysis:

> And whanne the goddesse this lesson hade tolde,
> Abouten me so as I cane beholde [looked around me]
> Right sore astonyed I stode, *as in a traunce,*

To seen the maner and the countenaunce
And al the chere of this woful man,
That was of hewe pale and dedly wan,
With dreed oppressid oonly in his thought[.]

(952–8, my emphasis)[46]

Not only is the dreamer gripped with empathetic immobility here, but additionally the narrator's remembrance of his dream becomes so vivid that, in the process of writing, he experiences the same feeling of aphasia and paralysis as the dreamer and the male lover, despairing that 'For rowth [pity] of whiche of his wo to endyte/ *My* [the narrator's] penne I feele qwakyng as I wryte' (966–7, my emphasis).[47] Through the transference of dread between lover, dreamer, and narrator, which serves as an extension of the light's pervasive influence, the poem registers its desire for escape from the affective convergences of the temple and its glass walls.

46   Here he seems additionally to reference the black knight in Chaucer's *Book of the Duchess*, whose 'sorwful hert' after he made his complaint 'gan faste faynt, / And his spirits wexen dede, / The bloode was fled, for pure drede, / Doune to hys hert to make hym warme – / For wel hyt feled the hert had harme – […] And that made al / Hys hewe chaunge and wexe grene / And pale, for ther noo bloode ys sene / In no maner [l]ym of hys' (488–92, 496–9). These male lovers experience shared physiological symptoms in response to their amatory tribulations.
47   Regarding this moment, Judith Davidoff notes that 'a certain empathy connects the dreamer and the lover', and observes that the narrator's lines are derived from Chaucer's *Troilus and Criseyde*: 'And now my penne, allas, with which I write, / Quaketh for drede of that I moste endite' (Book IV, lines 13–14), where the reference is to Criseyde's betrayal of Troilus (Davidoff, 'The Audience Illuminated, or New Light Shed on the Dream Frame of Lydgate's *Temple of Glas*', *Studies in the Age of Chaucer* 5 (1983), 103–26 (118)). Anna Torti remarks upon the 'parallel descriptions of the man's and the poet's sufferings' and notes that a similar passage appears in Lydgate's *A Complaynt of a Loveres Lyfe*: 'O Nyobe! Let now thi teres reyn / Into my penne and eke helpe in this nede, / Thou woful mirre that felist my hert blede / Of pitouse wo, and my honde eke quake / When that I write for this mannys sake' (Torti, *The Glass of Form: Mirroring Structures from Chaucer to Skelton* (Cambridge, 1991), 81; for the text see John Lydgate, *A Complaynte of a Lovers Lyfe*, ed. Dana M. Symons, in *Chaucerian Dream Visions and Complaints* (Kalamazoo, MI, 2004), 176–82). Notably, the narrator's involvement in the dream here directly refutes Spearing's claim that '[w]ithin the dream [the Dreamer] plays no part […] He is merely an observer, before whom the dream unfolds itself as a kind of pageant' (A. C. Spearing, *Medieval Dream-Poetry* (Cambridge, 1976), 174).

In the midst of this manic environment, accordingly, the central pair of lovers long for constancy and fidelity, and the assurance that the piercing work of love would be lasting, rather than perpetually in motion like the metamorphosing figures depicted in the glass walls around them. The Boethian ideal of patience is a prominent theme of the poem. Venus reassures the lady, for example, that the torment she endures is a necessary step towards joy and happiness, just like martyr saints who earn the reward of heaven (387–90). An even more persistent phrase than variants of the word 'pierce' is 'withouten chaunge', which appears eight times, reflecting an underlying anxiety about the mutable qualities of sacred spaces and the depth of penetration enacted by multimodal art.[48] Venus, divine arbiter, provides assurance to the lady that 'he that ye have chosen yowe to serve / Shalle bene right swich as ye desire / *Withouten chaunge*' (426–8, my emphasis); her instructions to the man reinforce this demand for constancy, asking him to be humble and meek, 'Withoute chaunge in partye or in al' (1175). The paradox of an image fixed in a wall that is nonetheless an image of transformation points to the way all the lovers in the temple desire a change of state: once changed and inhabited by their love-longing, they yearn for desire to be transmuted into fulfilment, misery into happiness or death. They wish to be bonded together, to allow love to both 'enbracen and constreyne' (1125) them, a dual image of comfort and restriction. The lady's explanation to the man that 'she [Venus] myn hert hathe in subjeccion / Whiche hole is youres and never shal repent' (1095–6) encompasses the paradoxical nature of love in *Temple*: the lady's heart belongs to Venus, a symbol of love, as much as it belongs to the man, and this state of servitude enables the lady to achieve fulfilment of her desires. Venus's advice to the distraught lover not to let any other beauty into 'thyn hert myne' (1208) further emphasizes the paradox of happy subjection across these love circuits: Boffey glosses 'myne' as the verb 'penetrate', but there is a clear dual meaning with the possessive pronoun 'mine'. The man's heart is as much Venus's as his own, because he has devoted himself to Venus and Venus, as the goddess of love, inhabits it.

Ultimately, the onus of satisfying this underlying need for stability rests on the shoulders of the lovers themselves; their chance of success depends on their ability to uphold their pact of love, to retain and internalize the transformative effects of the glass around them. And indeed,

---

48   In Boffey, lines 378, 428, 493, 752, 1015, 1175, 1315, and 1353; it appears one additional time in Mitchell's version (lines 365, 385, 435, 493, 732, 995, 1155, 1295, 1333).

by the end of the poem, the pseudo-marital union between the lovers allows their hearts to be 'bothe sette at rest / Withowten chaunge or mutability' (1314–5). But the dreamer's own fate is less certain. The noise of the heavenly music celebrating the union of the lovers wakes the dreamer up, removing him from the performative power of the walls of the temple. He characterizes this event as a 'sodeyne chaunge' (1387) that stands in direct contrast to the hoped-for state 'withouten chaunge' of the lovers. In this final moment he replicates the paralysed trance of the male lover and himself within the poem: 'Me thought I was ay ligging in a traunce / So clene awey was thoo my remembraunce / Of al my dreme' (1388–90). Because his trance replicates the dreamer's state within the dream, where the dreamer lies in yet another 'traunce', the passage paradoxically re-enacts and undermines the existence of the vision at the same time, as the dreamer loses track of the contents of the dream but retains its effects. This moment becomes an effective evocation of stained-glass aesthetics, their reliance upon expressive power rather than just instructional contents, and their manner of leaving observers transfigured. But unlike Chaucer, whose dreamer seems to embrace the consuming impact of glass even as he fails fully to understand it, Lydgate voices concerns about painted glass and its performative material, favouring perhaps a more tempered, detached engagement with instructional surfaces. Lydgate's dreamer is more unsettled by his lack of understanding after emerging from the temple than was Geffrey in *The House of Fame*. The narrator's final efforts to 'maken and to wryte' (1399) his dream not only represent attempts to re-establish contact with the lost lady, but also to re-establish contact with the vision itself.[49]

As I have argued, John Lydgate's *The Temple of Glass* incorporates an aesthetic of stained glass into its narrative as a means of embodied trans-formation, the characters within the poem absorbing and re-enacting the drama on the walls, and becoming changed through their penetrative encounters. The piercing effects of glass manifested through the lovers' gazes echo and cast doubt upon, in a secular context, the 'incarnational

---

49   In Mitchell's version he dispatches his 'litel rude boke' to '[his] ladi', perhaps a real-world equivalent of the lady within the poem (lines 1393, 1392). This alternative version, then, offers up the book itself as an extension of the love principles it contains, reminding readers of the concreteness of the text as an archived and manifested version of this multivalent vision. In addition, London, British Library, Add. MS 16165, and Cambridge, Cambridge University Library, MS Gg.4.27 both contain a complaint addressed to someone named Margaret (though Boffey doubts the complaint is Lydgate's; Introduction, 22–3).

aesthetics' that characterized fifteenth-century devotion, which was a celebration of the corporeal and the sensory above the didactic and detached, an attempt to 'transform the abstract and theological to the personal and concrete'.[50] But in this poem, the characters worship love rather than Christ, and Lydgate may then additionally be commenting on courtly practices that lead to impaired reason under love's consuming influence. While Geffrey's encounter with glass in *Fame* leaves him awestruck, in Lydgate the lovers yearn to escape the mutable environment of the temple and become paralysed with despair through their fluidly transferring identities. Thus we can in this poem glimpse Lydgate's 'unease with affective, unmediated visual experience', and the destabilizing effect of the initial transformations of love in Venus's glass perhaps becomes an indirect commentary on the embodied modes of devotion promoted by contemporary religious glass imagery.[51] *The Temple of Glass* thus becomes as much about the capacity of art to transform, and the inherent risks therein, as it is about the vicissitudes and exigencies of love.

In this article I have argued that a deeper appreciation of stained glass and its hermeneutic function in the late Middle Ages can help us to approach literary dream visions as affective texts that often exceed our logical comprehension but appeal to our senses and emotions, speaking more in feelings than in words. In the fourteenth and fifteenth centuries, stained glass was carried closer than ever before to viewers' perceptions, becoming subject to close scrutiny as well as sensorial stimulation, and both Chaucer and Lydgate set its affective power to work in their poems, though for Lydgate this affective power was a source of distrust. It may be that for these authors the aesthetic of stained glass proved consonant with the permeable poetics of dream vision. Stained glass, even though the product of careful planning and strategic deliberate choices, often registers as fractured and random even as it exudes expressive power (especially after having been subject to centuries of damage and shoddy Victorian restoration). Similarly, the events of late medieval dream visions tend to be disordered but captivating, replicating the random organization of dreams and casting the subjects of visions into emotional turbulence. I hope this study can provide impetus for examining other secular texts for their infusion of material aesthetics into their narratives, and for thinking through the fragmented yet enthralling nature of other dream-vision imagery.

---

50   Gibson, *The Theater of Devotion*, 7.
51   Gayk, 'Images of Pity', 177.

8

The Idle Readers of *Piers Plowman* in Print*

SPENCER STRUB

> *Rules as concerning Reading.*
> In reading, first; Take heede what Booke thou doest read; that they be
> not leawd and wanton, nor needlesse and vnprofitable, not sauouring of
> Popish superstition. But either the holy Scriptures, or other sound and
> godly Authors. In reading of the Scriptures, read not heere, and there
> a Chapter, (except vpon some good occasion) but the Bible in order
> throughout [...]
> 3 In reading of other good Bookes, read not heere a leafe of one, & a
> Chapter of an other (as idle Readers vse to do for nouelties sake) but make
> choyse of one or two sound and well pende Bookes; which reade againe
> and againe, for confirming of thy memorie, and directing of thy practise.
> 4 Before reading, pray vnto God to blesse thee in that action.
> 5 In reading, settle thy selfe to doe attention.
> 6 After reading, apply it to thy selfe for thy instruction, in thy practise
> and imitation.[1]

Some rules are made to be broken. These rules from the seventeenth-
century religious handbook *A Garden of Spirituall Flowers*, though
straightforward enough, are no exception. The idea that one should read
good matter in a thorough and linear fashion, in dedicated and repeated
stints, with eyes on 'one or two' books rather than distracted across

* I would like to thank Megan Cook, Taylor Cowdery, Ellora Derenoncourt,
Maura Nolan, R. D. Perry, and José Villagrana, as well as Wendy Scase and the
anonymous reviewers for this journal. Research for this project was supported
by the Friends of the Bancroft Library. An early version of this article was
presented at the Sixth International *Piers Plowman* Conference in 2015.
1 *A garden of spirituall flowers. Planted by Ri. Ro. Will. Per. Ri. Gree. M. M. and
Geo. Web* (London, 1610), STC (2nd edn) 21206, sig. G.3r–v.

many, has a history, of course. The emphasis on continuous attention reproduces an entire Protestant ideology of reading: unlike Catholics (especially *medieval* Catholics), who chopped up the Bible for liturgical and devotional convenience, Protestants read the Bible from start to finish, or so polemicists maintained. As these directions make clear, the same principle of continuous reading should be applied by extension to 'other good Bookes', which likewise require sustained attention for their lessons to be understood and applied in daily life.

But there are some wrinkles in these rules. Never mind that the evidence left by actual English Protestants almost always points to discontinuous Bible reading, as Peter Stallybrass has argued.[2] Never mind that these directions themselves are borrowed, abridged, and shoehorned together with tracts by half a dozen other Elizabethan Protestant writers, 'a leafe of one, & a Chapter of an other' – that this call for continuous reading is transmitted in a book *designed* for discontinuous reading.[3] And never mind that the form of this wildly popular book, reprinted twenty-nine times between 1603 and 1643, looks like nothing so much as a late medieval devotional miscellany (even the title betrays its ancestry in medieval florilegia): another wildly popular type, but one undoubtedly savouring of 'Popish superstition'. Such ironies seem lost on the compiler of *A Garden of Spirituall Flowers*, but they are nonetheless revealing for medievalists interested in the sixteenth- and seventeenth-century reception of Middle English literature. The normative force of those 'Rules as concerning Reading', and the contradictions they overlook, suggest just how many 'idle Readers' there might have been in early modern England, reading not only the Bible but also the archive of medieval culture in manuscript and in print.

This article addresses the ways in which such idle readers read and interacted with the early modern printed editions of *Piers Plowman* – a piece of that archive of medieval culture that was subject to especially intense interest from the mid-sixteenth century onward. Most of what

2   Peter Stallybrass, 'Books and Scrolls: Navigating the Bible', in *Books and Readers in Early Modern England*, ed. Jennifer Andersen, Elizabeth Sauer, and Stephen Orgel (Philadelphia, 2011), 42–79.
3   These directions are originally found at greater length in Richard Rogers's *Seven Treatises*, a popular work of Puritan-leaning religious instruction; see Rogers, *Seuen treatises containing such direction* [...] (London, 1603), STC (2nd edn) 21215. On the discontinuous reading facilitated by this type of book, see Matthew P. Brown, 'The Thick Style: Steady Sellers, Textual Aesthetics, and Early Modern Devotional Reading', *PMLA* 121 (2006), 67–86.

follows will address one specific book: a copy of Owen Rogers's 1561 *Piers Plowman* heavily annotated in the late sixteenth century, now Berkeley, Bancroft Library, PR2010 .A1 1561. (I will refer to this book as the 'Bancroft *Piers*' henceforth.) The readers of this book, and of several other books which I will refer to below, should be counted among the group that Heidi Brayman Hackel has termed the 'less extraordinary readers', or what Alison Wiggins calls in her survey of annotated printed copies of Chaucer 'casual and careless readers'. The former label points to these readers' relative historical obscurity – provincial and middling, they go unmentioned in the *Dictionary of National Biography*; the latter refers to their mode of engagement, the material trace of which appears considerably less thorough or consistent than the traces usually left by the learned humanist or devotional practices of reading and note-taking.[4] I have called these people 'idle readers', borrowing the *Garden of Spirituall Flowers*'s pejorative label, because the evidence generally points away from the clear and strongly motivated aims of many post-Reformation readers of *Piers Plowman*.[5] Idle readers pick up books and put them down; they doodle; they mark some pages but not all; they seem more curious than self-cultivating. But their idleness means that they respond to the poem in ways that are hard to predict from printed references to *Piers Plowman* or the traces left by better-known figures, the sources otherwise privileged in reception history. They are not, as I will argue, driven by confessional or polemical ends. Instead, this broad group of comparatively marginal sixteenth- and seventeenth-century readers seem to have come to this particularly difficult Middle English text without the sense of rupture or distance that we assign to post-Reformation readers of medieval literature; their responses speak to a comfort with the poem that more serious and scholarly approaches lack. When idle readers' responses are taken seriously, which means hazarding the reconstruction of intentions that lie behind notes that seem to resist 'close reading', the ongoing life of the poem becomes evident: these idle readers did not approach their books as artefacts but as everyday objects, suitable for both reading and use.

4 Heidi Brayman Hackel, *Reading Material in Early Modern England: Print, Gender, and Literacy* (Cambridge, 2005), 3; Alison Wiggins, 'What did Renaissance Readers Write in their Printed Copies of Chaucer?' *The Library* 9 (2008), 3–36.
5 I am grateful to Wendy Scase and Lawrence Warner for first proposing the term in response to an earlier version of this essay.

Early Modern Readers of Piers Plowman

Robert Crowley's letter to the readers of his edition of *Piers Plowman*, written sixty years earlier than *A Garden of Spirituall Flowers*, lacks the latter's explicit emphasis on completion and continuousness. But Crowley's letter shares with it a vein of moralistic instruction:

> Loke not upon this boke therfore, to talke of wonders paste or to come but to emend thyne owne misse, whych thou shalt fynd here moste charitably rebuked. The spirite of god geue the grace to walke in the way of truthe to Gods glory, & thyne owne soules healthe.[6]

Do not pick out the exciting bits of prophecy, Crowley insists, but read *Piers Plowman* for its holistic ethical value: an equation of right reading and spiritual emendation, of readerly difficulty and improvement of the self, not so different from that in the *Garden of Spirituall Flowers*. In Crowley's preface, the poem's charitable rebukes apply to 'thyne owne misse', just as the *Garden* encourages readers of any virtuous matter to 'apply it to thy selfe for thy instruction'. And just as that work's prescribed mode of Bible reading was rarely realized, so many readers happily disregarded Crowley's directions, annotating, compiling, and recopying the poem's supposed prophecies, as Wendy Scase and Lawrence Warner have shown.[7] Some such readers were, in fact, remarkably thorough in defying Crowley's instructions. London, British Library, C.122.d.9, a Crowley *Piers Plowman*, records a single reader's responses to the text on almost every page through passus 19 – one imagines the compiler of the *Garden of Spirituall Flowers* would admire their work – but as Jane Griffiths has recently observed, the reader of C.122.d.9 treated *Piers Plowman* specifically as a library of apocalyptic prophecy.[8] As Griffiths points out, the reader's indifference to Crowley's directions points out

6   Robert Crowley, *The vision of pierce Plowman nowe the second time imprinted* [...] (London, 1550), STC (2nd edn) 19907, sig. *ii verso.
7   Wendy Scase, '*Dauy Dycars Dreame* and Robert Crowley's Prints of *Piers Plowman*', *Yearbook of Langland Studies* 21 (2007), 171–98 (esp. 183–90); Lawrence Warner, *The Myth of Piers Plowman: Constructing a Medieval Literary Archive* (Cambridge, 2014), 72–86.
8   Jane Griffiths, 'Editorial Glossing and Reader Resistance in a Copy of Robert Crowley's *Piers Plowman*', in *Makers and Users of Medieval Books: Essays in Honour of A. S. G. Edwards*, ed. Carol M. Meale and Derek Pearsall (Cambridge, 2014), 202–13. This book was first discussed by Barbara A. Johnson, *Reading*

the '*de facto* limits on the authority of the printed word', the capacity for readers to appropriate and apprehend in ways that authors, editors, and printers can neither anticipate nor direct.[9]

But if we know that early modern readers disobeyed Crowley's editorial instructions, our critical histories have nevertheless privileged certain types of reading and reader. The story of *Piers Plowman*'s reception tends to emphasize two overlapping sixteenth- and seventeenth-century demographics: Protestant reformers and antiquarians.[10] My findings here lie in large part outside these categories, and I will suggest that the preponderance of such figures in the history of *Piers Plowman*'s reception has entrenched certain scholarly stereotypes of early modern readership that need to be revised. But there is nevertheless good cause for such a perception. Crowley's three 1550 editions of *Piers Plowman* are representative of the particular sixteenth-century English Protestant conjunction of historical recovery and ecclesiological polemic, for example. Crowley was undoubtedly a religious and political reformer and controversialist, and his editions reflect his convictions, but it is increasingly clear that his editorial work was sound, informed by a broader community of scholars that he did not hesitate to draw upon. It was, in other words, a project reformist in aims but antiquarian in methods.[11] Rogers's reprinting was likely intended for similar audiences, even if its production was more opportunistic than high-minded in aim.

Piers Plowman and the Pilgrim's Progress: Reception and the Protestant Reader (Carbondale, IL, 1992), 150–2.

9   Griffiths, 'Editorial Glossing', 213. On appropriation and readerly invention, see especially Roger Chartier, *The Order of Books: Readers, Authors, and Libraries in Europe between the Fourteenth and the Eighteenth Centuries*, trans. Lydia G. Cochrane (Stanford, CA, 1994), 1–23.

10   For example: 'Because *Piers Plowman* remained popular in the sixteenth century, especially within reformist and antiquarian circles, much sixteenth-century annotation relates to those particular concerns'. Simon Horobin, 'Manuscripts and Readers of *Piers Plowman*', in *The Cambridge Companion to 'Piers Plowman'*, ed. Andrew Cole and Andrew Galloway (Cambridge, 2014), 179–97 (192).

11   The foundational work on the reformist use of *Piers Plowman* is John N. King, 'Robert Crowley's Edition of *Piers Plowman*: A Tudor Apocalypse', *Modern Philology* 73 (1976), 342–52. King's arguments about Crowley have been convincingly challenged by R. Carter Hailey, '"Geuyng light to the reader": Robert Crowley's Editions of *Piers Plowman* (1550)', *Papers of the Bibliographical Society of America* 94 (2001), 483–502, and 'Robert Crowley and the Editing of *Piers Plowman* (1550)', *Yearbook of Langland Studies* 21 (2007), 143–70. Crowley's

More to the point, surviving records of readership suggest that by the middle of the sixteenth century many of the poem's readers came to it for its historical value, its anticlerical invective, or both.[12] Not all such readers were particularly attentive to the poem: the antiquarian Humphrey Llwyd's copy of the Rogers edition, now London, British Library, C.71.c.27, for instance, bears his ownership mark but is otherwise untouched.[13] The Protestant-reformist interpretation of the poem requires considerable bending of Langland's words and sentiments, and the evidence left by some such readers is therefore unsurprisingly inapt. A sixteenth-century reader of London, British Library, MS Cotton Vespasian B XVI (C-text sigil M), for example, labels Mede 'A roman harlot' – not exactly, it should be said, an accurate interpretation of the first vision, a court satire in which Mede stands for the corrosive rewards of wealth in both secular and religious contexts.[14] To read her as Roman requires a considerable degree of Protestant wishful thinking.

For the most part, though, the study of *Piers Plowman*'s early modern Protestant and antiquarian readers has shown their reading to be careful and thorough, and certainly not idle. Francis Aldrich, the Calvinist-leaning master of Sidney Sussex College, Cambridge, carefully annotated his Rogers copy, now Oxford, Bodleian Library, Malone 313. Aldrich underlines anticlerical and antipapal passages, even going so far as to argue with the poem: 'Perce here deceyved', he wrote beside the

scholarly networks are discussed in Thomas A. Prendergast, 'The Work of Robert Langland', in *Renaissance Retrospections: Tudor Views of the Middle Ages*, ed. Sarah A. Kelen (Kalamazoo, MI, 2013), 70–92.

12   The fullest discussion of the reception of *Piers Plowman* in the early modern period is in Sarah A. Kelen, *Langland's Early Modern Identities* (New York, 2007), especially 17–76. See also Johnson, *Reception and the Protestant Reader*.

13   The title page is inscribed: 'Humfre lloyd 1564 / Hwy pery clod na golud. / Lumley'. On Llwyd as antiquarian, see see R. Brinley Jones, 'Humphrey Llwyd (1527–68)', *Oxford Dictionary of National Biography*, ed. H. C. G. Matthew and Brian Harrison (Oxford, 2004).

14   London, British Library, MS Cotton Vespasian B XVI, fol. 22v. 'Mede mornede þo and made heuy chere' (C.4.160) is boxed by the same hand. Here and in what follows I will quote from the relevant printed editions of the poem in the form version, passus, line number; all references to line numbers in *Piers Plowman* are to the Athlone Press editions: *Piers Plowman: The B Version*, ed. George Kane and E. T. Donaldson (London, 1975); and *Piers Plowman: The C Version*, ed. George Russell and George Kane (London, 1997). All abbreviations will be silently expanded.

orthodox Catholic account of the Eucharist.[15] This copy has been largely overlooked, but it is representative of the thorough, intellectual, and rather truculent engagement that we expect of Langland's post-Reformation readers. Lawrence Warner and Simon Horobin have uncovered a number of manuscripts and printed editions associated with the Protestant scholar Stephan Batman and the broader antiquarian circles of Archbishop Matthew Parker. Like Aldrich, Batman carefully sorted through the poem with an eye conditioned by Protestant polemic and his priestly vocation.[16]

The exceptions to *Piers Plowman*'s Protestant reception seem, perversely, to prove the rule. The Catholic Andrew Bostock's copy of the Crowley *Piers*, which has been discussed recently by Rebecca Schoff and Christine Schott, show Bostock throwing rejoinder after rejoinder at Crowley's marginalia.[17] The Catholic courtier and martyr Adrian Fortescue's manuscript of the poem bears witness to a heated debate in its margins, as Fortescue and his wife Anne's notes were later challenged and overwritten by a Protestant inheritor of the book.[18] Though this line of study is still new, and ongoing work will no doubt bring to light further exceptions like Bostock and the Fortescues, the evidence they left behind nevertheless points to a poem whose meaning was inextricable from the wider cultural conditions of interconfessional strife. Moreover, even if these Catholic readers are diametrically opposed to the politics and ecclesiology of the main reformist current of *Piers Plowman* reception – which goes to Langland, as to Wyclif and Chaucer,

15   Oxford, Bodleian Library, Malone 313, sig. Gg.iiir. The line – 'Here is bread blessed, and gods body therunder' (B.19.385) – is spoken by Conscience, not Piers.

16   Lawrence Warner, 'New Light on *Piers Plowman*'s Ownership c.1450–1600', *Journal of the Early Book Society* 12 (2009), 183–94; Horobin, 'Manuscripts and Readers', and 'Stephan Batman and his Manuscripts of *Piers Plowman*', *Review of English Studies* 62 (2010), 358–72. Though Batman seems an exemplary reformist reader, there is little evidence of Parker's close attention to the poem.

17   Rebecca Schoff, *Reformations: Three Medieval Authors in Manuscript and Movable Type* (Turnhout, 2007), 204–6; and Christine Schott, 'Notes for Posterity: An Owner's Annotation in an Early *Piers Plowman* Printing', *Journal of the Early Book Society* 16 (2013), 195–202.

18   Karrie Fuller, 'Langland in the Early Modern Household: *Piers Plowman* in Oxford, Bodleian Library MS Digby 145, and its Scribe-Annotator Dialogues', in *New Directions in Medieval Manuscript Studies and Reading Practices*, ed. Kathryn Kerby-Fulton, John J. Thompson, and Sarah Baechle (South Bend, IN, 2014), 324–41.

in search of a Protestant English church before Luther – they still share a public-minded way of reading poetry with their antagonists.[19] Aldrich's dialogue with Langland and Bostock's dialogue with Crowley may resemble the poem's own fierce disputations, but they belong to a broader public conflict between Catholics, Calvinists, and advocates of the Established Church. Their annotations respond to the poem according to the terms and motives of a debate external to the poem, carried out in sermons and pamphlets, and they treat *Piers Plowman* at least in part as *material* for that debate.

These are active, not idle, readers. In their foundational article on Gabriel Harvey's annotations, Lisa Jardine and Anthony Grafton argue that early modern readers viewed 'action as the *outcome* of reading': reading and note-taking were prefatory steps to public engagement.[20] The Rogers *Piers Plowman* owned by Harvey's younger brother Richard may not reveal the same aims as Gabriel Harvey's copy of Livy, but it likewise attests to a *very* close reading to public ends. Every page of his book is annotated. Many of his marks simply pull out key terms, explain narrative turns, or offer tentative steps towards interpretation (serving a role similar to Crowley's marginal apparatus, which Rogers's mostly bare margins lack).[21] But other moments reveal a more heated and polemical reader: Richard actually participates in one of the poem's debates, responding to the Doctor of Divinity's dismissal of Patience's account of dowel, dobet, and dobest ('it is but a Dido') with the incredulous note, 'Dido? yea?'[22] In a note on the poem's first page, he praises the poem's stance 'agenst the Romish

19   There is a way in which these texts are private: both Fuller and Schott present the audiences of the annotations in MS Digby 145 and MS Douce L250 as the annotator's families. But that intimate audience does not preclude public ambitions, interests, or modes of engagement. See Fuller, 'Scribe-Annotator Dialogues'; and Schott, 'Notes for Posterity'.

20   Lisa Jardine and Anthony Grafton, '"Studied for Action": How Gabriel Harvey Read his Livy', *Past & Present* 129 (1990), 30–78 (40). Emphasis original.

21   Other marginal notes reveal more obscure interpretative aims: he tries to work out the succession of numbers in the dense symbolism of Piers's plough in passus 19, for example, marking 4. 4. 2. 1. 2. 3 in the margin alongside the respective parts of the image; whether he thought some numerological code lay behind it, or whether he was simply trying to clarify this part of the poem for himself is unclear. See New Haven, Beinecke Library, Id L26 550F, sig. Gg.i.

22   Beinecke Library, Id L26 550F, sig. S.iiii verso, at B.13.172.

Glory', and his marginal annotations unsurprisingly reveal interests in anti-Roman polemic.[23] Unlike his brother, Richard Harvey was not jockeying for advancement at court, but he *was* a clergyman, reading for sermon, education, and debate, his goals the pious obverse to his brother's secular ambitions. The same point can be applied more broadly: though antiquarian, reformist, and even recusant readers were not necessarily 'reading for action' in precisely the same way as Gabriel Harvey (their interests probably did not lie in policy or in political advancement, and Langland's cultural capital was different from Livy's), their reading points to a public outcome, an intervention in the world.[24]

These active readers, whose thoughts become manifest as public engagement, appeal to critics because they promise to solve interpretative problems endemic to the history of reading. Most readers' thoughts cannot be reconstructed: they are anonymous or semi-anonymous, their intentions are inaccessible, their social world only partially imaginable. But marginalia made by a 'known individual' like Harvey, Aldrich, or Batman – public figures with a textual record – 'can thus be considered within his particular social, theological and literary contexts', as Horobin notes.[25] Questions of meaning and intention in material traces otherwise resistant to interpretation (manicules, marginal lines, one-word notes) can be set aside if we can already guess what the reader was thinking. The meticulous work of scholars like Horobin shows how context really can make sense of such traces. But there is a risk of confirmation bias here as well, as there is in any literary-critical historicism.[26] There is also a risk of granting physical evidence

---

23   On this annotation, see also Johnson, *Reception and the Protestant Reader*, 153–5. Harvey's notes also reveal an interest in prophecy: see Warner, *Myth of Piers Plowman*, 83.

24   The active readership of *Piers Plowman* does not begin in the sixteenth century, of course, and in earlier periods it may well have played a role closer to Harvey's Livy than it did later. The fourteenth- and fifteenth-century recopying and imaginative rewriting of the poem in legal and bureaucratic circles proximate to court, as identified by Kathryn Kerby-Fulton and Steven Justice, suggest as much. See Kerby-Fulton and Justice, 'Langlandian Reading Circles and the Civil Service in London and Dublin, 1380–1427', *New Medieval Literatures* 1 (1997), 59–84.

25   Horobin, 'Stephan Batman', 360.

26   See the wide-ranging critique of such historicist confirmation bias in Derek Attridge, *The Singularity of Literature* (London and New York, 2004), 1–17.

an uncomplicated authority: as Alexandra Gillespie has cautioned, 'books – those ragged objects in our hands, the "soil" with which we work – are not just true', but are (or should be) as resistant to critical certainty as the text they transmit.[27]

So what happens when the readers for action are replaced by idle readers? When the readers of *Piers Plowman* are not reformers or antiquarians with official appointments and published tracts to their names, but provincial farmers and merchants otherwise unknown to history, whose reading left evidence that is confusing, incoherent, or partial? What kind of interpretative claims can be made about *those* books?

Piers Plowman in the Provinces

The welter of names in the Owen Rogers *Piers Plowman* now in the Bancroft Library points precisely to such obscure and middling readers, firmly anchored in the provinces.[28] The first owner may have been John Tynker (1542–98?), whose signature survives on the verso of the title page, dated to 1561 (Fig. 1).[29] Tynker lived in the village of Kirkburton in West Yorkshire, the son of a minor landowner of the same name.[30] His inscription may simply reproduce the edition's publication date (the same hand has written the impossible '1551' beside it), but given his dates and the book's later circulation, confined to cities further to the south, he remains the most likely candidate for earliest identifiable owner. However, Tynker left few traces in his book and no indication of how he obtained it. It seems more likely that he bought it locally than direct from London: by 1561 York no longer supported native printers, but aside from the university towns it was the major hub of the provincial

27   Alexandra Gillespie, 'The History of the Book', *New Medieval Literatures* 9 (2007), 245–86 (272).
28   A full transcription of annotations can be viewed at spencerstrub.com/bancroftpiers.
29   On Tynker, see *The Parish Registers of Kirkburton, Co. York*, ed. Frances Anne Collins, 2 vols (Exeter, 1887–1902), 1:3 and 1:156. Note, however, that several roughly contemporaneous John Tynkers are recorded in the parish registers, all apparently part of the same extended family based in Kirkburton.
30   See *Parish Registers of Kirkburton*, ed. Collins, 1:30, for John Tynker the Elder (d.1554).

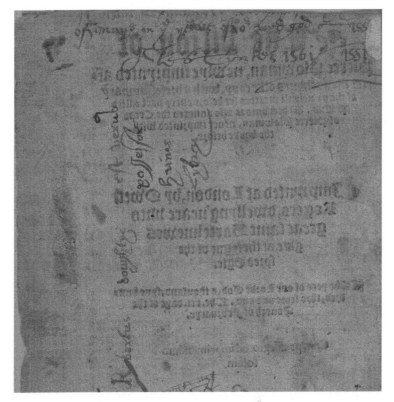

Fig. 1   Signature of John Tynker, dated 1561; Berkeley, Bancroft Library
PR2010 .A1 1561, title page verso

book trade.[31] Booksellers or pedlars may have met Tynker in Kirkburton,
or he may have travelled to York.[32]

31   See D. M. Palliser, *Tudor York* (Oxford, 1979), 169–70; Paul Morgan, 'The
Provincial Book Trade before the End of the Licensing Act', in *Six Centuries of
the Provincial Book Trade in Britain*, ed. Peter Isaac (Winchester, 1990), 31–9;
Stacey Gee, 'The Printers, Stationers and Bookbinders of York before 1557',
Transactions of the Cambridge Bibliographical Society 12 (2000), 27–54; and John
Barnard and Maureen Bell, 'The English Provinces', in *The Cambridge History
of the Book in Britain*, vol. 4: *1557–1695*, ed. John Barnard and D. F. McKenzie
(Cambridge, 2002), 665–86.

32   On itinerant pedlars in provincial England, focusing on broadsides but
indicative of book sales as well, see Tessa Watt, 'Publisher, Pedlar, Pot-Poet:
The Changing Character of the Broadside Trade, 1550–1640', in *Spreading the

The next marked owner is Richard Bynnyngley of Doncaster, South Yorkshire.[33] The Bynnyngleys were of yeoman rank and, like the Tynkers, minor landholders. Bynnyngley left considerably more evidence of engagement with the book than Tynker, all in a sprawling secretary hand particularly characterized by a u-like minuscule 'e' (Fig. 2). I will turn to that evidence of engagement in the next section. Though again it is impossible to know how or from whom Bynnyngley obtained the book (if Tynker's will or any relevant records of booksellers survive, I could not locate them), Doncaster was a natural destination for goods, as it was a transit centre, a river port and crossing-point for roads from Yorkshire to Derbyshire.[34]

From Bynnyngley, the book moved south along those roads to Robert Doughtie, a mercer in Derby from at least the 1580s on. Doughtie's work required travel, and unlike any of the other readers of the book, he had definite ties to London; when he died in 1603, he was buried there, though his descendants remained in Derbyshire.[35] When he made his will in 1588 he had substantial goods to dispense, though sadly no books are mentioned.[36] With Doughtie the clear transmission history ends,

---

Word: The Distribution Networks of Print, 1550–1850, ed. Robin Myers and Michael Harris (Winchester, 1990), 61–81. There *is* sound literary precedent for Yorkshiremen fetching books from London: the 1575 *Newes from the north* imagines 'Pierce Plowman', like Tynker a Yorkshire 'Countrie man', returning from London to Ripon 'bringing vnder his arme a fardel of Bookes'. *Newes from the north* is, of course, fiction, and the question of the value of those books – and Pierce's ability to secure a loan using them as surety – animates the opening of the dialogue. See *Newes from the north. Otherwise called The conference between Simon Certain, and Pierce Plowman* (London, 1579), sig. B.ii verso.

33   Richard Biningley and Alis Diconson, marriage record, 27 November 1573 (Rossington, Yorkshire); accessed via Ancestry.com. *England & Wales Marriages, 1538–1940*, 2008.

34   David Hey, *Packmen, Carriers, and Packhorse Roads: Trade and Communications in North Derbyshire and South Yorkshire* (Leicester, 1980), 16 and 114.

35   London Metropolitan Archives, St Dunstan and All Saints, Stepney, Register of burials, Jul 1603–Aug 1618, P93/DUN/275; accessed in Ancestry.com, *London, England, Baptisms, Marriages and Burials, 1538–1812* [database online] (Provo, UT, 2010).

36   Doughtie also had some local prominence: from 1583–4, he was warden of the Collegiate Church of All Saints, Derby. See John Charles Cox and William Henry St John Hope, *The Chronicles of the Collegiate Church or Free Chapel of*

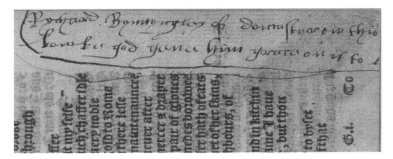

Fig. 2   Richard Bynnyngley's ownership mark; Berkeley, Bancroft Library PR2010 .A1 1561, sig. G.i recto

and it can only be picked up again four centuries later.[37] But a number of other hands in the book are likely contemporary with Doughtie's and can be placed in Derby or its surroundings. A sixteenth-century inscription by a 'husbandman[n]e' from Repton, Derbyshire, implies the book travelled there, for example.[38] It seems likely that the book was a lending copy: Doughtie hedged against its loss by leaving ten ownership marks in the book – there were probably more before the margins were trimmed – in some leaving a note to anyone who finds it mislaid, 'I praye you restor [it] to my agent' (Fig. 3).[39]

In addition to the nameable series of owners, an unnamed secondary audience read and, in some cases, wrote in the book. Attempts to reconstruct *that* audience must remain speculative. But even the identifiable owners of the Bancroft *Piers*, coming from the provincial middle class, constitute an understudied readership for the printed *Piers Plowman*. All of the identifiable people associated with the book were laymen, based in

All Saints, Derby (London and Derby, 1881), 35. Doughtie's will was proven in London in 1588; see the National Archives of the UK (TNA): PROB 11/72/247.

37   The book came up for auction at Christie's in 2005. It remained in private collection from 2005 to 2013, when Paul Dowling of Liber Antiquus purchased and sold it to the Bancroft Library. I am grateful to Paul Dowling for sharing this information in private correspondence, 15 August 2015.

38   PR2010 .A1 1561, sig. F.iii recto. I have not been able to trace this husbandman, as with a number of other one-off names in the book (a surnameless Francis, and a 'Robte Priise' who may be one Robert Pryce, married in Derby in 1602).

39   PR2010 .A1 1561, sig. H.iv recto. On antecedents to Doughtie's gentle anathema, see Glending Olson, 'Author, Scribe, and Curse: The Genre of Adam Scriveyn', *Chaucer Review* 42 (2008), 284–97.

Fig. 3   Robert Doughtie's ownership mark; Berkeley, Bancroft Library
PR2010 .A1 1561, sig. H.iv recto

Derbyshire or Yorkshire (Map 1). None was titled and none has left any
record of higher education. Aside from gender, these 'less extraordinary'
men share little with the scholars and churchmen, based in London and
the universities, who are most often attested in the surviving records of
Piers Plowman's early modern readership.

Now, the Bancroft *Piers* is not exceptional in the early modern
history of reading full stop. Its owners should probably be counted
among the local mercantile elite, especially Doughtie. David Cressy's
reconstruction of early modern literacy rates suggests that mercers were
among both the wealthiest and most literate of early modern trades-
people.[40] The yeoman rank in general was considerably more literate
than husbandmen and labourers, among whom at most one of the
book's readers can be counted.[41] Slightly later records from York and
Derbyshire suggest that merchant literacy included book-reading as well
as pragmatic or documentary literacy.[42] Moreover, bibliographers have

40   David Cressy, *Literacy and the Social Order: Reading and Writing in Tudor
and Stuart England* (Cambridge, 1980), 132 (literacy) and 140 (wealth). Cressy's
figures for writing ability likely underestimate rates of reading ability, however;
see Margaret Spufford, 'First Steps in Literacy: The Reading and Writing
Experiences of the Humblest Seventeenth-Century Autobiographers', *Social
History* 4 (1979), 407–35. It is also worth noting that sixteenth-century Doncaster,
Derby, and Repton were comparatively prosperous agrarian-mercantile counterparts to the poorer Peak Country nearby, the 'pastoral, industrial north' of
Derbyshire dominated by the lead-mining industry. On the history of that
division, see Andy Wood, *The Politics of Social Conflict: The Peak Country,
1520–1770* (Cambridge, 1999), 41.
41   Cressy, *Literacy and the Social Order*, 136.
42   The debtors of the early seventeenth-century York bookseller John Foster
are 'almost two-thirds' clergymen, but include nine merchants. See John Barnard
and Maureen Bell, *The Early Seventeenth-Century York Book Trade and John*

Map 1   Towns associated with the Bancroft *Piers.* Underlying GIS data
for map from H. R. Southall and N. Burton, *GIS of the Ancient Parishes of
England and Wales, 1500-1850* [computer file] (Colchester, 2004)

found evidence of exchanges among this class that strongly resemble
the various movements of the Bancroft *Piers*: as Maureen Bell writes
of Leonard Wheatcroft, 'the tailor and sometime yeoman of a small
Derbyshire town had plenty of opportunities for buying books or

Foster's Inventory of 1616 (Leeds, 1994), 17. Rosemary Milward's analysis of
seventeenth-century Chesterfield probate inventories turns up a mercer, a cloth-
worker, a tanner, a widow, and two unspecified yeoman among the book-owners
who died before 1650; the fact that Doughtie's will mentions no books, like others
discussed below, suggests book ownership well beyond what can be reconstructed from such probate evidence. See Milward, 'Books and Booksellers in
Late 17th-Century Chesterfield', *Derbyshire Miscellany* 10 (1985), 119–45 (130–1).

exchanging them with others'.[43] The same must have applied to Doughtie, Bynnyngley, and the other readers of the Bancroft *Piers*, though they antedated Wheatcroft by a century.

Especially given the low rate of survival for 'popular' books, it is entirely possible that the Bancroft *Piers* is representative of a broad sixteenth-century provincial readership for the poem.[44] *Piers Plowman* certainly made it out of southern England and urban centres: the Yorkshire preacher Walter Stonehouse may have owned a manuscript of *Piers Plowman*, while in the rural West Midlands, Frances Wolfreston owned a copy of Crowley's second edition.[45] But these cases are not perfect analogues to the Bancroft *Piers*. Stonehouse was an Oxford-educated clergyman; Wolfreston, an exceptionally book-loving member of the country gentry. Both gathered their collections in the seventeenth century. Most importantly, neither of their books can be traced, and whatever styles of reading they disclose must remain unknown.

43 *A Catalogue of the Library of Titus Wheatcroft of Ashover*, ed. Maureen Bell (Chesterfield, 2008), 73.

44 Books in institutional and otherwise stable libraries tend to survive at much higher rates than books outside of them, such as the Doughtie *Piers*, a fact that may account for the presumed prevalence of religious and academic figures in the reception of medieval poetry. See Paul Needham, 'The Late Use of Incunables and the Paths of Book Survival', *Wolfenbütteler Notizen der Buchgeschichte* 29 (2004), 35–59 (39–41 especially). Note, however, that Needham's general estimates for rates of survival are based on the figure of 20 million European incunables, which has been questioned by Joseph A. Dane, *The Myth of Print Culture: Essays on Evidence, Textuality, and Bibliographical Method* (Toronto, 2003), 32–56. More directly apposite to my claims here, however, is the discussion of the low survival rates of provincial early modern manuscripts in Steven W. May and Arthur F. Marotti, *Ink, Stink Bait, Revenge, and Queen Elizabeth: A Yorkshire Yeoman's Household Book* (Ithaca, NY, and London, 2014), 7. A rather surprising analogy is worth making here: the surviving manuscript copy of the *Book of Margery Kempe* is likewise first attested in Yorkshire before moving to Derbyshire. Unlike the Bancroft *Piers*, it was held in a major institutional library (the library of the Carthusians of Mount Grace) and by the prominent recusant Digby family; its survival is nonetheless somewhat miraculous, as described in Julie A. Chappell, *Perilous Passages: The Book of Margery Kempe, 1534–1934* (New York, 2013).

45 On Stonehouse, see Sebastiaan Verweij, '"Booke, go thy wayes": The Publication, Reading, and Reception of James VI/I's Early Poetic Works', *Huntington Library Quarterly* 77 (2014), 111–31 (118). On Wolfreston, see Paul Morgan, 'Francis Wolfreston and "Hor Bouks": A Seventeenth-Century Woman Book-Collector', *Library* 6 (1989), 197–219.

So if the Bancroft *Piers* is not unprecedented, it does offer a unique opportunity to discern how the poem was read in the post-Reformation provinces: though they may represent the early modern reading majority, people like Bynnyngley and Doughtie are hard to find in studies of medieval reception. Neither univocally reformist nor clearly antiquarian, the traces left by these identifiable but comparatively marginal readers disrupt existing narratives of the early modern *Piers Plowman*.

Idle and Intentional Marks

Reaching interpretative conclusions about the Bancroft *Piers* is rather more difficult than reconstructing its movements through Yorkshire and Derbyshire. Digital genealogical registries and archival records can fill in birthdates and professions for the names in books, but they cannot tell us what those people thought of the books they handled. The Bancroft *Piers* is marked throughout by the thoughts, such as they are, of Doughtie, Bynnyngley, and at least two other consistent and repeated hands. Taken collectively, those markings point to an engagement with the text that falls short of the *Garden of Spirituall Flowers*'s instructions: it is partial, distracted, intermittent, and sometimes incoherent. That incoherence is interesting on its own terms, however. These idle readers responded to *Piers Plowman* in diverse ways, some consistent with the evidence in other copies, others very unlike it. Carl James Grindley's taxonomy of readers' marks in manuscripts of the C-text is useful here. He identifies three broad categories of annotation: the first, those with 'no apparent relationship to the book' (such as ownership marks and pen-trials); the second, those particular to the book (tables of contents and copied letter-forms); the third, those that respond to the works therein (reading aids, responses, and other commentary).[46] All three categories are amply attested in the Bancroft *Piers*. Such diversity of reception shows the poem being reinterpreted as it met new audiences, even two or more centuries after its composition.

---

46 Carl James Grindley, 'Reading *Piers Plowman* C-Text Annotations: Notes toward the Classification of Printed and Written Marginalia in Texts from the British Isles, 1300–1641', in *The Medieval Professional Reader at Work: Evidence from Manuscripts of Chaucer, Langland, Kempe, and Gower*, ed. Kathryn Kerby-Fulton and Maidie Hilmo (Victoria, B.C., 2001), 73–141.

As might be expected, the more academic kinds of markings in many surviving copies of the Crowley and Rogers *Piers* – corrections to the editorial text that imply access to manuscripts, for example, or substantiating marginal comments on specific historical references – are nowhere to be found here. These readers were not mining the poem for its documentary value, nor engaged in any sort of humanist textual scholarship. The first of Grindley's types is widely attested. Someone in Doncaster, for example, repeatedly drafted an indenture in the margins. At four points throughout the book, a Derby reader – not Doughtie, probably, but someone who borrowed or bought the book from him – has practised writing the salutation for a letter to Anthony Bate, a wealthy cloth-worker and one-time bailiff of Derby.[47] In both cases, the writer tested a formal engrossing secretary hand (the first shows particularly elaborate embellishments) in a book otherwise marked in relatively sloppy, casual, and untutored hands. These kinds of pragmatic marks that make a notebook of a printed book – capitalizing on otherwise-scarce paper conveniently at hand – are indicative of the use of the book rather than its reading.[48] The copious ownership marks left by Doughtie and Bynnyngley, and the single signatures left by Tynker and the Repton husbandman, are more ambiguous cases: as Daniel Wakelin has argued of the far more prolific reader and annotator William Worcester, the *ex libris* should be read within the 'practices of representation and self-presentation in texts', the limit of a continuum of fiction and autobiography.[49] Doughtie – the 'verus possessor huius lybry', as one of his ownership formulae puts it – marks his ownership, reinforcing the claim to his property.[50] But the husbandman's signature makes no such claim, simply noting his place and profession ('rapton in darby / shyre in the conty of darby husband / man[n]e'). These kinds of marks may just

47   On Bate, see *The History and Gazetteer of the County of Derby*, ed. Thomas Noble, vol. 1 (Derby, 1831), Appendix, 20; W. G. Dimock Fletcher, *Leicestershire Pedigrees and Royal Descents* (Leicester, 1887), 81; TNA C 1/1403/3–4.

48   On the distinction between use and reading (and a call to return to studies of reading), see Jennifer Richards and Fred Schurink, 'Introduction: The Textuality and Materiality of Reading in Early Modern England', *Huntington Library Quarterly* 73 (2010), 345–61. For a nuanced account of use and non-reading, see Leah Price, *How to Do Things with Books in Victorian Britain* (Princeton, 2012).

49   Daniel Wakelin, 'William Worcester Writes a History of his Reading', *New Medieval Literatures* 7 (2005), 53–71.

50   PR2010 .A1 1561, title page verso.

register a reader's presence and literacy, a self-assertion on the order of
the modern graffiti tag, as Jason Scott-Warren has argued.[51]

Such marks reveal a social world, and they help us see the book being
put to use within that world. But they do not say much about how the
book was read, or what meanings were made of it. The poem *was* read,
though, and there are marks that reveal readers' thoughts about the
poem in their hands. But even those marginalia that directly engage
with the texts – Grindley's type three – refuse to align with any one
narrative of reception. In part, that resistance is simply characteristic of
the kind of reading the text records. The Bancroft *Piers* lacks evidence
of the kind of sustained engagement found in Richard Harvey's copy
or in British Library C.122.d.9, which are marked throughout by a
single hand. Though the Bancroft *Piers* is also marked throughout, no
such single coherent presence can be read into it: its margins are a riot
of different hands, belonging to people who were reading the book
probably over a series of decades. Nor is there much evidence of the
basic interpretative annotations, such as narrative markers or glosses
to 'hard words', found in C.122.d.9 and other printed copies of *Piers
Plowman*. In the sole exception, a reader has copied 'sum rex' beside the
Angel's speech in the Prologue, marking its opening line: 'Sum Rex, sum
Princeps, neutrum fortasse deinceps' ('I am king, I am prince; [you will
be] neither perhaps hereafter').[52] The marginal identification of sententious or sacred Latin is common enough in early modern readers' notes
on *Piers* in manuscript and print – as Warner has pointed out, Beinecke
Library Id L26 550c is particularly obsessive in this regard, going so far
as to create a primer of Langland's Latin on a blank leaf – but there is no

---

51   Jason Scott-Warren, 'Reading Graffiti in the Early Modern Book', *Huntington
Library Quarterly* 73 (2010), 363–81. The analogy has limits: graffiti culture is
both internally self-governing and subject to legal and extralegal repression;
early modern marginalia was neither. The elevation of graffiti (and its formal
reflex, street art) and its commodification in the art market over the past several
decades *does* make an interesting parallel to critics' and booksellers' attitudes
to annotations in books, however: what was once defacement or 'dirt' is now
valorized in a discourse that treats it as particularly spontaneous and 'real'. On
those attitudes, see Susan Stewart, '*Ceci Tuera Cela*: Graffiti as Crime and Art', in
her *Crimes of Writing: Problems in the Containment of Representation* (Oxford,
1991), 206–33.

52   PR2010 .A1 1561, A.iii recto. B.Prol.132. On these lines, see Andrew Galloway,
The Penn Commentary on 'Piers Plowman', vol. 1: *C Prologue–Passus 4; B
Prologue–Passus 4; A Prologue–Passus 4* (Philadelphia, 2006), 127–8.

follow-up in the Bancroft *Piers*.[53] If an attempt was made to construe the
text or index its *sententiae*, it ended rather swiftly. Perhaps a sixteenth-
century reader found these lines on the evanescence and responsibility
of kingship particularly compelling, but again, if so, the poem's many
other passages on kingship and governance go unmarked. 'Readers for
action' closely attended to the first vision, for example, even if they bent
its meaning according to their own motives; these readers show no such
engagement.

   That said, the book does not entirely resist interpretative judgment.
One consistent interest is unsurprising: at least one annotator, writing
in a comparatively formal and careful engrossing secretary probably
in the early seventeenth century, was drawn to the poem as a reformist
document. Though satires of pilgrims and monks get a few lines in the
margins,[54] his or her interest mostly bends towards the antiepiscopal
and antiprelatical, cued in part by the preface in Rogers's edition, which
describes how the poem 'declareth the great wickednes of the Bishoppes,
that spareth not to hange their seales at euery Pardoners boxes, and what
shameful Simonye raigneth in the church'. (The reader drew a line after
this paragraph.)[55] The prediction of dispossession voiced by Anima in
passus 15 has been marked several times, with emphasis hinging on the
poem's account of the donation of Constantine, when the church 'dronke
[the] venym' of temporal wealth. When Anima exhorts, 'take her landes
ye lordes, & let hem liue by decymus', this annotator has written: 'questio
orietur' – the question will arise.[56] While this ominous note undoubtedly
draws on some vein of Protestant critique, whether it should be read
more specifically as retrospective crowing over the dissolution of the
monasteries or a Puritan's comment on the future of the Church of
England is unclear. The Reformation was famously belated in the
diocese of York, but the early seventeenth century saw a concerted attack
on recusancy, driven by the archbishop and picked up by pamphleteers
and preachers.[57] But by the end of Elizabeth's reign, there was also a

53   Warner, *Myth of Piers Plowman*, 67–71.
54   PR2010 .A1 1561, sig. h.ii recto.
55   Ibid., sig. *.ii recto.
56   Ibid., sig. z.iiii verso; 15.364.
57   On the reformation of York, see Claire Cross, 'Priests into Ministers:
The Establishment of Protestant Practice in the City of York, 1530–1630', in
Reformation Principle and Practice: Essays in Honour of Arthur Geoffrey Dickens,
ed. Peter Newman Brooks (London, 1980), 203–25. On the campaign against
recusants after 1606, see Barnard and Bell, *John Foster's Inventory*, 28–31.

substantial Puritan presence in Derbyshire; the 'notoriously disobedient' Puritan Arthur Hildersham preached in Repton in the early seventeenth century, for example.[58] Taken alongside the apparently antiepiscopal sentiments of the reader, the annotations to passus 15 certainly suggest a more radical reformist reader: though Constantine was an object of admiration for earlier Protestants like John Foxe, the critical fourteenth-century tradition of the Donation, which this section of *Piers* shares with the *Confessio Amantis* and the *Plowman's Tale*, was often cited by Puritan writers as historical justification for their positions against the Established Church.[59] That suggestion is hard to substantiate, however. The *loci classici* for reformist readings of *Piers Plowman* – passus 10's prophecy of the abbot of Abingdon, for example – go unmarked. If there is a Calvinist reader, his or her reading is not so cranky or energetic as Aldrich's, and nowhere are the poem's doctrinal errors pointed out. One does not get the sense that a polemicist or preacher has gone looking for evidence in this book.

It is worth underlining this point: these readers do not participate in the interconfessional debates that 'readers for action' might. The book's marginalia generally reveal religious interests more ecumenical than polemical. Passages of straightforward moral or religious instruction, equally appealing across confessional divides, are marked more often than the reformist satire described above: Holy Church's lecture on moderation in food and drink in passus 1 has been noted, for example, and her instruction in passus 2 to turn to 'ye psalter' for 'how ye shoulde saue your selfe' has been starred.[60] In such reactions, the

---

58   On Calvinist writers in Yorkshire, see A. G. Dickens, 'The Writers of Tudor Yorkshire', *Transactions of the Royal Historical Society* 13 (1963), 49–76. On Calvinists in Derby, see Christopher Haigh, 'Puritan Evangelism in the Reign of Elizabeth I', *The English Historical Review* 92 (1977), 30–58. On Hildersham, see Roland G. Usher, 'The Deprivation of Puritan Ministers in 1605', *The English Historical Review* 24.94 (1909), 232–46 (240). On 'Puritanically-inclined' Chesterfield, see Wood, *Politics of Social Conflict*, 271.

59   See, for instance, Henry Barrow's quotation of the *Plowman's Tale* in *A petition directed to her most excellent maiestie...* (Middleburg, 1591), STC (2nd edn) 1521, 34–5 (sig. E.i^v–E.ii^r). Barrow's quotation is lifted by William Prynne, *A breviate of the prelates intollerable usurpations. Edition 3. much enlarged* (Amsterdam, 1637), 26–7; and John Milton, *Of Reformation Touching Church-discipline in England: And the Causes that hitherto have hindred it* (London, 1641), 31.

60   PR2010 .A1 1561, sigs. B.i recto and B.iv verso.

poem becomes a pragmatic work of religious instruction, a response continuous with the fifteenth-century scribes and readers who compiled the poem with catechetical works, and annotated and rubricated it for ease of ethical use.[61] Like those earlier readers, though, the readers of the Bancroft *Piers* did not come to the poem exclusively for practical instruction. Some more metaphorical devotional passages also earn attention: there seems to have been an effort to work out Langland's image of the Trinity as a candle in passus 17, for example, though that note has been trimmed beyond legibility.[62] Less ambiguous marginal markers point to the foundation and roofing of the Barn of Unity and Conscience's two commands to delve a ditch around it, perhaps indicating a particular receptivity to Langland's agrarian metaphor in an audience more proximate to farm-work than others.[63] Taken together, these marks point to readers making the poem useful and legible for themselves, as a piece of Christian instruction rather than ammunition for interconfessional battle.[64]

Invention in the Margins

More surprisingly, some readers not only made an effort to construe Langland's poetry but also contributed their own to the book's margins. The first instance comes in Bynnyngley's hand in passus 8. What remains of it is fragmentary: 'Sere knaue and take up your beter', he writes, 'name is Johne name les / because I woulde be blamles' (Fig. 4).[65] It is not uncommon to encounter doggerel like this in the margins of Renaissance books, but these lines are unusually evocative and are

---

61   On the catechetical works that accompany *Piers Plowman*, see A. I. Doyle, 'Remarks on Surviving Manuscripts of *Piers Plowman*', in *Medieval English Religious and Ethical Literature: Essays in Honour of G. H. Russell*, ed. Gregory Kratzmann and James Simpson (Cambridge, 1986), 35–48 (47).
62   PR2010 .A1 1561, sig. C[c.]iii verso.
63   Ibid., sig. Gg.ii recto–verso.
64   For similar evidence of the ongoing post-Reformation devotional use of Middle English religious writing (both Wycliffite and orthodox, often in the same book), see also Margaret Connolly, 'Sixteenth-Century Readers Reading Fifteenth-Century Religious Books: The Roberts Family of Middlesex', in *Middle English Religious Writing in Practice: Texts, Readers, and Transformations*, ed. Nicole R. Rice (Turnhout, 2013), 239–62.
65   PR2010 .A1 1561, sig. L.iii recto.

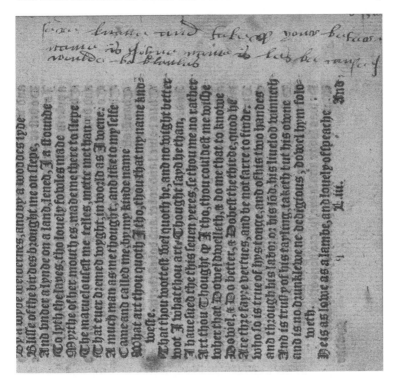

Fig. 4 'Sere knaue and take up your beter / name is Johne name les be cause I / woulde be blamles', in Bynnyngley's hand; PR2010 .A1 1561, sig. L.iii recto

impossible to place precisely. They do not come from *Piers Plowman* itself, though they have a broad thematic affinity with the poem, which is unquestionably interested in directing knaves to do better. Their immediate prompt is probably Will's anxious question to Thought on the same page: 'What art thou', he asks of the figure who just called him by his 'kinde name', 'thou that my name knowethe?'[66] Bynnyngley may answer Will's question with a little free association, or with a snatch of a song otherwise lost or so misremembered as to be unrecognizable. But the lines are also strikingly reminiscent of the third of John Ball's 1381 letters, as recorded in Walsingham's chronicle:[67]

66 B.8.71–2.
67 I am grateful to Adin Lears for first suggesting this connection.

Johon schep som tyme seynte marie prest of ȝork. and now of colchestre. Greteth wel johan nameles and johan þe mullere and johon carter and biddeþ hem þat þei bee war of gyle in borugh and stondeþ togidere in godes name. and biddeþ Peres plouȝman. go to his werk. and chastise wel hobbe þe robbere [...] be war or ȝe be wo knoweþ ȝour frend fro ȝour foo. haueth ynow. & seith hoo. and do wel and bettre and fleth synne. and sekeþ pees and hold ȝou þer inne. and so biddeþ johan trewaman and alle his felawes.[68]

If Bynnyngley is thinking of this letter, he is not quoting it directly.[69] Rather than reproducing a document from a chronicle as evidence for a historical claim, as other readers do, Bynnyngley's doggerel seems to share what Steven Justice calls the 'slogans and apothegms' of the letters, recalling and remixing them as the writers of the letters seem themselves to have done.[70] Bynnyngley's 'name is Johne name is les' particularly calls to mind Ball's 'johan nameles'; the truncated command to 'take up your beter' recalls the various hortatory statements of the letter (the familiar 'do wel and bettre', for example). The rebel letters and Bynnyngley's doggerel can be differentiated from the versified 'when' prophecies, conventional in late medieval evil-times satire, on the basis of such hortatory statements. That satire and the early modern poetry modelled on it share with the letters a vein of gnomic complaint, but lack their coded bidding and chiding.[71] Bynnyngley therefore seems to be looking further back. With no direct textual connection, however, this resonance could be incidental. There is no evidence of Bynnyngley's historical interests or politics that would provide a reason for quoting a half-remembered snatch of Ball's letter. Lawrence Warner has recently argued that a common corpus of proverbial figures and slogans lies behind Ball's letter and *Piers Plowman*.[72] If that is the case, then Bynnyngley's verse

68   This edition of the letter comes from Steven Justice, *Writing and Rebellion: England in 1381* (Berkeley and Los Angeles, 1994), 14–15.
69   The letter was printed in Holinshed's *Chronicles*, but there is no other reason to think that Bynnyngley had access to a copy of Holinshed. See Raphaell Holinshed, *The firste [laste] volume of the chronicles of England, Scotlande, and Irelande* (London, 1577), STC (2nd edn) 13568b, 1035.
70   Justice, *Writing and Rebellion*, 20.
71   On 'when' prophecies, see Scase, 'Dauy Dycars Dreame', 173–4.
72   Lawrence Warner, 'Plowman Traditions in Late Medieval and Early Modern Writing', in *The Cambridge Companion to Piers Plowman*, ed. Andrew Cole and Andrew Galloway (Cambridge, 2014), 198–213. Warner's suggestion should be

may be another piece of evidence for the continuing circulation of those proverbs. Whether proverb, quotation, or invention, the lines read as a surprising echo of Langland's idiom, a clear moment of reader response that cannot be assimilated to patterns found in the other printed copies of *Piers Plowman*.

A similarly evocative note is appended by the seventeenth-century reformist hand to the description of the collapse of the Barn of Unity in passus 20 (Fig. 5). 'Amidst the stonie rocks I say', it reads, 'I sawe a man enclined to wickednes'.[73] This note, like Bynnyngley's, seems to be the writer's invention. 'Wickednes' and 'stonie rocks' are unsurprisingly ubiquitous in early modern translations of the Hebrew Bible and New

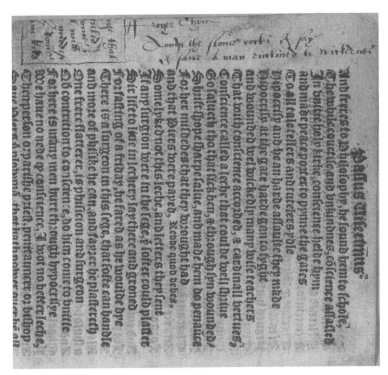

Fig. 5 'Amidst the stonie rocks I say / I sawe a man enclined to wickednes'; PR2010 .A1 1561, sig. J[j].i verso

weighed against the complex interaction of oral and literate cultures mapped by Justice, *Writing and Rebellion*, 13–66.

73 PR2010 .A1 1561, sig. J[j].i verso.

Testament, but I have not been able to find this precise formulation
anywhere. It may allude to an episode in the Gospels: Christ's exorcism
of the mountain-dwelling 'man with an unclean spirit' in Mark 5, or
perhaps the temptation of Christ in the stony desert.[74] Regardless, it is a
fitting comment for its context, given that it sits in the margin of *Piers
Plowman*'s final apocalyptic episode, the storming of Unity by men
'enclined to wickednes'.

   On the other hand, the collapse of the Barn of Unity happens to fall
on the verso of the penultimate leaf, whose margins would therefore
be the first blank space a seventeenth-century user of this book would
find when opening from the back cover. (Doughtie's ownership marks
fill the margins of the final pages.) Unlike Bynnyngley's little verse –
which clearly responds, however loosely, to passus 8 – the placement of
this note may be random, its inscription in a copy of *Piers Plowman* an
accident of convenience rather than an intentional act. Other markings
in the book are similarly intriguing but ultimately uncertain. One reader
has written 'Abraham' below Ymaginatif's retelling of Trajan's exceptional
salvation in passus 12.[75] That reader may have been collocating standard
knowledge of the redemption of the patriarchs in the Harrowing of Hell
with Langland's more idiosyncratic vision of a virtuous pagan emperor
'broken out of helle'. Or he was named Abraham and was just signing his
name. If the latter, he wrote his name nowhere else, but the possibility of
simple coincidence cannot be ruled out. What this 'Abraham' tells us is
that trying to imagine otherwise-unrepresented readers on the basis of
their marks is dangerous. One reader marks the question posed to Piers
during the organization of the half-acre in passus 6, 'What should we
women worke, in the meane whyle?'[76] The same annotator has marked
Conscience's condescending rebuke to Mede for reading 'like a lady'
with a 'non' in the margin.[77] Whether or not this reader bridled at the
misogyny in this passage, it is an oddly fitting comment from an idle
reader, because Conscience rebukes Mede by pointing out that she fails
to achieve the clerical standard of continuous reading: 'This text that
ye haue told, were good for lords', he says, but 'you failed a conning
clerk, that coud ye lefe haue turned'.[78] Mede's counsel and her learning

74   I am grateful to José Villagrana for the first possibility.
75   PR2010 .A1 1561, sig. S.i recto.
76   Ibid., sig. H.iv recto.
77   Ibid., sig. E.i recto.
78   Ibid.; at B.3.346–7.

are impugned at once; the female speaker and idle reader are conflated. But understanding what the 'non' reader's objection *means* ultimately depends on guesswork. Whatever follows that 'non' is trimmed, and if this actually is a case of a reader talking back to the book, it is frustratingly isolated.

As I noted near the beginning of this article, the absence of interpretative certainty is inevitable when trying to construct the history of books read by 'idle', 'unimportant', or anonymous people. Such resistance to interpretation is in fact consistent with material book history in general, regardless of the reader. Near the start of his recent survey of Renaissance marginalia, William Sherman comments on the 'ineluctable specificity of readers and readings', a specificity that makes evidence of readership difficult to assimilate to broader theories and historiographical narratives.[79] One way to overcome that difficulty is to build a bigger data set, to look for patterns across many books: the studies by Brayman Hackel, Sherman, and Wiggins, built on surveys of entire printed runs and whole libraries, have done just that.[80] Work on that scale has provided crucial contributions to the sociology and history of reading. But attention to particular books and particular readers – to singular events of reading and response rather than patterns or categories – remains useful. A single book has a particular capacity to surprise.

Vulgar Readers

By way of illustration of this power of surprise, I would like to turn to one more copy of *Piers Plowman* and its idle readers. The readers of New Haven, Beinecke Library, Id L26 550, a first-edition Crowley *Piers Plowman*, do not share a precise profile with the readers of the Bancroft *Piers*. The volume should be localized to Suffolk rather than anywhere further north.[81] Those who left records in the book are later

79   William Sherman, *Used Books: Marking Readers in Renaissance England* (Philadelphia, 2009), xvi.
80   See also the more provocative promise of 'a more rational literary history' via large-scale quantitative methods, with the uncertainty generated by single points of evidence dispelled by analysis at the level of the 'collective system', in Franco Moretti, 'Graphs, Maps, Trees: Abstract Models for Literary History – 1', *New Left Review* 24 (2003), 67–93 (68).
81   One seventeenth-century reader, Thomas Withers, was based in Walsham,

than the readers of the Bancroft *Piers*: the earliest who can be traced read the book in the seventeenth century, and the book continued to be annotated into the eighteenth.[82] At least one of those eighteenth-century readers, the religious controversialist Thomas Herne, has left a textual record outside the pages of this book.[83] But there are at least four other hands in the book, two of which sign their names. Like Bynnyngley and Doughtie, those readers would be otherwise unknown in literary history, and they come from the same echelon of the provincial yeomanry. More importantly, the accreted traces of their reading point to a similarly heterogeneous range of interests. As with the Bancroft *Piers*, some readers are idle and distracted, and their marks are indicative of the surprising variety of uses and responses that Langland's poem elicited well after its brief sixteenth-century return to canonicity.

The book is littered with the predictable residue of pragmatic use: pen-trials, ownership marks, and drafts of salutations for letters.[84] Some of the annotations are the work of a quite literally idle (and perhaps bored) reader: the running titles are copied repeatedly at the bottom of pages in the middle of the book, for example, an exercise that produced results that are clearly just experiments in handwriting, unhelpful as

Suffolk. See his will, TNA PROB 11/294/118. There are a number of references in the book itself to places in Suffolk, as at Id L26 550, 1r (sig. A.i recto) and 103v (sig. Cc.iii verso).

82   Because my interest here is in the seventeenth-century readers, in what follows I will not discuss the book's substantial scholarly annotation by an eighteenth-century hand, especially in the early pages of the book. That hand defines individual words with reference to their Old English antecedents ('likam' is glossed as 'A. S. body, flesh' on fol. 1 / sig. A.i recto, for instance, and a half-dozen other words are glossed in the same fashion on the same page). This hand cites Tyrwhitt on Chaucer, and thus must have marked Id L26 550 sometime after 1775. A number of other copies of *Piers Plowman* are glossed in similar ways by eighteenth-century readers: Cambridge, MA, Houghton Library, Hou Gen STC (2nd edn) 19907, for example, makes similar lexicographical connections to Old English, while Boston Public Library, G.406.32 perhaps works from a Chaucer glossary for its notes.

83   See W. C. Sydney, 'Herne, Thomas (d.1722)', rev. S. J. Skedd, *Oxford Dictionary of National Biography*, ed. H. C. G. Matthew and Brian Harrison (Oxford, 2004).

84   For the salutations, see: in Thomas Withers's hand, at Id L26 550, 74v (sig. T.ii verso) and 79v (sig. U.iii verso); in the earlier Henry Adams's hand, at 64v (sig. N.iiii verso) and 87r (sig. y.iiii recto).

finding aids.[85] But other notes reflect more careful consideration. A seventeenth-century hand appended vaguely apposite Latin *sententiae* to passages in the poem, for example. Langland's first articulation of a vision of kingship in the Prologue, which begins with Christ the king and proceeds to an idealized account of a king at the top of an ordered society, occasions the comment 'regum longe manus' ('the hands of kings are long'), somewhat eccentrically translated by the writer as 'kinges haue longe fingers'.[86] The same reader copied out relevant courtroom quotations from Cicero and Terence in the margins of Conscience's denunciation of Mede; that reader also copied a line from Bunyan's *Pilgrim's Progress*, providing the definite and rather late *terminus a quo* of 1678 for his or her annotations.[87] These references, drawn from school Latin and Bunyan, are by no means recondite for a seventeenth-century reader, but they do point to the slightly more literary and educated approach available to a late seventeenth-century yeoman. Other hands, which appear roughly contemporaneous, are similarly serious in approach: one copies out Langland's Latin, while another copies out Proverbs 24.21: 'My son feare thou the Lord & the King: / & meddle not with them that are given to change.'[88] The inter-confessional brutality that characterizes sixteenth-century reformist readings of *Piers Plowman* is absent here, but there is tone of fear and trembling. It crops up elsewhere in the margins, too, suggesting a series of devout readers.[89]

It is all the more surprising, then, that the first impression the book gives is of an anarchic and jocular group of readers. The same hand responsible for the admonitory verse of Proverbs asked earlier in the book, 'And art thou he that did the bottle bring', the good-timing question arranged around a grotesque image of a man's head.[90] A similar

---

85   Ibid., 36v (sig. J.iiii verso), and 37r (sig. k.i recto).

86   Ibid., 2v (sig. A.ii verso).

87   'Da mutuum testimonium', 'animus tibi pendet', and 'ask my felaw if I be a thefe', respectively. Ibid., 14r (sig. D.ii recto).

88   Ibid., 25r (sig. G.i recto) and 96v (sig. Z.iiii verso).

89   One reader copies out 'Amend yor liues for the kingdome of heuen' several times on 71r (sig. S.iii recto). Another writes 'Lett Hobkins Come & Sternhold with', unfortunately fragmentary; Hopkins's and Sternhold's metrical psalter was widely used and massively reprinted, but also often lampooned, so this comment may be intended to mock. See Beth Quitslund, *The Reformation in Rhyme: Sternhold, Hopkins, and the English Metrical Psalter, 1547–1603* (Aldershot, 2008).

90   Id L26 550, 37v (sig. L.i verso).

grotesque head on the first leaf is labelled, 'Old Nitker of Westerfeild in the countie of Suffolk coockold'. An image of a woman sticking her tongue out on the same page is accompanied by another message, apparently so incendiary as to merit scratching out. (Only the beginning, 'a tounge is a womans', is legible.)[91] Thomas Withers, a wealthy seventeenth-century Walsham yeoman, obsessively practised his signature in the margins of the book; some subsequent reader saw this as an opportunity for added commentary (Fig. 6):

> *Thomas Withers*
> is a little knaue [...]
> *Thomas Withers*
> is an arrant knaue
> *Thomas Withers*
> that boy[92]

Such marginalia – or, to return to Scott-Warren's consciously anachronistic term, especially appropriate here, 'graffiti' – are not unusual in early modern books.[93] There is, needless to say, nothing in *Piers Plowman* that would occasion *these* kinds of comments. Thomas Withers and his antagonist could be writing in any book. As with the 'man enclined to wickednes' at the end of the Bancroft *Piers*, sorting accident from intention here is impossible. But the accretion of accidental and intentional acts nevertheless affects the way a book signifies, because later readers – including modern critics – cannot help but notice both. Read through the marginal comments of the readers of Beinecke Id L26 550, *Piers Plowman*'s moments of low humour – the moments when the poem bends towards the 'leawd and wanton' and 'needlesse and vnprofitable', to return to the *Garden of Spirituall Flowers*'s categories of literature – come into focus. The confession of the Deadly Sins in B passus 5, a locus for such low humour, earned two readers' attention. In one notorious

91   Ibid., 1r (sig. A.i recto).
92   Ibid., 72r (sig. S.iiii recto), and 104v (sig. Cc.iiii verso).
93   Scott-Warren's relevant comments are worth quoting in full: 'One fairly common type of graffiti in early modern books is the praise or defamation of individuals [...] It tells of a world in which books were adjuncts to everyday sociability. They were passed around, and as they circulated, aspects of communal life – the negotiation of relationships, the debating of reputations – rubbed off on them' ('Reading Graffiti', 378–9).

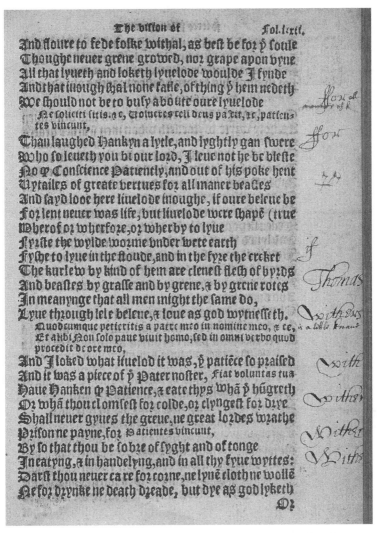

Fig. 6   'Thomas Withers is a little knaue'; New Haven, Beinecke Library, Id L26 550, 72r (sig. S.iiii recto)

moment, Glutton, lured off the path to church by gustatory pleasures, ends his drinking-bout with a series of bodily eruptions:

> He pyssed a pottell in a Pater noster whyle
> And blew his round rewet at his rugge bones ende
> That al that harde that horne, helde his nose after
> And wished it had bene wyped in a wyspe of firses.[94]

One reader copies a selection out in the margins of this page: 'blew his round rewe[t] att his rugg[e] bones ende'. This annotator was perhaps trying to construe the passage. Another, however, wrote a simpler message directly beside these lines: 'fart' (Fig. 7). The gloss is eloquent in its simplicity: whether it records a surprised response or provides a finding aid for future reference, it seems clear that the annotator found the passage funny. This marginal enthusiasm for Glutton's flatulence, transmitted alongside the rude doodles and the defamation of Withers and in the same hand as pious annotations, are reminders that early modern readers could easily hold the sacred and profane, the humorous and deadly serious, in close proximity. We tend not to go to *Piers Plowman* for humour, but these idle readers seem to have found it there.

Conclusion

The successive readers of the Bancroft *Piers* and Beinecke Id L26 550 left ample evidence of engagement with the book and the poem it contains, but no single 'reading' of the poem emerges from that evidence, as it might from the traces left by more systematic contemporaries such as Richard Harvey, Francis Aldrich, or the reader of C.122.d.9. In part, this heterogeneity simply has to do with the history of repeated resale and circulation that the idle readers' books share: many readers make many readings. It may also proceed from the issues of class and education that I noted at the outset. More systematic annotations reflect learned methods of note-taking and reading that may not have been available to Doughtie and Bynnyngley. Regardless of the material conditions that obtained, however, these copies of *Piers Plowman* testify to a different approach to the poem. These books were not studied – they were picked up and read, scribbled in, marked, and put down again, to be passed

94   Id L26 550, 26r (sig. G.ii recto); B.5.341–4.

The visson of   Fol.xxi

And blew his round rewet at his rugge bones ende
That al that harde that horne, helde his nose after
And wished it had bene wyped with a wyspe of firses
He might neyther stepe nor stand, or he a staffe had
And than gan he to go, lyke a glewe mans bytch
Sometyme a syde, and sometyme arere
As who so layeth lynes for to latche foules
And whan he drough the dore than dimmed his eyen
He stombled on the thyrsholde, & threwe to the earth
Clement the cobler caught hym by the myddle
Forto lyft hym a lofte, and laied him upon his knees
And Gloto was a great churle & a grymne in the lifting
And bought up a candle in Clementes lappe
There is none so hongry hounde in Hertforde shere
Durst lap of tho levinges, so unlovely they smaughte
With al the wo of thys world, his wife & hys wench
Bare hym home to hys bedde & brought him therin
And after al this excesse he had an accidie
That he slope saturday & sonday, til sunne wet to rest
Than waked he of hys wynking, & wyped hys eyes,
The first word that he warped was, wher is the bolle
Hys wife ganedwite him tho, how wickedly he lived
And Repentaunce right so rebuked hym that tyme.
As in wordes & workes thou wroughtst yll in thy lyfe
Shryue the & be ashamed therof, & shew it with thi mouth
I Gloton quod the grome, gylte me yelde
That I have trespaced with my tog, I can not tel howe
Sworne gods soule, & so god me helpe & the holidome
There no nede was nyne hundred tymes
And over seme at my soupe, and sometyme at nones
That I Gloton gyrte up, ere I had gone a mile.
And I spilt that might be spared & spet on some hungry
        G.ii.   Over

[marginalia: blew his round now at his rugge bones end / this is / that I / faide / and / is / a b c d e / f g h i / l m n o p / q r s t u v w / x y z & / people]

Fig. 7   Notes on Glutton's drinking-bout; New Haven, Beinecke Library, Id L26 550, 26r (sig. G.ii recto)

on to someone else. As should be clear from the preceding discussion, it is nearly impossible confidently to read a unifying intention into this kind of engagement. Just as *Piers Plowman* refuses to fit to the unities of message, character, purpose, or genre that we might like to assign it, these particular copies resist the kind of conclusions we would ascribe to a single educated reader, to figures like Harvey or Aldrich.

Even while it does not suggest a single intention, however, the idle readers' fragmentary use of the two copies of *Piers Plowman* discussed above does ultimately accommodate a broader narrative: it shows that Langland's poem could be more of a living document in the sixteenth and even seventeenth centuries than we might think. Against Puttenham's complaint that Langland's 'verse is but loose meetre, and his termes hard and obscure, so as in them is litle pleasure to be taken', some of these readers seem to have found something pleasurable or at least imitable in its style.[95] Others found humour in it, or instructions, or provocations to devotion. As with almost any annotated early modern book, many others simply treated it as a drafting pad or notebook. The encounter with historical alterity – the mixed utility and pleasure that come from an encounter with something too old to be fully inhabited – in antiquarian responses to medieval poetry, and to a lesser extent in the more mercenary reformist uses of it, are not really in evidence in either the Bancroft *Piers* or among the seventeenth-century readers of the Beinecke copy. There is little evidence that these readers, otherwise under-represented in the history of *Piers Plowman*'s reception, set themselves 'to doe attention' as the *Garden of Spirituall Flowers* demanded. Rather, both sets of idle readers approach the poem not from across a distance, nor as a source of difficulty, but as something vital and present, suitable for casual use and reuse.

As I have argued throughout this article, idle readers present a healthy challenge to certain enabling assumptions in book history and reception studies. The readers of the Bancroft and Beinecke *Piers* are not 'active' and they are not polemical, but they are not entirely disengaged from the poem, either: they seem to have read in a state of intermittent focus and distraction, with a multiplicity of interests – like many readers, that is, both modern and historical, who read for pleasure or edification and who lack the desire or ability to carry out a sustained programme of careful notation. The challenge they present might be conceptualized

---

95   George Puttenham, *The arte of English poesie* (London, 1589), STC (2nd edn) 20519, 50.

along the same lines as current debates in literary criticism, particularly the recent antihermeneutical turn. Harvey and Aldrich would fill the role of 'symptomatic reader', whose strong reading strives to uncover some truth absent from the page. Idle readers, on the other hand, take their books as they come, not freighting them with the recessive traces of some offstage drama of history or ecclesiology – so they have a broad sympathy with 'surface readers', as Stephen Best and Sharon Marcus have described them.[96] There is something to this idealized picture: James Simpson has argued that bad-faith periodization and the study of English literary history emerged simultaneously and intertwined in the Protestant project of rupture and recovery.[97] Unlike idle readers, the active reading of people like Harvey and Aldrich, and Bale and Foxe before them, was intended to reiterate a bigger truth outside the text. Best and Marcus suggest in turn that attending to the surface – of one work or object, or across many via digital methods *à la* Moretti's 'distant reading' – can free critics from having to carry out such reiteration of a single master discourse, a process that a hermeneutics of depth supposedly requires. And as I have suggested, taking idle readers seriously *does* upend certain types of 'circular' analysis in reception studies.[98]

But such a comparison is fraught with its own difficulties. Idle readers are *not* surface readers, insofar as surface reading requires 'slow pace, receptiveness, and fixed attention'.[99] These are practical values shared with the *Garden of Spirituall Flowers*, despite the centuries and radically different epistemologies that separate the *Garden* from contemporary criticism. Idle readers' approach is discontinuous and associative: it displays *neither* careful attention to the textual surface nor

96 Stephen Best and Sharon Marcus, 'Surface Reading: An Introduction', *Representations* 108 (2009), 1–21.

97 James Simpson, *The Oxford English Literary History*, vol. 2: *Reform and Cultural Revolution* (Oxford, 2002), 7–33. The hermeneutics of depth is of course much older than the Reformation, a point made in reference to contemporary critical debates by Julie Orlemanski, 'Scales of Reading', *Exemplaria* 26.2–3 (2014), 215–33 (227–8).

98 I draw here on Timothy Bewes, 'Reading with the Grain: A New World in Literary Criticism', *differences* 21 (2010), 1–33 (5–6). But see the critique of 'surface reading' in Randy Schiff, 'Resisting Surfaces: Description, Distance Reading, and Textual Entanglement', *Exemplaria* 26.2–3 (2014), 273–90.

99 Best and Marcus, 'Surface Reading', 18.

a searching investigation of the depths behind it, but instead surprises with juxtaposition and invention.

Articulating a *method* to account adequately for idle readers, no matter their numbers or importance, presents yet more difficulties. Though Best and Marcus suggest that one mode of surface reading might be book-historical, attending to the 'literal surfaces of books themselves', the historical traces that idle readers left on the literal surfaces of books cannot be read according to the codes of a singular aesthetic object.[100] Most of the fragmentary textual detritus left by idle readers defies critical modes of reading, whether 'close' or 'surface'. They cannot be 'just read': they are both too opaque and too humble for that. They lack the kind of internal complexity that demands a critic's careful attention, but they wear almost nothing on their sleeves, either. But idle readers cannot be shunted aside: when we set them in their context, glean what empirical data we can from them, and collocate them with other texts, new possibilities for understanding how texts made meaning in history open up. And so I propose a delicate critical two-step, with Best and Marcus's salutary call for critical humility in mind. One *must* wager that an idle reader's note means *more than it says* – the characteristic sin of the suspicious reader – for it to be worth discussing at all. But one must also acknowledge that the reconstruction of such latent meanings out of fragmentary traces will inevitably be tentative, subject to revision, and potentially resistant to the historical or critical narratives with which we approach it. Making literary-critical meaning of idle readers, in other words, requires moving past the surface – without diminishing the uncertainty of what lies beyond it.

---

100   Best and Marcus, 'Surface Reading', 9.